The Complete Guide to Retail
Management

Alan Fiber

Penguin Books

Penguin Books Ltd, Harmondsworth,
Middlesex, England
Penguin Books Inc., 7110 Ambassador Road,
Baltimore, Maryland 21207, U.S.A.
Penguin Books Australia Ltd, Ringwood,
Victoria, Australia

First published as *The Independent Retailer*, Heinemann 1964
This completely revised and expanded edition
published in Penguin Books 1972
Copyright © Alan Fiber, 1972

Made and printed in Great Britain by
Cox & Wyman Ltd, London, Reading and Fakenham
Set in Monotype Plantin

Penguin Handbooks
The Complete Guide to Retail Management

Alan Fiber, qualified in law, has written extensively for businessmen, often under certain well-known pseudonyms. His writings have been translated for businessmen abroad, he has judged national retailing competitions, has participated in ITV programmes about business, and he is often asked to lecture at business seminars. By his early thirties he had held multiple directorships in an international organization concerned with management consultancy and business training. His army service was with Military Intelligence, working much of the time in the Malayan war. He writes from thorough experience as Managing Director of Business Management Advisory Services Ltd, which advises public and private concerns and trade associations of all sizes on improving business. The retail-management division, which he personally supervises, helps in every major trade.

This book is dedicated to H.A.F.
and the memory of the late J.R.F.

Contents

Checklists

List of Tables and Diagrams

Foreword to the Original Edition

J. W. Stevenson, F.C.C.S., *General Secretary of The National Chamber of Trade*

I have read Mr Alan Fiber's book *The Independent Retailer* with very considerable interest, and I am pleased indeed to commend it to anyone who obtains or is likely to obtain his or her living in the retail distributive trades.

The book, while being comprehensive in its coverage, is nevertheless quite detailed in its sections and is very easy to read. Of particular value to those contemplating buying a business are the various appendices, and the facts which are there put forward would amply repay a close study by any shopkeeper.

In these days when there are so many books on so many subjects it is refreshing to read one which actually does what its author sets out to do: to give the reader a really sensible and worthwhile grasp of the principles which govern the actual operations of a retail business.

J.W.S.

Acknowledgements

The author gratefully acknowledges his indebtedness to the following organizations who have kindly given permission for use of diagrams and tabular information:

Department of Trade and Industry (Tables 1–5)
Electricity Council (Diagram 5 and Table 15)
Central Statistical Office (Tables 16 and 17)
The Controller, Her Majesty's Stationery Office

Why Read This Book?

All concerned with every kind of shop need to know about the best in retail management, principles and practice. It is vital to existing retailers, whether considering expansion or wanting to check on making best use of financial and other assets; to would-be shopkeepers, as an appreciation of what to prepare for; to students of retailing, as well as to practising managers and assistants in shops, to help in their work and career advancement.

This handbook of retail management, designed for easy reading and permanent reference, applies to all kinds of shop. While of direct and major relevance to every independent shopkeeper, almost all equally applies to staff of chain and department stores, because the same basic principles apply to all forms of trading, and also because even the largest organization depends ultimately on a series of branch shops or departments, in each of which scale of operation and most retailing problems are remarkably similar to those of an independently owned shop.

Big changes are taking place in retailing. Some of the more significant are referred to at the start of Chapter 1. But in addition, retailing is becoming much more scientific.

The larger retailing firms employ specialist staffs to deal with specialist activities such as property location, stock purchase, display, staff matters, method study, and ensuring best use of capital, though everyone else in the organization needs to understand the main problems and methods if all are to work harmoniously. The independent retailer has to be his own series of specialists. He has to become much more proficient in business management than his predecessors and in addition have a deeper knowledge of the skills that produce the successful trader at the very time when the necessary range of skills is widening.

This book deals practically and in considerable detail with the many specialist aspects of retailing affecting all shops. Principles and techniques for all trades are dealt with. That techniques are altering is obvious, but the very principles of retailing are also undergoing change, as will be seen from the following chapters.

Many years' experience as a director of a management consultancy enables the author to appreciate the problems of retailing concerns of all sizes. As many are covered here as is possible within the confines of a single volume.

The retailer has been referred to throughout as 'he', though the term applies equally to the many women who are shopkeepers or retail managers. Similarly, the shopper has been referred to as 'she', the term normally covering masculine customers also.

The checklists are an aid to memory and reference, often containing material additional to that in the text. They do not attempt to summarize whole chapters.

Accuracy is essential in a book of this nature if the retailer, would-be shopkeeper, manager, assistant, or student is to extract from it the greatest benefit. No effort has been spared, therefore, in checking and cross-checking information and in obtaining advice from many people and organizations of importance to retailing. Thanks are due particularly, and are most gratefully given, to the several people who voluntarily gave up their time and offered invaluable comments to the improvement of the manuscript on which this edition is based.

Mr J. W. Stevenson, F.C.C.S., then General Secretary of the National Chamber of Trade;

Mr J. B. Turner, D.L., J.P., Secretary and Education Officer of the Retail Trades Education Council;

Mr K. A. E. Sears, M.A., D.P.A., of the City and Guilds of London Institute;

Mr J. G. Simpkins, F.C.A., a Chartered Accountant;

Mr S. Aarons, an experienced and successful independent retailer;

Mr L. Leventhal, director of a publishing company, whose advice on many aspects of this book, and encouragement over a number of years, have directly helped in its creation.

Valuable assistance has been given also by the Secretary of the

Institute of Chartered Accountants in England and Wales; representatives of the Law Society, the Royal Institution of Chartered Surveyors, and the many other professional, educational and trade bodies referred to in this book. Mr Peter Browning, B.Sc. (Econ.), also contributed useful comments on certain parts of the manuscript.

The aim has been to produce a volume that is both a practical guide and a handy work of reference which will benefit retailing in general and its readers in particular. There is still ample scope for successful retail trading despite the increasing competition and changing patterns, but only those prepared to give attention to all the facets of present-day retailing can hope to reap the greatest rewards.

1. Retailing Today

Important changes are taking place in retailing. With the ending of resale price maintenance, pricing has become more flexible. There is greater use of a variety of sales incentives, such as discounts to special groups of customers, trading stamps, and consumer competitions. Shops offering personal service find this facility a more distinct weapon against competitors. There has been a marked increase in the amount of selling on credit. The consumer protection movement grows in size and importance.

The general picture is of rather fewer shops as each year passes. Those that remain tend to sell more than formerly, to be better equipped, to be of larger floor area on average, and to require a greater capital investment. Self-service and self-selection techniques are being adopted in many different trades. The former distinctions between trades are becoming blurred.

Manufacturers are taking a much greater interest in retailing, directly through controlling their own shops and indirectly by such methods as premium promotions and teams of special merchandising and display men. The balance between small shopkeepers and large chain organizations is changing. There has been growth in the practice of retailers selling goods under their own brand name. The volume of retail sales completely bypassing shops has increased vastly.

The trading hours of shops are becoming more flexible. The working week for shop staff is growing shorter, sometimes to five days. Working conditions are being improved. A higher proportion of shop assistants are part-time employees, often married women, frequently with previous experience of retail selling.

Staff selection and training are becoming more important for retailers. Government-sponsored training boards for the distributive trades have been set up, as has an economic development committee, or 'Neddy', to help increase retail efficiency.

Voluntary buying groups have become more popular among shopkeepers and are spreading from the food trade, where they have grown to major importance. More and more retailers are buying from cash-and-carry warehouses. Evening deliveries to shops have been introduced. In a host of ways shop layout, display, and sales promotion techniques are being greatly improved. Among the substantial new legislation of recent years affecting many shopkeepers has been introduction of capital gains tax, corporation tax, and the 'close company' rules.

But perhaps most important of all, there are now better methods of measuring retail efficiency. Shopkeeping is becoming more scientific. Despite many trends favouring the larger organization, there is still ample scope for the smaller retailer, as long as he is efficient. These trends, their implications, and many associated matters are what this book is about. Before considering the individual shop and department in detail it is as well to look at the general trading situation.

GENERAL TRADING SITUATION

A considerable amount of useful information can be found in the official censuses of distribution. These were taken in 1950, 1957, and 1961, after which it was decided to take a full census concerning retailing every ten years – in 1971, etc. – with a sample census sufficient to reveal any major changes every ten years intermediately, in 1966, 1976, and so on. Results are published, around two years after the year of the census.

The growth in retail trade and the decline in the number of shops is shown in Table 1, though much of the apparent increase in the turnover of shops is attributable to higher prices of goods rather than to greater volume. The statistics in Tables 1 to 5 are intended to offer only a general impression: definition of terms and other technical matters need to be considered when examining census figures in detail.

Rather more detail for individual trades is given in Tables 4 and 5. It is important to realize that shops are classified in these tables according to the main goods dealt in. There are for most trades many more shops handling similar goods, counted in

Table 1. Total retail business and number of shops

Year	Total trade through shops (£ thousand)	No. of shops
1950	5,000,130	583,132
1957	7,587,154	577,405
1961	8,918,860	577,307
1966	10,954,134	498,477

(*Source:* Board of Trade 1966 census of distribution)

these tables as another trade because lines of that other trade predominate.

Although many larger retail organizations have made headway in recent years and some of the less efficient independent shop-keepers have been forced to close, the smaller trader will always be an important element in retailing. Too much should not be read into published statistics. Prospects for any particular shop are not wholly dependent on national trends: the future lies to a great extent in the retailer's own hands by his becoming more efficient in his selection of stock, choice of location, methods of sales promotion, use of capital, and the many other aspects of retail business management dealt with throughout this book.

NEED FOR ENTHUSIASM

At the personal level, it is important for the retailer or assistant to be enthusiastic about shopkeeping if he is to be successful and happy in his work. Most people in retailing have a preference for dealing with the goods of a particular trade, usually that in which they have practical experience. Without a liking for his trade, it is difficult for anyone to be happy with the type of articles handled all the time and the kinds of customer constantly dealt with.

Enthusiasm about a trade and its products makes the discovery of facts about merchandise to be sold – their suitability and un-suitability for various purposes, their proper care, their method of manufacture, and so on – a pleasant exploration. These facts are essential to up-to-date retailing because many shopkeepers are being asked more and more by customers for advice. This is the natural result of the wider choice of products available in most trades, and often of their greater complexity. Self-service and

Table 2. Independent, multiple, and Co-operative shops: the competitive position

	1957		
	Establish-ments	Turnover (£'000)	Persons engaged
Total Retail Trade	**577,405**	**7,587,154**	**2,529,602**
Co-operative Societies	28,945	904,796	197,625
Multiples	59,105	1,883,809	531,160
Independents	489,355	4,798,548	1,800,817
Percentage of total retail trade			
Co-operative Societies	5·0	11·9	7·8
Multiples	10·2	24·8	21·0
Independents	84·8	63·2	71·2

(*Source:* Board of Trade 1966 census of distribution)

self-selection shops increasingly draw away customers for products where no advice is necessary.

An up-to-date knowledge of products is also essential if a retailer is to buy his stocks wisely. He can then assess the advantages and disadvantages of new lines, realize whether they will sell well to his particular clientele, judge if they are well made and in all respects represent value for money, and whether they are appropriate to his shop. Knowledge of the value of what he has to offer customers, of retailing, and of competitive activity is also necessary if the retailer is to price his goods and services to produce the greatest profit. Without proper knowledge a retailer can make many mistakes that, with competition intensifying, will quickly put him out of business.

Normally, a fair amount of technical knowledge is necessary for a successful retailer and it takes some time to acquire. If, however, one has a real zest for retailing, even without any specialist knowledge of any trade, there may still be scope for trading successfully on one's own by selling goods that are well advertised and thus already known to customers. Cigarettes, confectionery, and some of the more usual groceries are obvious examples. But

1961			1966		
Establish-ments	Turnover (£'000)	Persons engaged	Establish-ments	Turnover (£'000)	Persons engaged
577,307	8,918,860	2,524,084	498,477	10,954,134	2,530,928
29,396	959,339	195,144	26,436	1,013,112	172,383
67,299	2,580,073	633,029	73,933	3,858,391	748,343
480,612	5,379,448	1,695,911	398,108	6,082,632	1,610,202
5·1	10·8	7·7	5·3	9·2	6·8
11·7	28·9	25·1	14·8	35·2	29·6
83·3	60·3	67·2	79·9	55·5	63·6

even in such trades there is a certain amount to be learnt, and anyone thinking of opening his own shop for the first time would be well advised to take a job in that trade for a while to gain experience, regardless of his age, or the wage he may command.

Table 3. The progress of independent, multiple, and Co-operative shops compared

	Percentage change in turnover		
	1950–57	1957–61	1961–6
Total Retail Trade	+51·7	+17·6	+24·2
Co-operative Societies	+58·3	+ 6·0	+ 5·6
Multiples	+72·3	+37·0	+49·5
Independents	+43·9	+12·1	+15·3

(*Source:* Board of Trade 1966 census of distribution)

REDUCING CAPITAL REQUIRED

The position of the smaller retailer is a little more secure against competition when he offers personal service rather than goods, for example hairdressing or electrical appliance repairs, though

Table 4. Retail business: key figures for each main trade

Kind of business	1957		
	Establish-ments	Turnover (£'000)	Persons engaged
Grocers and provision dealers	**151,859**	**2,038,374**	**556,706**
Other food retailers	**123,295**	**1,544,703**	**490,866**
Dairymen	7,534	322,921	72,314
Butchers	41,698	549,893	149,550
Fishmongers, poulterers	8,108	73,142	26,279
Greengrocers, fruiterers (including those selling fish)	39,515	270,451	108,093
Bread and flour confectioners	17,644	215,889	111,039
Off-licences	8,796	112,408	23,591
Confectioners, tobacconists, newsagents	**77,437**	**702,996**	**285,163**
Clothing and footwear shops	**97,656**	**1,180,212**	**411,631**
Boot and shoe shops	14,451	178,785	60,882
Men's and boys' wear shops	14,892	244,209	67,793
Women's and girls' wear, household textile and general clothing shops	68,313	757,217	282,956
Household goods shops	**62,115**	**795,566**	**259,603**
Furniture and allied shops	16,278	294,369	86,369
Radio and electrical goods shops (excluding hire)	13,498	235,335	70,314
Radio and television hire shops	352	15,242	3,655
Cycle and perambulator shops (including 'radio and cycle' shops)	7,497	61,344	21,448
Hardware, china, wallpaper and paint shops	24,490	189,277	77,817
Other non-food retailers	**61,360**	**563,050**	**237,597**
Bookshops and stationers	6,818	81,577	36,007
Chemists, photographic dealers	18,129	269,690	96,158
Jewellery, leather and sports goods shops	20,380	137,532	61,402
Other non-food shops	16,033	74,251	44,030
General stores	**3,683**	**762,253**	**287,946**
Department stores	718	453,912	169,156
Variety and other general stores	2,965	308,342	118,790

(*Source:* Board of Trade 1966 census of distribution)

	1961			1966	
Establish-ments	Turnover (£'000)	Persons engaged	Establish-ments	Turnover (£'000)	Persons engaged
151,154	2,366,805	556,953	122,336	2,871,544	519,773
127,304	1,770,600	489,438	103,296	2,055,956	454,738
6,580	363,740	73,600	4,473	440,071	67,577
44,248	630,660	152,309	38,087	716,824	137,976
7,857	80,687	23,532	5,557	80,753	20,466
42,072	320,749	112,122	26,779	307,518	87,753
17,549	234,224	103,396	17,849	289,100	113,128
9,000	140,539	24,479	10,551	221,688	27,838
70,662	799,622	250,717	63,015	1,035,064	296,112
96,612	1,384,576	405,079	81,544	1,675,325	398,080
14,583	220,678	63,220	13,451	258,562	64,539
14,060	270,780	63,823	14,534	346,431	70,324
67,969	893,118	278,036	53,559	1,070,331	263,217
69,133	993,660	281,376	68,339	1,267,127	294,749
17,038	372,664	91,443	19,273	510,841	104,158
16,653	270,169	76,200	15,695	291,814	72,784
2,225	71,350	15,829	3,800	129,468	23,309
5,657	38,545	13,835	3,776	30,646	9,465
27,560	240,931	84,069	25,795	304,357	85,033
58,692	673,909	227,776	57,028	972,091	257,968
6,284	84,008	29,043	5,887	126,918	34,859
18,392	347,423	102,464	17,934	498,390	114,782
19,277	164,655	57,063	18,586	240,890	63,960
14,739	77,824	39,206	14,621	105,895	44,367
3,750	929,687	312,745	2,919	1,077,026	309,508
784	545,421	181,757	778	661,959	180,992
2,966	384,266	130,988	2,141	415,068	128,516

Table 5. Retail business in 1966: the competitive position between kinds of organization

Kinds of business	All retail establishments		
	Establishments	Turnover (£'000)	Persons engaged
Total Retail Trade	**498,477**	**10,954,134**	**2,530,928**
Grocers and provision dealers	**122,336**	**2,871,544**	**519,773**
Other food retailers	**103,296**	**2,055,956**	**454,738**
Dairymen	4,473	440,071	67,577
Butchers	38,087	716,824	137,976
Fishmongers, poulterers	5,557	80,753	20,466
Greengrocers, fruiterers (including those selling fish)	26,779	307,518	87,753
Bread and flour confectioners	17,849	289,100	113,128
Off-licences	10,551	221,688	27,838
Confectioners, tobacconists, newsagents	**63,015**	**1,935,064**	**296,112**
Clothing and footwear shops	**81,544**	**1,675,325**	**398,080**
Boot and shoe shops	13,451	258,562	64,539
Men's and boys' wear shops	14,534	346,431	70,324
Women's and girls' wear, household textile and general clothing shops	53,559	1,070,331	263,217
Household goods shops	**68,339**	**1,267,127**	**294,749**
Furniture and allied shops	19,273	510,841	104,158
Radio and electrical goods shops (excluding hire)	15,695	291,814	72,784
Radio and television hire shops	3,800	129,468	23,309
Cycle and perambulator shops (including 'radio and cycle' shops)	3,776	30,646*	9,465
Hardware, china, wallpaper and paint shops	25,795	304,357	85,033
Other non-food retailers	**57,028**	**972,091**	**257,968**
Bookshops and stationers	5,887	126,918	34,859
Chemists, photographic dealers	17,934	498,390	114,782
Jewellery, leather and sports goods shops	18,586	240,890	63,960
Other non-food shops	14,621	105,895	44,367
General stores	**2,919**	**1,077,026**	**309,508**
Department stores	778	661,959	180,992
Variety and other general stores	2,141	415,068	128,516

* Figures combined with those for radio and electrical goods shops to avoid disclosing information about specific undertakings.

(*Source:* Board of Trade 1966 census of distribution)

Co-operative Societies			Multiples			Independents		
Establish-ments	Turnover (£'000)	Persons engaged	Establish-ments	Turnover (£'000)	Persons engaged	Establish-ments	Turnover (£'000)	Persons engaged
26,436	1,013,112	172,383	73,933	3,858,391	748,343	398,108	6,082,632	1,610,202
12,757	484,181	71,745	14,119	1,058,993	157,321	95,460	1,328,370	290,707
8,176	265,366	47,109	18,493	589,424	103,470	76,627	1,201,166	304,159
659	147,165	22,065	604	193,825	25,390	3,210	99,082	20,122
5,313	65,202	12,496	4,306	116,410	18,790	28,468	535,213	106,690
120	1,262	320	270	11,625	2,019	5,167	67,867	18,127
1,112	11,290	2,689	1,325	30,870	7,208	24,342	265,358	77,856
793	35,522	9,142	6,259	107,519	35,642	10,797	146,059	68,344
179	4,926	397	5,729	129,175	14,421	4,643	87,587	13,020
134	5,298	363	6,111	147,577	30,511	56,770	882,189	265,238
2,538	57,003	12,800	17,487	858,440	152,721	61,519	759,882	232,559
630	10,534	2,462	6,664	172,974	40,151	6,157	75,054	21,926
426	9,417	1,793	4,704	181,645	31,332	9,404	155,370	37,199
1,482	37,052	8,545	6,119	503,821	81,238	45,958	529,458	173,434
1,214	41,120	6,673	10,668	374,178	70,806	56,457	851,828	217,270
559	25,183	3,691	2,227	139,574	25,844	16,487	346,084	74,623
251	9,054	1,497	2,860	87,035	16,182	12,624	196,340	55,232
17	518	116	3,078	109,161	18,066	705	19,789	5,127
*	*	*	*	*	*	3,736	30,031	9,338
387	6,365	1,369	2,503	38,407	10,714	22,905	259,585	72,950
1,108	24,879	5,445	5,138	284,350	67,937	50,782	662,862	184,586
10	249	48	830	47,436	12,389	5,047	79,233	22,422
1,000	22,883	4,949	2,692	189,309	45,704	14,242	286,198	64,129
59	1,238	286	1,146	39,068	7,715	17,381	200,584	55,959
39	509	162	470	8,538	2,129	14,112	96,849	42,076
509	135,265	28,248	1,917	545,429	165,577	493	396,333	115,683
238	117,998	25,059	213	156,864	42,442	327	387,097	113,491
271	17,267	3,189	1,704	388,565	123,135	166	9,236	2,192

there is still need to gain experience in shopkeeping before setting up, and success will ultimately depend on the degree of skill in the chosen trade. Although not an invariable rule, where personal

---

Checklist 1. Why shops fail

---

1. Insufficient trade.
2. Lack of capital.
3. Absence of certain personal qualities.
4. Inadequate knowledge of retailing and the specific trade.
5. Reluctance to work profitably.

---

skills are necessary to carry on a trade, as distinct from the retailing aspects, there tends to be slightly less need for substantial capital to open a shop.

For the would-be shopkeeper with limited capital and perhaps little retailing experience, the practice of 'franchising' may offer a solution. In several trades, including snack bars, self-service laundry and dry cleaning, and car washing, some companies running a chain of similar shops offer a franchise, or agreement to the exclusive use of the company's trade mark and services within a reasonable area.

The shopkeeper is in many respects free to operate as he wishes, and in return for a franchising fee, often a percentage of turnover, for obtaining supplies and equipment from a firm nominated by the franchising company and for keeping to stipulated minimum standards for customers, he obtains free advice on running the business and the benefit of the franchising company's general sales-promotional activity. The scope for profit is usually somewhat less than for completely independent retailers: the position of the owner of such a shop is somewhere between that of an independent trader and a manager.

The many ways to minimize the capital required to start or run any shop are dealt with throughout this book, but, as can be seen from Appendix 3, the necessary amount is still often more than novices expect.

PANORAMA OF RETAILING FUNCTIONS

Those not already experienced in running their own shop, of any trade, size, or type, may welcome a bird's eye view of the whole process. Of course, shops exist in society to pass goods and, often, advice to those wishing to buy, but to do this involves a good deal more. The right goods must be in stock, which means that they were bought at some earlier time and, even though cash may not have been paid then, finance and administration must have been thought about. Few goods sell themselves; sales have to be promoted, which in turn means a study of one's likely customers and probably also the employment of some assistance in the shop. Thus the seven main functions of a retailer are to provide finance for the whole operation; institute a profit-earning system of administration, including paying accounts; employ staff; buy goods; stock them; sell them; and devise ways of increasing net profit.

The main object of opening a shop of one's own is to make a profit, but this does not mean that every retailer is a money-mad tyrant. Often shopkeepers need to do tasks which bring in no profit, sometimes which in themselves even make a loss. But such building of goodwill among customers is also necessary if a business is to thrive.

Nevertheless, a successful retailer must keep at the back of his mind the overall financial arrangement of his business. If he is not in business for profit but because he likes dealing with the goods of the trade and selling to people, he would be far better off working as an employee in a similar shop, leaving to someone else the headaches – and they can be considerable – of small-shop management. So, the object of owning a shop is to make as much profit as possible and at the same time enjoy the work (after all, it occupies about half one's waking life); to gain fulfilment from satisfying the needs of many people; to make friends in the course of time with a number of customers and other retailers; and to give the opportunity to one or more assistants to develop their careers and perhaps eventually run their own shops – possibly, a branch of one's own if all goes well.

Anyone thinking of setting up shop for himself should carefully analyse his reasons for doing so and objectively consider his aptitudes and attitudes of mind before committing himself. Any existing retailer who is not doing as well as he had hoped might with advantage do likewise. In addition to the need for enthusiasm for the goods and likely customers of the chosen trade, it is vital to be able to take important decisions without wavering, to be able to deal with employees – and set an example – and to be candid with oneself at all times. If on reflection it appears that the main reason for setting up for oneself is to take life rather more easily than when working as an assistant, the full implications of running one's own shop have not been realized.

WHY SHOPS GO OUT OF BUSINESS

Many shops, especially small shops, go out of business every year. There are five main reasons: insufficient trade in the district because either it simply does not exist for the goods being offered or it is being taken away by competitors; lack of capital; the absence of certain personal qualities, such as enthusiasm, or the ability to think in terms of the other person – customer, staff, or anyone else – or willingness to adapt to changing circumstances; an inadequate knowledge of one's business as a shopkeeper, or of the trade; and a reluctance to work hard enough to good purpose – perhaps through greater concentration on administration rather than on actual retailing.

To know these factors is as important to established shopkeepers as to those thinking of starting their own shop. The dangers are always present. Trading conditions and the state of competition continually alter; firms of all ages and sizes on occasion find themselves acutely short of capital; personal attitudes vary from time to time; and the whole business of retailing is currently undergoing greater changes than at any time in this century.

2. Finance

Good financial management is of vital importance to existing and intending retailers alike. Financial mismanagement not only causes business failures, it also prevents otherwise successful traders from achieving their full potential. In a sense this is worse, because mismanagement is not obvious and can therefore continue, sometimes, for years; meanwhile opportunities are thrown away and the fateful day when efficient competition overtakes the less efficient shopkeeper is merely postponed, not avoided. This is the position of many independent retailers today: their profits are being sharply reduced because of the more skilled business management of competitors. The solution is not to complain of 'unfairness' but to become better retailers.

BASIC FINANCIAL IDEAS

Advice on financial management is to be found throughout this book and especially in Chapters 8 and 9, but at this stage it is important to understand the basic financial concepts and terms, even before one calculates how much capital may be required to set up in business, how best to plan expansion, or how to set about checking up on existing retailing methods.

Mark-up is the amount added by the retailer to the cost price of an article to arrive at the selling price. This is usually expressed as a percentage of the COST price. For example, an article costing a retailer 20p and selling for 25p has a mark-up of 5p or 25 per cent, 5p being 25 per cent of 20p.

Margin is the difference between the cost to the retailer of an article and the price at which he sells it (that is, the same as the mark-up) expressed as a percentage of the SELLING price. To take the same example, an article costing 20p and selling at 25p has a margin of 5p or 20 per cent, 5p being 20 per cent of 25p.

Turnover is the total value of sales at selling prices over the period mentioned in association with the word.

Stockturn rate of a line of goods is the number of times a year that capital invested in the line is turned over, that is, reinvested in further similar items after a sale has been made. Every line of goods has its own rate of stockturn; the average of all is the average stockturn rate for the business. Each shop has its own average stockturn rate because no two shops stock exactly the same lines and sell them in the same proportions, but the type of trade carried on determines the average rate of stockturn to an even greater extent: a newsagent turns most of his newspaper stock over every day; an ironmonger may count himself lucky to average four stockturns a year because many items, such as gardening equipment and fires, sell during a limited season only and even then some models may remain in stock for weeks before being chosen by a typical customer as just what he wanted. To calculate the shop's average stockturn rate, divide its annual sales, at selling prices, by the average value of stock at selling prices.

Net profit is gross profit less overhead costs, but with the addition of any discounts received from suppliers.

Capital in ordinary language is money and other assets such as shopfittings, a lease, debtors, and stock. But the shopkeeper who realizes that his capital is not just so much money and assets but these used over a period of time is already over the first hurdle to becoming an above-averagely-shrewd retailer. If one can develop this two-dimensional view of capital, the amount of money and the time during which it is employed, two important factors immediately stand out.

The first brings us back to stockturn. The quicker capital tied up in stocked goods can be changed into cash – that is, on making a sale – and, after deductions for overheads and profit, reinvested

Table 6. Percentage return on selling price

To find the percentage return on selling price, divide the selling price into 100 times the profit: for example, if an aerosol moth spray costs 23p and sells for 30p, a hundred times the profit, in pence, is 700. The percentage profit on selling price is, therefore,

$$\frac{700}{30} = 23 \cdot 3 \text{ per cent}$$

To find the selling price giving the required percentage profit:

$$\text{Selling price} = \frac{100 \times \text{cost price}}{100 - \text{rate of profit}}$$

Thus if dress material costs £1 a yard and a margin of 33⅓ per cent is required, selling price will be

$$\frac{100 \times 1}{100 - 33\frac{1}{3}} = \frac{100}{66\frac{2}{3}} = £1 \cdot 50 \text{p}$$

A useful ready reckoner can easily be compiled along the following pattern:

Mark-up's proportion of cost price	Resulting gross profit's proportion of selling price
One half	One third
One third	One quarter
One quarter	One fifth
One fifth	One sixth
etc.	etc.

in goods for sale, the more profitable will be the business. For example, a shop using £2,000 worth of stock at selling prices that brings in a net profit of 10 per cent on selling price with an average of five stockturns a year makes £1,000 per annum net profit ($£2,000 \times 5 \times \frac{10}{100}$). If, by good management, the retailer can increase his stockturn rate to six times a year with the same net profit he will earn £1,200 net profit ($£2,000 \times 6 \times \frac{10}{100}$).

No more capital is being employed in the business but because it is being worked more intensively it is producing much more profit. The factor of time has entered into consideration of the amount of capital; in practice, it means that a shopkeeper must be acutely aware of his stockturn rates and must make every effort to increase them. How to do this will be considered later.

Checklist 2. Leasehold versus freehold premises

Leasehold entails smaller initial outlay and, therefore, is easier to sell, but:

1. There is always the risk, however small, that the lease may not be renewed (see page 71).
2. It is unlikely that major alterations to the structure will be allowed by the landlord.
3. There may be restrictions in the lease on use of premises for certain trades or associated equipment which, while not affecting the original purchase of the lease, may inhibit desired expansion into associated lines.
4. There is no possiblity of capital appreciation on short leases as a bonus on the finance invested, although the possibility, usually less likely, of capital depreciation is equally removed.

INTEREST RATES

The second factor that becomes apparent when developing a two-dimensional view of capital concerns interest rates. These can never be expressed as merely a percentage. They can only be a percentage over a period of time. That period is often one year, and so the time is not always stated; this is where lies danger for an unwary shopkeeper calculating the cost of borrowing money. It can make an enormous difference to the cost of a loan.

A phrase such as 'It costs only five per cent extra each month' by a glib salesman sounds reasonable, especially if the charge for bank overdrafts happens to be higher than five per cent at the time. But this phrase might mean 'five per cent to be paid each month on the sum originally advanced': on £100-worth of, say, shopfittings with repayments spread over one year, this means £5 interest payable every month – £60 in all, equal to almost 116 per cent effective interest on the average amount on loan, which is the figure to compare with the rate charged on bank overdrafts.

Later in this chapter it will be seen that there are several sources from which a retailer can borrow to finance his business. Each source charges interest and if the shopkeeper is to be able to compare one with another all interest charges must be reduced to the same basis. It is unlikely that they are all expressed in the same way at the outset: the phrase 'interest rate' is totally ambiguous. The easiest method is to express all interest charges as a percentage per annum effective interest on the average amount on loan.

The time factor, the period on which interest charges are calculated, has just been discussed; the second major possibility of error in comparing the cost of loans from different sources lies in whether interest is charged on the average amount on loan or on the sum originally advanced. If a loan is paid off by regular instalments, it can be seen that the average amount on loan is a little over half the sum originally lent, the whole amount being outstanding at the beginning and only the last instalment just before the loan is paid off. An example may make the position clearer.

The cost of a £400 loan at ten per cent per annum for four years to be repaid in equal annual instalments will be:

(i) If the interest charge is based on the sum originally advanced, the sum payable equals 10 per cent of £400 × 4 (years) =   £160

(ii) If the interest charge is based on the actual amount on loan, the sum payable equals (10 per cent of £400 × 1) + (10 per cent of £300 × 1) + (10 per cent of £200 × 1) + (10 per cent of £100 × 1) = £40 + £30 + £20 + £10 =   £100

The position is illustrated by Diagram 1, where the total shaded area represents the interest payable if the charge is based on the

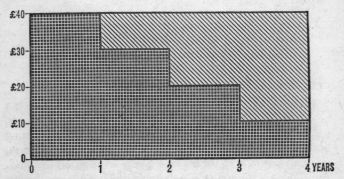

Diagram 1. Interest based on the sum originally lent is almost double that based on the diminishing outstanding balance

sum originally advanced, while the heavily shaded area illustrates the amount payable if it is based on the actual amount on loan. So, if the sum originally lent is the basis of the loan, the effective rate per cent per annum will be almost double the rate quoted by the lender.

The third possible source of error in computing the cost of buying with borrowed money lies in the original price. It is dearer to buy, say, shopfittings costing £100 with interest on the outstanding balance charged at six per cent per annum payable in two annual instalments, than to buy the same equipment for £90 and to pay interest at ten per cent per annum on the same terms, as Table 7 shows. It is a common trick of salesmen to offer a relatively low rate of interest and at the same time raise the original price: this does not affect a retailer comparing interest rates on borrowed capital, but it might catch him out when he is buying equipment for his shop.

Table 7. Basic price as well as interest rate affects total cost

	Interest at 6 per cent per annum (£)	Interest at 10 per cent per annum (£)
Basic price	100·00	90·00
First year's interest	6·00	9·00
Second year's interest (half purchase price having been repaid)	3·00	4·50
Total cost	£109·00	£103·50

CAPITAL REQUIREMENTS

With these basic financial concepts in mind, attention now can be given to calculating capital required to start a shop or branch, and ways of raising finance for this or for expanding an existing business. Broadly, capital is required for premises, equipment, stock, money to keep the business going, and possibly goodwill. Appendix 3 sets out a typical example which illustrates the following paragraphs;

Premises are either leasehold or freehold. As a shop is chosen mainly for its position and price, once he has decided on his property, the retailer rarely has any choice, but other factors being equal, it is better to start in leasehold premises. The initial outlay is much less and this is a useful way to cut down considerably the minimum capital required to start a shop or branch. A leasehold shop also tends to be easier to sell because the same considerations will apply to any purchaser, a point worth bearing in mind as the retailer may wish to sell after a few years to move to a larger or better-positioned shop.

Living accommodation also must be allowed for in calculating the cost of setting up a shop. Some business premises contain living accommodation, its cost being included in the price of the lease or freehold, but if the retailer has to live away from his shop, leasehold living accommodation has the advantage of tying up less capital than freehold premises. Allowance must be made also for keeping property decorated and in repair. In addition, alterations may be required to the premises before setting up business and the estimated cost should be included in the calculation of capital outlay. A lease may stipulate or allow for an increase in the rent after the first few years: this too should be considered when calculating the cost of particular premises.

Although some of these expenses will not occur until after the shop has been trading for some time and, presumably, producing clear profit, it is unwise to rely on trading income to pay for such exceptional items. It is far wiser to look ahead right at the start and make provisions for every possible major expense.

In buying a shop it is prudent to employ an accountant, a solicitor, and a surveyor; in addition, the stock and equipment may have been valued by professional advisers. How all these people can help a retailer is detailed in the next chapter, but at this point it is important to remember to allow for their fees. If a limited liability company (also discussed in the next chapter) is to be formed, a further allowance has to be made in calculating the starting capital required.

Equipment. Fixtures, fittings, and loose effects are normally sold with a business, and a separate sum agreed. Their value is the value to the incoming retailer, and has nothing to do with the original or current purchase price, nor with what the outgoing shopkeeper thinks they are worth. It may be that most of it is outdated or unsuitable, so consideration of what equipment will be required should be given before any is bought. The buyer is under no legal responsibility to buy equipment from an outgoing shopkeeper: it is entirely a matter for negotiation between the seller and buyer of the shop. Even if most of the equipment is bought from the outgoing retailer, additional items may be needed; their cost should be allowed for in calculating capital required.

Stock. The same principle applies if the outgoing shopkeeper offers his stock. Some of it may be outdated, damaged, or extremely slow moving; only worthwhile items should be purchased and these at a price thought reasonable by the incoming retailer. A sum should be agreed separately from payments for property, goodwill, or anything else.

The approximate amount of capital which will be tied up in stock is the average weekly turnover multiplied by the average number of weeks that goods remain in stock. The latter is of course also the number of annual stockturns divided into fifty-two. The next chapter shows how an accountant can help in arriving at these figures.

It should be remembered that any purchase tax on merchandise increases its cost to the retailer and thus ties up extra capital in stock. Also, the incoming shopkeeper must not overlook the fact that new goods have to be delivered and perhaps paid for before the old stock is completely sold out.

Running costs. It takes time to build up trade to the full potential of a shop. In addition, the retailer may be starting at a quiet period of the year so that weekly turnover consistently falls below the theoretical average arrived at by dividing anticipated annual turnover by fifty-two. Yet bills should still be paid promptly and to ensure that this can be done it is necessary to start business with sufficient funds in the bank to cover all normal running costs for the first period of trading. The length of this period varies according to speed of stockturn: for grocers or confectioners, eight weeks may be sufficient; for ironmongers, six months is more prudent.

Biggest of these expenses is wages which, in this context, includes money drawn by the retailer for himself and any of his family employed in the business. Wage costs also include compulsory national insurance contributions, and should cover wages for replacement staff, if any are employed during the paid holidays of regular staff.

Advantages and disadvantages of allowing credit to some customers are discussed later; if any credit trading is done, it is necessary to allow for the average amount likely to be owed by customers during this first trading period.

Other costs to be met in this period may include rent, if the premises are leased; charges for rates, heating, lighting, telephone, insurances, water, shop- and window-cleaning, stationery, postage, wrapping materials, printing billheads and letterheads, and so on.

It is certain that the retailer will want to do some advertising when he begins. This may be as simple as merely putting up a notice in the shop window saying 'Under new management', or it may be something more elaborate such as distributing leaflets to all houses in the district, arranging for a well-known personality to declare the shop open, or giving away a small item with all purchases over a certain amount during the first week or two. This is dealt with in more detail in Chapter 14, but the expected cost of any initial advertising should be added to the capital required.

Goodwill may be payable if the incoming retailer intends to take over an existing business and carry on the same type and class of trade. The goodwill may be extremely valuable provided it is not all vested in the outgoing retailer. If, however, it is intended to change the trade and name of the shop, goodwill may be worth nothing except, possibly, a good trading position. Assuming full goodwill is payable because the shop is to continue very much as before, a reasonable sum to allow in any preliminary calculations of the amount of capital required to start a shop might be three times the average yearly net profit, before tax, that the outgoing retailer has made over the last five years. The next chapter will show how an accountant can help to assess a fair figure and perhaps obtain a reduction in the price asked.

One final figure must be added to the capital requirements list: the safety-margin reserve. Its size depends upon the individual retailer's own judgement but it has three purposes: to meet any unexpected costs or temporary dips in sales; to give the retailer relative peace of mind; and to enable the business to continue if a loan is suddenly called in or if a supplier reduces the period of credit. The former is important: it is essential to be able to carry out special sales promotion if it is felt that a small investment would do a lot of good. Also, this reserve may be the only way in which advantage can be taken of a supplier's special offer. On the second point, it is obvious that there are plenty of other potential sources of trouble when starting a shop: any retailer will want to give of his best instead of fearing that he will not receive supplies of a good line in time because he was late in paying his supplier the previous month. The paramount importance of the third purpose is self-evident.

Although Appendix 3 sets out a typical example of costs involved in buying a business it can be a rough guide only. Several items are liable to wide fluctuations according to circumstances: location of the community served, position of the shop in relation to the main shopping centre, whether the same type and class of trade is being continued by the purchaser, whether structural alterations are necessary before the new retailer can open, the size and structural condition of the premises, the amount of stock required, and so on.

SOURCES OF FINANCE

The estimated cost of setting up a shop or branch may well be higher than was expected; luckily it is not all needed in cash. There are several possible sources of additional finance, but borrowing always incurs liability to repay interest as well as capital, so it is imprudent to borrow unless essential. Thus before borrowing, the retailer should ask himself, and answer with all honesty, what the precise advantages are of borrowing for any particular purpose and whether it would not be better to wait until more of his own money had been saved to reduce the loan required. The cost of borrowing must be considered, all comparisons being made on the basis of per cent per annum effective interest on the average amount on loan, and whether the advantages of having the finance make it worth that price. Thought also should be devoted to how payment of interest and repayment of capital can be afforded and the position if repayments cannot be sustained, for example, because of illness.

There is nothing bad about trading on borrowed money so long as good use is made of it and the loan repaid when due. Some retailers borrow to protect their own credit: by obtaining a long-

Table 8. Some comparative costs of borrowing

Interest charges vary, from time to time and with circumstances, but the following gives a broad comparison. Bank rate is assumed to be 6 per cent per annum.

	Per cent per annum effective interest on the average amount on loan	After tax relief on interest payments*
Bank overdraft facilities	8	5½
Bank 'personal' loan (7½ per cent to 8 per cent nominal, based on original sum)	14–15	9–10
Hire purchase (9½ per cent to 13 per cent nominal, ditto)	18–25	12–17

*Interest charges do not qualify for tax relief for individuals but are allowable in business accounts.

term loan they are able to pay their suppliers promptly, thus obtaining discounts and building up suppliers' goodwill – valuable when goods are wanted urgently or when popular lines are in short supply.

The bank is the most common source of borrowed finance, after suppliers. Naturally, every retailer needs to have a bank account so that he can conveniently pay his suppliers and make other large payments by cheque, and also as a safe place for his takings until they are used for stock once again. The methods adopted and the services given by all the major banks are roughly the same, as are their charges. To open an account, the retailer merely chooses his bank, often the one whose branch is nearest the shop, and asks to see the manager about opening an account. Everything else will then be explained to him.

The following paragraphs mention finance possibly available from the bank. In each instance a chat with the bank manager will reveal whether a loan will be granted and, if so, on what terms. It is necessary to be a customer of the bank, that is to have a current account for trading transactions, before any loan will be considered.

Normal bank loans are usually available at relatively low rates of interest both to help in getting a business going and to finance expansion. Banks like security, such as a life assurance policy or mortgage on the shop, to cover at least part of the money advanced, but they will generally offer some finance to established and credit worthy customers without any other security than the potential of the retailing business: that is, the prospect of steady trade and eventual growth. Their reward is the interest on the loan, usually charged at two per cent per annum above the prevailing bank rate, with a minimum of six per cent per annum, and the hope that the retailer will continue to be a customer with his current account. Bank rate varies, usually between three per cent and eight per cent per annum, although changes are never large and on the whole are infrequent.

Loan interest is charged periodically on the outstanding balance of the loan account. Apart from overdraft facilities, discussed below, this is the cheapest borrowed finance normally available. But due to government policy, bank loans are sometimes difficult to obtain, even if reasonable security can be provided. If granted, a loan account is opened and run separately from the current account. Repayment terms are by prior agreement with the bank manager. Normal loans are not offered by the bank as permanent finance: they are reviewed every half year and may be called in by the bank at any time, but in practice they often continue for several years.

Overdraft facilities permit a client to withdraw more from his current account than he has deposited, up to an agreed limit. Repaying this type of loan takes the form of reducing the outstanding debit balance. Interest rate is often the same as for a normal bank loan, but as interest is assessed on the daily balance an overdraft is cheaper than a loan. Overdrafts are usually taken to tide traders over short periods, often only a week or two: for example, just after paying suppliers' monthly accounts and before much of the new stock has been sold. They help by enabling the retailer to trade with a smaller current-account balance than would otherwise be necessary, and by leaving his capital free for financing other aspects of the business.

Term loans may also be available. They are granted for a definite term, hence the name, on security of specific assets such as shopfittings, and are not subject to earlier recall. Repayments are spread equally over the loan period, often three to five years. Interest is charged at two per cent per annum above bank rate with a minimum of six per cent per annum on the outstanding balance.

Personal loans, offered by some banks, are intended to finance the purchase of certain personal assets, but exceptions are made, sometimes to help small businesses, as in the instance of a van used partly for business. Security is not required, other than the reliable character of the borrower being known to the bank. From £50 to £500 may be lent in this way, repayments being made over six, twelve, eighteen, or twenty-four months. Interest charges, being based on the original amount advanced, are at a comparatively high effective rate. The rate is fixed at the beginning of the loan and does not fluctuate.

The estate agent or business transfer agent handling the sale of the particular shop often offers to arrange a personal loan to make purchase easier. It is important that the solicitor of the intending buyer agrees that the loan terms are fair before the retailer commits himself.

Merchandise suppliers are an important source of finance for all retailers. Most suppliers allow a period of credit on their accounts once they have obtained references regarding the retailer's financial standing and character. This can reduce considerably the amount of capital required for starting a shop and for keeping it going while expansion takes place. How to choose and deal with suppliers is discussed in Chapter 6 and Appendix 4.

Specially extended credit is sometimes allowed for the first year or two. Occasionally, and by special arrangement, a major supplier may loan a fixed sum for an agreed period, in addition to the normal month's credit for fresh supplies, charging interest around two per cent per annum above the prevailing bank rate. Where they particularly want to continue to supply the shop they may agree to advance a sum covering much of the starting stock from all suppliers. Alternatively, they may agree to such special terms provided the retailer pays off the loan piecemeal, but within perhaps two years, when settling the monthly account for new supplies. For such arrangements, suppliers require good evidence of character and of proved previous ability in the trade, preferably in a shop where they were also the major supplier.

Credit facilities are also frequently available to lessen the burden of finding cash to buy shopfittings, cash register, delivery van, and so on. Many firms selling this type of equipment offer easy-payment terms, and some trade associations also have schemes to aid such purchases. Charges vary, so it is always best to inquire from several sources to find the most suitable terms. Charges are usually expressed as a percentage of the original amount loaned, so the effective rate of interest on the average amount borrowed is nearly double what it may at first appear to be. Rates tend to be slightly higher if the purchase is met over a relatively short period, but bearing in mind the two-dimensional view of capital, this does not mean that it is cheaper to buy equipment over a longer period if sufficient cash is available to purchase more quickly. For example, the total amount of interest paid on £100-worth of shopfittings at seven per cent per annum on the purchase price repaid over two years is £14; at eight per cent per annum over one year it is only £8.

'Leasing' equipment is an additional means of making limited

capital go further. Equipment, notably delivery vans, is hired out for a monthly charge with the proviso that it is replaced with the latest model every, say, two years. A replacement is also provided whenever breakdown occurs. Unlike hire purchase, the equipment never becomes the retailer's property. Leasing is more expensive than hire purchase and considerably dearer than outright cash purchase, but it has the advantage of providing an expensive asset without tying up capital, charges being met out of monthly trading profits.

Life assurance policies can be used to finance the opening or expansion of a shop. The amount of the loan is not likely to differ much whether it comes from an insurance company or bank. Ninety per cent of the surrender value of an endowment policy and eighty per cent of that of a whole life policy is usually advanced, but the surrender value may be considerably below the amount already paid in premiums.

Mortgages can sometimes be raised on freehold or long leasehold premises, thus reducing the amount of capital required to start or expand a business. Most mortgages are granted on living accommodation; it is not always easy to obtain a mortgage on a shop, even if the retailer's living accommodation is attached. This is because shops offer less security: there is always a demand for living accommodation but that for specific shops varies, especially as over the years shopping centres tend to move. The majority of mortgages are arranged when the move into new premises takes place, but it is possible to raise this form of loan at any time.

The best terms usually come from a building society. Banks are often more conservative in their valuations while private sources expect higher rates of interest. A building society is likely to offer between seventy per cent and eighty per cent of their valuation of a shop, and a higher percentage on living accommodation. A small local building society is more likely to grant a mortgage on a shop than the larger national societies. Interest rates vary from time to time; in recent years they have usually been around five per cent to eight per cent per annum on the outstanding balance for living accommodation, an extra half per cent per annum on shop and attached living accommodation, or an extra one per cent per annum on a lock-up shop. Although local authorities often lend up to 100 per cent of their valuation on living accommodation, they do not offer mortgages on shop premises.

Leaseback arrangements. Any retailer who has bought the freehold or really long leasehold of his premises can turn his large fixed capital investment into ready cash by arranging to sell this asset in return for a lease, or a shorter lease as the case may be, plus a cash sum. Estate agents, solicitors, accountants or bank managers may know of willing investors. This 'leaseback' arrangement is economic only if the need for additional capital to be employed actively in the business is likely to be permanent. Even then, if it seems that the value of the property is likely to increase in the next few years, for example, because the street is becoming an important shopping centre, it may be better to retain the freehold or long lease and to try to raise a mortgage instead. In this way, the capital invested in the property may show a worthwhile increase in value over a few years, after which the interest in the premises can be sold, if then necessary, at a better price.

Second mortgages may be obtained from private investors to cover some of the difference between the amount actually advanced by the first mortgagee, that is, the building society or similar source, and the property's full valuation. A building society may offer only seventy per cent of their valuation as a safeguard against decline in the value of the shop and against overvaluation by the surveyor. As the second mortgagee has much less security he expects a higher rate of interest, often over twelve per cent per annum on the outstanding balance.

Individuals willing to invest in second mortgages may be contacted through an accountant, solicitor, or bank manager. A small fee, which should be agreed beforehand by the retailer, may be charged by the professional man for the introduction and two or three pounds a year may also be payable for his work in periodically rendering accounts of payments. Terms of the loan should be put into a simple legal contract.

In the same way, loans are sometimes available without the

security of a second mortgage, although they are more likely to be provided for financing established shops wishing to expand than for newcomers to retailing. The lender prefers to see trading accounts for each of the last few years so that he can better assess his risk. Interest rates, corresponding to the risk, are usually high.

A partner may be one possible means of raising finance either initially or for expansion. It depends on circumstances whether he takes an active interest in the business or merely puts up some of the finance. If a partnership is decided on, a solicitor should draw up a deed of partnership stating the nature of the business, amount of capital to be put up by each, how profits and losses are to be shared, what interest is payable on capital, what salaries each may draw, and how the partnership can be ended.

After paying all expenses, including salaries and any agreed sum as financial reserve for the business, profits or losses are shared equally, unless the partnership deed states otherwise. But it can be arranged that profits are paid out in any agreed proportion, and interest on capital can be at any agreed rate. A partnership, which, if necessary, can have more than two partners, has a disadvantage in that if the business fails, the partners are liable to pay debts to the full extent of their personal estate.

Company formation. It is, therefore, safer for a retailer, and easier to find a person to put up some of the finance, if a limited company is formed instead of a partnership. Other advantages of a company include the possibility of borrowing on security of the fixed assets of the business (assets acquired for continuous use in the business, such as property, shopfittings, and delivery van) by issuing debentures; the death of a director does not force the winding up of the company (whereas, unless specifically provided for in the partnership deed, a partnership must end with death, whereupon the deceased's executors may call for repayment of some of the capital, making it difficult for the business to continue); and security can be offered to investors, in addition to limiting any possible loss to the sum advanced, by issuing shares that take precedence in payment of dividends or in repayment in the event of liquidation.

Perhaps one of the greatest advantages is that more potential sources of finance become available: local professional men and people in retirement can be approached to take shares in the company, each putting up fairly small amounts, for example, £500, alongside the much larger sum of the retailer. But although the retailer is allowed to approach friends, he must not, by law, ask for finance from the public. Corporation tax, which applies to all companies irrespective of size, but not to partnerships, gives a tax disadvantage to forming a company because it is charged on all profits made, while dividends paid by the company to shareholders are charged with income tax in addition. The advantage of limiting shareholders' liability in the event of a serious loss usually outweighs this tax drawback, but an accountant or solicitor can advise what is best in particular circumstances, and if necessary give more detailed information about company formation. Finance from the general public can be solicited only in certain circumstances, on which a solicitor can advise.

It is not always easy to find a partner or co-director willing to contribute the required capital, and it is even harder to find one with the appropriate business ability as well. The bank manager, accountant, solicitor, or other acquaintances may know someone; otherwise, a retailer can only advertise or ask a firm specializing in these matters. An advertisement in a local paper may be seen by an investor who already knows the shop and, therefore, may be more willing to be a sleeping partner or director than would a complete stranger. As it is illegal for a private company to advertise specifically for finance, any advertisement must offer a directorship so that it can be claimed that it is primarily the personal ability of the man which is sought. In practice, it is necessary only for the new director to be present at company meetings without performing any other duties, unless a working director is required.

To find an investor who is prepared to work in the business and who is experienced in a particular trade, it is best to advertise in the papers of that trade. Investors often prefer to offer their personal services rather than merely put up money, as in this way they can claim earned income tax relief on their salary.

There are a few firms which arrange to bring together working or sleeping investors and suitable businesses but there is no recognized professional qualification for running such a business. Some firms of business transfer agents, who also need no particular qualifications, sometimes offer to find investors for shopkeepers. A fee of ten per cent of the capital raised is common.

The terms on which a likely partner or co-director will offer his capital vary, but are governed by three factors: the degree of risk involved in financing the shop, what work he has to do, and income rates available from other comparable investments, such as mortgages or through a stock exchange. Forming a public company and seeking a stock exchange quotation to raise the finance is not practicable for a small retailer: this is possible only with very much larger businesses.

Local authorities may be a further source of finance by making standard discretionary grants available to owners of old-fashioned houses to help modernize them. While this does not provide finance for a shop, it does mean that where the grants are available, money which would otherwise be spent on living accommodation remains free for use in the business. Local authorities provide full details on request.

The Industrial and Commercial Finance Corporation (I.C.F.C.) sometimes provides finance for shop expansion, although not for original setting up. The usual minimum loan is £5,000, although each application is considered on its merits. Formed by the principal banks, I.C.F.C. caters for private and the smaller public companies and has dealt with unincorporated concerns. Loans, sometimes with no security, are advanced for from ten to twenty-two years in exchange for ordinary or preference shares. Full details are available from I.C.F.C. (for their address see Appendix 8).

Building contractors. As building alterations or repairs are sometimes a major expense when starting or expanding a shop, it is useful to remember that contractors are occasionally willing to wait for payment in return for a higher contract price, especially if the work can be offered when the builder is not busy.

Checklist 3. Investment policy

1. See that business is not starved of total capital.
2. Keep correct proportion of capital free from long-term commitments (consult accountant).
3. Consider whether further investment in the business would be justified (e.g. new equipment, or to finance some of own hire purchase trading).
4. Keep savings safe, but available when necessary, and earning reasonable interest, e.g.
    (a) available immediately or at a few days' notice: bank deposit account, interest usually 2 per cent per annum below bank rate; National Savings Bank $3\frac{1}{2}$ per cent per annum, the first £15 interest tax free; Trustee Savings Bank $3\frac{1}{2}$ per cent per annum, ditto; building societies (interest rates vary; their special tax concession may be valuable);
    (b) available at three months' or six months' notice: building societies; local authority loans; reputable investment trusts;
    (c) available at longer notice: loans, properly secured, through accountant or solicitor, or possibly investment in unit trusts or quoted stock exchange securities. National savings certificates may be attractive if it is unlikely they will have to be encashed before the end of their stated term.
5. Always seek competent advice, e.g. from accountant and bank manager.

Moneylenders should not be used as a source of business finance: if a retailer cannot raise sufficient capital through normal channels he should reconsider his decision to open a shop or to expand.

Own profits. A most important source of capital has been kept till last: self-finance through reinvestment of some of the profits of a shop in improvements and expansion. By drawing out less to live on than has been earned, some finance becomes available and there are no problems of repayment. Until a sufficiently large sum is accumulated the money can be earning interest by being invested in, for example, a building society or a bank deposit account. No prudent businessman runs an unnecessarily large current account, on which no interest is earned. Instead, the money will be invested where it can be withdrawn easily when required and, subject to the degree of risk involved, will be earning as much interest as possible.

FINANCIAL PLANNING

Having reviewed the usual financial requirements and possible sources of finance, the retailer can match up one with the other for his own circumstances. The arrangement of this 'mixture' is worth careful thought and subsequent checking to make certain that the most advantageous solution has been found. Prime considerations include sufficient funds to maintain and build up day-to-day trading, obtaining all capital on the most advantageous terms, and maintaining maximum flexibility by not tying up too great a proportion of capital in fixed and intangible assets like property and goodwill.

Any asset securing a loan should be used to obtain the greatest amount possible. Any asset remaining unmortgaged is then free to provide finance for expansion if later required. It is not nearly as easy to obtain the equivalent sum by the apparent alternative of increasing the amounts advanced on assets already partly mortgaged.

Although it may be counsel of perfection, it is better for the retailer not to use the mortgage on his house or his life assurance policy for his business, particularly if this involves a fair degree of risk, as this could conceivably affect his family's future adversely. It is better to use these assets as the safety reserve already referred to, backing the few hundred pounds, or whatever is deemed advisable, for those occasions where a little extra ready cash, which can be repaid quickly, is required. This is not to say it is wrong to buy a property on mortgage – it is usually very wise financially and from every other viewpoint – but that it is preferable that it is not linked directly with the progress of the business.

The first year of trading is usually the most difficult: credit is harder to obtain as the retailer's skill is unproved; not all potential customers have yet become aware of the good service, advice, and range of goods available; and the retailer is not yet fully experienced in managing the particular shop. But trading improves with good management. Great reliance has to be placed on borrowed money at first but this considerable liability should be progressively reduced.

To borrow finance when it is not fully justified means tying up assets unnecessarily to provide security, or denying oneself a slice of future profits by having to pay interest; but not to increase capital when it is prudent is equally bad management. Capital should be increased when what it can earn is noticeably greater than its cost. So ruling rates of interest are not the determining factor: it may be wise to borrow at ten per cent per annum at one time and bad management to borrow at five per cent per annum at another. The net profit that the borrowed capital earns is what matters. But the prudent retailer always sees that he chooses the most advantageous source, remembering that each must be compared on the same basis.

When the retailer has matched costs of setting up a shop or branch with sources of finance available for his own circumstances and checked that his solution is the best, he knows roughly what size and position of shop he can afford. The procedure in finding and buying a shop is discussed in the next chapter.

3. Buying a Shop or Branch Premises

The intending or expanding retailer already knows roughly what price he can afford to pay for his shop and the type of goods it will sell. Probably he also has a preference for working in one particular town, or area of a city, so the choice is narrowed considerably. Where living accommodation is sought attached or close to the shop it is all the more important to find premises in a district in which the retailer feels he can happily invest his money and mortgage his assets. Especially for the intending retailer, the shop will be a place in which to enjoy life, not merely a location for earning enough to scrape a living.

When beginning the search for a specific shop, the first step is to list all the requirements, including the limits of the acceptable alternatives. Important points listed will be whether permission to trade in the desired range of products can be obtained; whether scope to earn a target profit exists; the limit of purchase price; the size of the shop and whether it will cover any special needs, such as extra large storage space; and the type of living accommodation, attached or located nearby. Except for scope to earn a target profit, which is dealt with throughout this book, answers to all these points are purely factual and can be found out easily.

The retailer is faced immediately with the choice of buying a shop already in his line of business, or empty premises, or a shop dealing in some other trade that would have to be changed. Individual circumstances determine whether the advantages outweigh the disadvantages of buying a going concern in the chosen trade, but it is important to bear in mind that the shop may be badly located, that it may have a bad name in the district, that some people in the neighbourhood may have the habit of deliberately not frequenting the shop, and that the purchaser may be saddled, at least for a time, with the seller's unwise choice of fittings and stock.

On the other hand, it may be possible to get a bargain because the seller, for personal reasons, is in a hurry to leave – but a convincing story is often told to make personal reasons appear to be the excuse for selling a badly located shop. If the seller is a good retailer he passes on the benefit of his experience about fittings and what to stock. Usually, there is less risk of failure for the new retailer because most of the existing customers are likely to continue to use the shop. But this last advantage may not be so great as it first appears: the changing pattern of retailing may be affecting the shop's trade. Ways to check on this point are dealt with later in this and the next two chapters.

If the purchaser concludes that the price asked for goodwill (it will be seen later how an accountant assesses the value) is reasonable he can make an offer. Even if his estimation of goodwill value is far below the stated price, he should still make his offer, just in case it is not refused. But rather than pay an unrealistic price, he may well do better to buy an empty shop, or a shop in another line of business with a low goodwill price, and change its trade. If it is hoped to change a shop's trade to one of those listed in the penultimate section of Chapter 16 it will be necessary to obtain planning permission. It can be noted at this stage also that before a retailer can sell certain merchandise or offer certain services, such as those listed in an earlier section of Chapter 16, he may be required to notify the appropriate authorities mentioned there.

But whether or not a going concern is bought, the procedure in purchase is very similar. In either case it is vital to have professional help from an accountant and a solicitor, and usually a surveyor also, as well as checking with one's own market research. Each professional man employed should act solely for the buyer: it never pays to use the same man as the seller. Such an outlay of a few pounds in fees is vastly offset by having experienced specialists working solely in one's own interest. Not only do they check the accuracy of many of the seller's statements, but they can often provide the ammunition for negotiating a reduction in various elements of the purchase price. Fees are often charged according to a fixed scale laid down by the appropriate professional body (see

Checklist 4. Going concern or not?

Consider:

A. Personal factors:

  1. Experienced and skilled in retailing?
  2. The trade and merchandise well known?
  3. Energetic and enthusiastic?

The stronger the 'yes' to each question the more likely are well-sited empty premises or a suitable shop for sale in another trade to be best.

B. Business factors:

  1. Decide best sites in the area suitable for desired trade.
  2. Vacant premises available in any of these positions?
  3. Any other premises available in another trade in these positions where goodwill asked is small?
  4. What going concerns are on offer?
  5. Are they about the right price, size, etc.?
  6. Do they offer scope for improvement in their trading prospects?
  7. Are they fairly priced?
  8. Is the extra potential from a well-sited shop for sale in another trade likely to be worth the lowest 'goodwill' price acceptable to seller?

Appendices 1 and 3). What various professional qualifications mean and how to find suitable professional men in any particular district are detailed in Appendix 1.

FINDING A SHOP

There are several possible ways of finding a shop in any given district. Most businesses are sold through estate agents or business transfer agents who know of most shops on the market within their area. Agents' addresses can be found from the classified telephone directory of the required area, or as detailed on page 265. Some agents specialize in certain trades rather than a particular locality: they usually advertise in the journals of the appropriate trades. Advertisements in the trade press announcing businesses for sale are common. The names, and sometimes publication dates and prices, of all trade papers can be obtained from most public libraries by consulting one of the reference books listed on page 278.

Bank managers sometimes know of businesses in their district that are about to change hands. If the retailer already runs an account with a bank which has a branch in the desired area the approach can be made through one's own bank manager. Local authorities are worth a visit when looking for premises as they usually own shops, especially on housing estates. It is also a good idea to contact private firms of estate developers if one of their estates falls within the retailer's selected area as they may have premises to offer.

The nationally circulating property journals, publications of the trade or local papers of the area are further possible sources of information. It is possible also to place one's own advertisement in such publications but sometimes this attracts failing businesses, or business transfer or estate agents of dubious character. If one is already in the desired trade, even if only temporarily to learn the business, it is worth while asking various suppliers of goods to that shop : they may know of another retailer who is thinking of moving, or quitting the trade.

THE PROSPECTUS

Whenever the search for a business is conducted through an estate agent or business transfer agent, the prospective buyer will be presented with sheets called prospectuses, containing details of available businesses. Prospectuses rarely give complete details. What is omitted can be almost as revealing as what is put in, as a prospectus is only an advertisement for the business, drawn up by a man experienced in selling businesses. He is paid by the seller and therefore does his best for the seller; he is interested in getting as high a price as possible because his fee is a percentage of this price. So any buyer must expect to find that the business for sale has been described in its most attractive light; in a prospectus, every item ought to be checked. Its only value is that it gives a rough indication of the business so that possible buyers can decide whether to consider it more closely.

Estate agents belonging to one of the recognized professional organizations mentioned in Appendix I have passed various examinations, gained practical experience over a minimum period, and conform to a basic code of professional conduct. There is still no powerful professional body of business transfer agents to enforce similar minimum standards.

It is incorrect to say that anyone not belonging to one of the bodies listed in Appendix 1 is not a suitable person with whom to deal, just as it is fallacious to say that all who do belong guarantee never to make a mistake and never to give less than brilliant service. However, starting or changing a business is fraught with sufficient risks without taking any unnecessarily, and the chances of good service and fair dealing are greater from members of professional bodies. Some unqualified agents are little more than glib salesmen; a few are rogues; many are perfectly reputable and honest men. The safest method is to use them, if at all, merely for bringing together seller and buyer, leaving all verification of accounts – which sometimes they offer to do – to a qualified accountant.

NEGOTIATING WITH THE SELLER

Whether a retailer finds a prospective shop through an estate agent, business transfer agent, or by other means, fullest details must be obtained. No potential buyer ever need be shy about asking questions: it is his right, and no good businessman would leave any doubt in his mind unanswered before committing himself to such a major purchase. Furthermore, a businesslike approach wins respect from the seller and his advisers. Small shops are declining more than ever in the face of big-business competition. To purchase a business in such circumstances without checking every important aspect that can be checked would be foolish.

Sellers, and even more so their agents, frequently try to rush a buyer into making a purchase by speaking of other interested parties who are in a hurry to buy. Often this is untrue, but if they exist, they too will want to investigate and check the details. The chance of being beaten in a race to buy is extremely slight compared with the risk of rushing into an unfavourable purchase. It is not suggested that the necessary information should not be gathered, and negotiations conducted, as quickly as possible, but that lack of time should never be used as an excuse for avoiding a full investigation. Buyers are usually in a strong position. They are not forced to buy any particular shop at any particular time, but the seller is normally in a hurry to sell.

A purchaser can do a little exploratory work before calling in his professional advisers, with the advantage of not incurring professional fees until he is somewhat more certain that the desired shop has been found. Appendix 2 shows a typical good prospectus for a shop: few are in fact so detailed. A potential purchaser should start by obtaining such information: he cannot make decisions without it.

If the shop has come to his notice through an estate agent or business transfer agent he will have to contact the agent because the precise address is normally withheld to ensure that the purchaser deals through the agent, who can then claim commission. This is of course reasonable if his efforts have brought buyer and seller together. In other cases, except where the business has been advertised under a box number, the contact can be made directly with the seller who can then be asked for full details.

An appointment should be made to meet the seller at the shop, preferably during trading hours. But this may be inconvenient for the seller, especially if he has no one to serve customers calling during the meeting. It is not important for the potential purchaser to visit during trading hours: if it seems later that this is the shop the purchaser is looking for, he will return, as the next chapter explains. It is preferable, however, to visit the shop during daylight hours so that the locality, the immediate competition, and the outside of the premises can be seen before the meeting.

A notebook or sheets of paper pinned together should be taken to the meeting, the first pages listing such information as contained in Appendix 2, leaving space for answers to any unknown points. This notebook will be produced very early in the meeting and the potential purchaser will quite unashamedly ask the seller to verify any information the buyer may have already and proceed to ask for the remaining answers, point by point. Having the questions ready and on paper saves time during the meeting and ensures that none is overlooked.

Further information gathered during the meeting thought worthy of note can be added, ensuring that each note is legible and gives full details. There is no reason at all to be embarrassed in taking notes of important matters, nor about the time it takes to write down details. This is the businesslike approach, certain to impress the seller and of great use to the potential buyer. It is more than embarrassing, and in fact worrying, to find on one's return home that certain parts of the notes are illegible or do not make sense because incomplete details were taken down. Buying a shop is an important and intricate affair: there is no need to be shy about asking questions, nor to worry about being thought foolish for doing so.

The meeting should take place in a cordial but businesslike atmosphere. Both men are present for a particular purpose and both want to get down to brass tacks, so it is unnecessary to spend too long on preliminary generalities. An observant and unhurried look at the premises, inside and outside, will be a great help in fixing details of layout in the purchaser's mind. Sketch plans can be drawn, if thought necessary. If the seller suggests the look-round immediately after the introduction, or if the light is failing, it can take place before the 'notebook' session; otherwise it is probably best done afterwards.

The look-round will have enabled the potential purchaser to estimate very roughly what sums he must allow for redecoration, the dilapidations reserve, and alterations to the premises before taking over, and an assurance should be obtained from the seller that the premises are in good structural condition. Any defects found on later inspection by the buyer's surveyor can then be used as bargaining counters to reduce the purchase price. The seller will also have been asked his intentions concerning the shop equipment and stock, and the possible buyer will have noted, probably mentally, which equipment he would like to take and which of that being offered would be of little value. It should be confirmed during this visit also, if required, whether any of the existing staff will be prepared to remain.

CHECKING PROFIT CLAIMS

The central problem at this stage is to obtain a rough check of the figure quoted for gross profit; expenses can be verified fairly easily, so once gross profit is known with reasonable accuracy, a good guide exists to real net profit. During the meeting the seller should be asked to justify his turnover and gross profit claims by listing major lines, grouped according to the approximate profit margin, and giving the approximate annual turnover of each of these lines, possibly expressed as a rough proportion of total turnover. These figures should be entered in the potential buyer's notebook and may look something like Table 9, assuming a confectionery, tobacconist, and newsagency shop with a claimed annual turnover of £30,000 per annum is under consideration.

Table 9. Calculating approximate gross profit of a shop

Major product groups	Approximate percentage of total turnover	Approximate percentage gross profit on selling price	Calculation (£)	Approximate gross profit per annum (£)
Cigarettes and tobacco	50	10	$\frac{50}{100} \times 30,000 \times \frac{10}{100}$	1,500
Papers and magazines	25	25	$\frac{25}{100} \times 30,000 \times \frac{25}{100}$	1,875
C'fectionery; ices; toys	15	20	$\frac{15}{100} \times 30,000 \times \frac{20}{100}$	900
Cards;books; stationery; sundries	10	35	$\frac{10}{100} \times 30,000 \times \frac{35}{100}$	1,050
Seller's claimed approximate total gross profit per year				£5,325

The seller should be able to give such approximate details from memory if he has a good grasp of his business. The potential buyer can then ask for these figures to be substantiated by spot checks. The total turnover figure can be verified from the seller's accounts prepared for the tax inspector, or if the visit takes place during the weeks between the end of the trading year and submission of accounts, the figure can be arrived at from the seller's takings book which he is certain to have kept for his own and his accountant's use. The possible buyer should check as far as possible that the takings book is genuine and not prepared specially for the sale.

Any comments by the seller to the effect that a percentage of the takings does not appear in the book to avoid tax should be completely ignored: this of course is illegal and may well be untrue; in any case it is not checkable. Non-disclosure by the seller to his accountant and inspector of taxes of some of the shop's takings would reduce the gross profit percentage on sales as well as affect other figures in the accounts of the business. If the seller claims to have taken sums out of the business regularly without informing his accountant, the purchaser should ask him directly whether the accounts are true or false: he will then be forced to say that they are not completely truthful, giving the purchaser all the more justification, and cause, for thorough investigation of the business.

If the meeting occurs towards the end of a trading year it would be wise to take the figure for the completed months of the current year, compare them with those for the same period of the previous year and adjust the figure for the whole of the previous year in the same ratio. For example, if turnover in the first nine months of the current year is £18,000 and was £20,000 during the same period in the previous year, with a final total for the previous year of £24,000, the calculation would be $\dfrac{£18,000 \times 24,000}{20,000} = £21,600$.

It will be noticed that an estimate of the last three months of the current year is not made by taking a proportion of the turnover during the earlier part of the current year: this is to allow for seasonal variations in trade. Neither are figures for the previous year alone taken, to allow for improvement or deterioration in business since then. Even so, the figure arrived at remains only an estimate of annual turnover.

The seller's figures should be substantiated by spot checks on some invoices or statements of account. It is clearly more important to pay most attention to those lines earning the major proportion of gross profit. It is usual for a few suppliers to handle the bulk of a shop's trade: examination of these figures alone often provides a sufficiently accurate check on proportion of total turnover and on margins.

The potential purchaser can then return home, arranging to contact the seller in due course if he is interested in taking the matter further. Once home, he can arrive at the estimated net profit of the present owner by deducting all expenses from the estimated gross profit.

ELUSIVE DETAILS

All expenses will have been listed in the notebook but four items may be missing unless the potential buyer has particularly asked the seller for details. The first is the extent to which the business has been charged with wages or salary for work done by the owner, and possibly his family also. All work performed on behalf of the business should be charged against gross profit at a reasonable rate. If, for example, the owner serves in the shop full-time, doing all his other duties in slack periods and when the shop is shut, it is fair to charge the business the equivalent cost of a full-time manager. If the wife serves, say, all day Saturdays, but is not otherwise employed, the business should be charged with the cost of a part-time helper of equivalent ability and honesty, whether or not the wife actually receives payment.

The second of the four items frequently missing from a retailer's accounts, and thus not appearing on any prospectus nor mentioned by the seller without prompting, is the cost of rent when the shopkeeper owns the freehold of the property. Freehold property is a capital asset and it is necessary for any retailer to charge his business, for accounting purposes, a fair rent for accommodation; either for the business premises alone, or, if living accommodation is being sold at the same time, for that also.

The third item not always found is interest on capital. To run any shop requires substantial capital: some of the profits from the trading must pay for the 'hire' of the capital employed. After all, if the retailer had no business of his own he could employ his capital to earn interest. He might leave it in the bank on deposit account, buy national savings certificates, invest in a good building society, or in other ways get several per cent per annum on his capital; but in fact he has invested it in an enterprise carrying a fair degree of risk. He should, therefore, charge the business with a rate of interest he could obtain, after tax, from investment elsewhere involving roughly the same degree of risk. This may be five per cent per annum, possibly much more. So that the business is not charged twice for use of the same capital, interest should not be charged on capital used to purchase freehold premises: 'hire' of this capital is accounted for by the charge of rent mentioned above.

Fourthly, depreciation on equipment should be charged against gross profit. The shop is a going concern and equipment has to be replaced periodically if it is to continue. Finance must be available for this at appropriate times, which means setting aside a proportion of the replacement cost so that it is spread evenly over the life of the equipment. Depreciation rates vary, but ten per cent per annum is a fair average figure for shop equipment, while twenty per cent per annum might be justified for certain contemporary equipment.

CONSIDERING THE PROPOSITION

The result of these calculations is that a fairly up-to-date approximate figure for annual net profit has been arrived at. Knowing this figure, having seen the premises, having had a glance at the neighbourhood, and also having obtained a vague idea about competitors, the potential purchaser can decide whether to take the matter further. So far he is completely uncommitted and no professional fees have been incurred. If the net profit seems a fair return for his expected efforts and everything else seems satisfactory he will then ask an accountant to help him investigate further. How to find an accountant is dealt with in Appendix 1; an indication of his fees is given on page 270. The relatively small cost of professional advice is now beginning to be incurred but there is a very long way to go yet before the retailer is committed to purchase any shop.

At this stage the retailer must consider as objectively as he can his own abilities as a businessman. If subsequent investigation reveals that although the purchase price of the shop is fair and everything else satisfactory, the business is already trading near the maximum possible for the district, an energetic retailer who has good grounds for considering he is above average as a shop-keeper may think twice about the purchase. No matter how hard he works he will be able to improve his business only marginally, while he will have paid the seller for having built up the trade. A business running below its potential offers such a man greater scope.

No available shop is likely to be perfect from every point of view. Making a wise purchase depends on a correct assessment of what is offered in relation to the price, and this involves knowledge of the general price level and peculiarities of a number of similar shops, and the advice of professional advisers. The final decision to purchase or not has always to be taken by the retailer himself.

ACCOUNTANT'S SERVICES

It is unnecessary to detail how an accountant goes about his investigations, but it can be seen from the following that the results he produces make his fee well earned. There is a big risk in buying a business without such information.

He will check the seller's claims concerning gross profit, each of the expenses, and the proportions of total turnover and individual margins of all major lines. The potential purchaser will have done this roughly already; the accountant will calculate accurately, and also check that nothing in the intending buyer's favour has been forgotten. He will then produce similar figures for each of the previous few years to establish the trends of turnover, margins, and expenses. It may be, for example, that turnover and net profits have been declining; or possibly turnover increasing but net profits falling. An accountant can suggest reasons for such changes and also give his opinion on whether the new owner could remedy them and, if so, by what methods. One point to bear in mind is the fluctuating, usually diminishing, value of the pound: if the purchasing power of a pound declines by three per cent in a year (such figures are computed annually by the government: Appendix 9 shows where to find the statistics) net profits must show a corresponding rise merely for the business not to be losing ground.

He will be able to explain also which major lines have grown in turnover and which have declined, thereby suggesting possible

good directions in which to encourage trade further should the
potential buyer purchase. If sales of major non-seasonal lines vary
greatly he will ask the seller for the reason, possibly uncovering
some disadvantages for anyone buying the shop. He will also demand explanations from the seller of major variations in wages and
in stocks. He will check whether any stock is mortgaged, whether
any negotiable instruments have been guaranteed by the seller's
company (if one has been formed), whether there is any tax liability owing from previous years, what capital allowance is made
by the inspector of taxes, and whether allowances for repairs to the
property have dropped recently, indicating that the seller has
been neglecting the premises.

Money may be owing to the business if the seller has allowed
credit to some customers. An accountant will ascertain the amount
and back up the purchaser in refusing to buy these book debts.
Instead, it should be agreed that the purchaser will collect them in
due course, either free or for a commission, and pay them to the
seller as collected.

The accountant can also make independent checks on the shopkeeper's reason for wanting to sell by asking creditors, suppliers,
bank, trade association, and any other possible sources. There is
added suspicion if a shop is being sold after only two or three
years: it suggests that having tried everything to increase trade,
the retailer is giving up as a bad job. It does not matter if the cause
of failure is lack of ability, but there may be a more fundamental
reason, such as poor position or increasingly stiff competition.

Where a going concern is being sold, the accountant can assess a
fair value for goodwill, which reflects many factors and varies
considerably. Goodwill depends mainly on the recent net profit
earned by the business but this must be modified by the degree to
which the shop has been run with maximum efficiency; the potential trade in the area, after allowances for probable changes in competition and population over the next few years; the amenity
value of the premises and location to the prospective buyer; and
the supply and demand of shops in the trade and of that type, in
that kind of location at the time that the purchase is being considered.

For a sound and conveniently run business, three years' net

profit before tax is often reasonable; for one not so sound or convenient, proportionately less. Using a super-profits basis, one of several possible bases, the importance can be seen of having all costs, including owner's wages, hypothetical rent if premises are freehold, interest on capital, and depreciation of equipment, charged against gross profit before arriving at net profit: net profit before these items might be £2,000 per annum, so that goodwill, assuming only three years' net profit is a fair price, might appear to be £6,000; but after charging them, true net profit may be only £500 per annum, giving a goodwill value, on precisely the same basis, of merely £1,500.

A retailer buying a similar business to one he has sold within a year previously is exempt from capital gains tax, but in all other circumstances this tax has to be paid on selling a shop. Any retailer moving to a new shop will want to take advantage of this fact.

There is always the possibility that the seller has been preparing his sale for a long time, for example, by ordering goods which he disposes of other than through his shop, so that it seems that the shop is selling more than it really is. The seller has to pay income tax on the profit he would have received if he had sold the goods normally, and he may even make a loss on resale: he hopes to recover these losses by inflating the price of goodwill.

It is not easy to overcome this deceit but an accountant may be able to detect such an occurrence through sudden and unexplained increases in purchases of certain lines a few months before the sale. If the retailer has been preparing his sale for a long time, increases may occur even more than a year before the shop is to be put on the market. In addition to the accountant's help, the intending purchaser may be able to uncover such falsehoods by roughly checking the true rate of sale of important lines during his market research investigations. These should be carried out after the accountant has produced his figures and a sum for goodwill, subject to solicitor's and surveyor's reports and the result of market research findings, has been agreed.

Market research will be carried out primarily to ascertain the state of competition and scope for development of trading. The results may alter considerably the value of the shop. Although these investigations should take place while solicitor and surveyor are working on the buyer's behalf, details have been left until the next chapter, so that they provide easy reference during actual market research.

SOLICITOR'S SERVICES

It is essential to employ a solicitor when buying a shop. How to find one is detailed in Appendix 1; an indication of his total charges is given on page 270. Solicitors' fees may be reduced if purchase of stock and equipment are dealt with separately from purchase of the rest of the business. Among his many duties are checks on the seller's right to sell, whether any restrictions exist on the use of the shop, whether the property is mortgaged or charged in any other way, and whether the local authority has any development plans for the area affecting the premises or possible future trade.

If the property is leasehold, he will explain implications of the various clauses in the lease and the position regarding dilapidations and compensation for any major improvements the purchaser may make. He will check that the landlord will accept the purchaser as a tenant, and that an extension of the lease will be granted if it has less than, say, ten years to run. This precaution is necessary to save the purchaser having to find a new shop after he has worked up his business, although a shopkeeper who has been a good tenant is protected by law and can be refused a new lease on only a few specified grounds, such as the landlord's need of the premises for his own business or residence being greater (as decided by the court), or that suitable alternative accommodation is available which will not diminish the goodwill value of the business. He will also say whether any premium being asked for the lease is reasonable. A premium is legal for business premises and is often required for a long lease of a good site, it being usual to write off its cost over the length of the lease as if an additional rental payment.

The solicitor will also draw up any partnership agreement which may be necessary, form a limited liability company if this is advantageous, and may advise on the choice of a trading name for the shop. He can also explain how a business in the joint names of husband and wife can save death duties. Where a going concern is being sold, he will insert in the agreement to purchase a clause to the effect that the seller must not set up business within, perhaps, two and a half miles of the shop during, say, two years from the date of sale, as a safeguard against the seller taking away some of the trade and attracting his former customers. He will also make arrangements for paying the deposit, making this 'subject to contract', and when it comes to the actual purchase of the shop, he will apportion the payments, such as for rates, made in advance or arrear of the date of sale.

SURVEYOR'S SERVICES

Unless the premises are being taken on a lease which is not fully repairing, it is worth employing a surveyor to report on the structural and decorative condition. How to find a suitably qualified man is detailed in Appendix 1; an indication of his fees is given on page 270. He will carry out his inspection and submit his report while the solicitor is dealing with the legal aspects of purchase. Many structural defects are not obvious, for example, dry rot and bad drains. The surveyor should be instructed to report thoroughly on every part of the premises, and to note against any item which in his opinion is not sound whether it requires urgent attention or if it could wait, and for how long, without running risks. He should also estimate against each unsound item the approximate cost of putting matters right.

A surveyor's report of defects can be used by the solicitor as a basis for negotiation to reduce the purchase price of the property or lease, especially if the seller assured the prospective buyer during his visit to the premises that all was in good condition. This applies to both freehold and leasehold property. Leaseholders usually must surrender the premises in the same state of repair and decoration at the end of the lease as that when it was first let. At the end of any lease a sum of money is usually paid by the retailer based on the report of the landlord's surveyor to cover dilapidations incurred from the start of the letting. Where a shop-keeper takes possession during the course of a lease he assumes

Checklist 5. Buying a shop

---

1. List requirements.
2. Start market research (see page 76).
3. Contact agents and other sources.
4. Investigate several possible shops to see general standards and current prices.
5. If a going concern is being bought and a likely business is offered, obtain fullest details, including rough check on profit claims.
6. If all appears correct and suitable, call in accountant.
7. If still satisfactory, instruct solicitor.
8. Obtain surveyor's report.
9. Value stock and equipment.
10. Take possession.

---

the responsibility for dilapidations incurred from the start of the original letting, therefore the purchase price should reflect the cost of repair and redecoration at the date of his purchase.

An estimate of any alterations and building work that would be necessary should also be obtained at the same time either from the surveyor or from a builder. Structural alterations should be supervised by a surveyor acting for the retailer, unless they are minor; if the property is leasehold, the landlord's consent to the work will be necessary.

A builder's estimate should not incur a fee as the builder hopes to do the work, although, if asked to estimate for more than one property because the first proposition fell through, he may not be happy about producing a second estimate for nothing. In any case, when a shop is finally bought and it requires more than very minor building alterations, at least two competing estimates should be obtained. Knowledge that a competitive quotation is being obtained is often sufficient to reduce the price; the builders should be made aware of competition but preferably not told which firm.

If the surveyor's report mentions doubtful or old wiring, or if substantial additions to the existing installation are required by the incoming retailer, it is worth obtaining a detailed report from an electrical contractor. Rewiring can be very expensive: its cost can be used by the solicitor as a further bargaining point against the purchase price. Similarly, the surveyor may suggest calling in a builder to help check the drains, for which it is usual to charge about a further five pounds.

STOCK VALUATION

When the decision to buy a particular shop has been made and the price and date for possession agreed, the only remaining point to consider is the value of the stock. As previously mentioned, the purchaser is often in a strong position and can dictate the terms on which he will buy the stock. He need only take what he wants and, sometimes, at less than cost price if any item is damaged, outdated, or not suitable for the shop. The minimum age of any item in stock is revealed by the latest date of invoices or delivery notes for those lines. The buyer should ascertain fairly early in his negotiations whether the seller is likely to insist on disposing of all the stock, at the price that he paid, together with the business. If he does, and the buyer wants the shop sufficiently to continue negotiations, he should instruct his accountant to adjust the valuation of goodwill accordingly. So long as the seller accepts the amount offered for goodwill the buyer will not have overpaid for the business, while the seller will be satisfied.

Valuation of stock may be performed by any of several methods. It is common in some trades to use a firm of valuers specializing in that trade; the same people often value the equipment also. If a village grocery changes hands, the buyer and seller themselves are more likely to assess the value, together with a representative from the local supplying wholesalers to advise them on fair prices. Estate agents and business transfer agents also sometimes offer to value stock for an additional fee though usually they are not the best people for the job because a competent valuer must have accurate up-to-date knowledge of all products in the trade and their current value – both the normal value and that depending on their condition and potential resale in that particular shop.

If the incoming retailer has the necessary trade experience and knowledge it may be best for stock to be valued by buyer and seller together and, if possible, in the presence of an impartial third party who knows the trade, and whose opinion would be helpful in any disagreement. Scale fees for professional valuation are sometimes unduly expensive in relation to the work involved: if a professional valuer is to be employed it may be possible to agree a smaller sum before he is given the job. The valuation is made on take-over day. An all-in price should not be agreed beforehand for 'all stock at time of change' as shelves previously laden may mysteriously empty on the actual day.

Although it may be possible for buyer and seller to agree between themselves on prices to be paid for stock and equipment – the latter being common – thereby saving valuation fees, it is important for the buyer's accountant to be informed of the proposed total prices before the buyer accepts irrevocably. Both sums will affect the incoming retailer's accounts, and inaccurate valuation could lead to the buyer paying tax rightfully due from the seller.

4. Market Research

Market research sounds intricate, highly specialized and expensive. For manufacturers it can be, but for the small retailer there is much that is common sense and that can be carried out by the intending or expanding shopkeeper himself, at virtually no more cost than a little of his time. The purposes of market research are:

1. To know the existing trade (if a going concern is being considered): who the customers are, where they come from, when they buy, what they buy, perhaps why they buy, and to estimate what more could be sold;
2. To assess the potential class and volume of trade, if it is intended to change the business of the shop or to check that assets and efforts are being used to the full;
3. To judge likely changes in the area itself, and in the income and tastes of potential customers;
4. To review existing competition and its probable future developments.

Thus market research is as relevant to practising retailers as to those considering a shop for the first time or opening a branch of a thriving business. Market research begins when a shop is first thought about: details come to light as the search for the right premises narrows down the choice; more information is disclosed when a potential shop is visited; further facts emerge from the investigations of one's professional advisers; but perhaps most data are collected once it seems probable that the right shop has been found and that agreement on terms is likely – but before any irrevocable step is taken in the purchase.

SOURCES OF INFORMATION

The order in which facts are obtained varies, but the following shows how much information is available by judicious probing:

Maps. If the selected district is not well known to the retailer, a study of a good street map will show not only streets but also bus routes, stations, open spaces, and so on.

A walk around a residential neighbourhood can be revealing. Some assessment of the residents can be obtained from the size, type, and age of the houses. Do they tend to sub-let? Are the houses kept in good, average, or bad repair? Are there many decorators' boards outside or does it seem to be a do-it-yourself district? Do the houses have gardens and, if so, are they well kept, well stocked or large? Do many houses have their own garages or are cars left in the streets overnight? Make, size, and age of cars are not the only visual indication of approximate incomes: other signs include prams, window curtains, and the kind of national newspapers that are read. The dress of residents may also be some guide and it may be possible to guess whether many wives go out to work.

Signs of growth. It is an asset for a shop to be located in a progressive community, as these tend to grow rapidly, thus increasing the number of potential customers. Some of the signs of a go-ahead area are steady increases in the number of banks, in transport facilities, and in the certified circulation of local newspapers.

Major shopping streets. Each major shopping street serving the area should be studied, observing the proportion of non-multiple shops and, if possible, whether they are long-established, but paying particular attention to shops selling goods or services contemplated by the retailer himself. Neighbouring competition is not necessarily harmful: similar shops often congregate to their mutual advantage. The street becomes known as a good place to buy certain goods and so draws customers from a wider radius than would the same shops sited some distance apart. But of course there must be a larger potential to tap. So long as adjacent competing shops offer slightly different goods, either in range or price, they are complementary: if a potential customer walks out of one shop without buying, there is every likelihood that he will buy from the neighbour.

Library research. A good public library, especially if one exists near the trading area under consideration, contains publications useful in assessing a district's potential. If, for example, the retailer's problem is knowing how much local families are likely to spend on the kind of goods he is thinking of selling, he can turn up the 'Income and expenditure analysis' section of the *Family Expenditure Survey*. This annually revised government publication includes regional and income-group variations. Guided by a trained librarian, other publications may help him define the district's effective trading area – often not the same as its administrative area – local communications, industries, and so on. The Board of Trade's census of distribution, carried out in detail every ten years and on a sample basis at each intervening five years, is likely to be available and may offer further useful guidance: some of its contents are referred to in Chapter 1 of this book.

Conversation in public houses, cafés, with estate agents and others may indirectly provide a clue about future trading prospects in a certain district by drawing the retailer's attention to the rumoured arrival of new multiple shops, moving of a street market, and so on. Of course, any such information must be checked from official sources before being considered seriously.

Local authorities can provide useful details of town planning schemes, already scheduled or proposed for some future period, which may affect the trade; for example, shopping centres may be moved, extensive residential areas rearranged, new housing or factory estates created. They may be planning to widen the streets, build new roads, or provide new car-parking facilities. Statistics about the local population and its rate of growth (or shrinkage) can be obtained, although this trend may not continue. The size of the local population within defined age groups is important in assessing the potential for certain trades. The local authority can usually provide the necessary estimate. At the local authority office it can also be ascertained whether a high or low proportion of the population depends on a small number of industries or firms, and if so, their general future prospects. Some indication of whether local industry or commerce is attracting work-people from far outside the proposed shop's normal trading area can also be obtained: it may be possible to turn such work-people into customers. Information may also be available about the movement of residential, industrial, or office districts, whether changes in bus routes or the siting of stops are contemplated, how early closing day is enforced, and whether many private schools exist in the district.

County council. Such information can be augmented by a visit to the town planning department of the county council, who initiate certain plans which may not come to light at local council offices.

ASSESSING COMPETITION

A list should be made of all shops likely to compete with the intending retailer, together with notes about the lines they cover, their general price range, and their specialities. Correct interpretation of such information depends on circumstances: a near-by shoe shop, for example, in the medium- to high-class range, may indicate that the retailer should aim at the medium- to low-price range so as not to compete directly. On the other hand, the type of district may not call for a shoe shop with a cheaper range but may provide greater scope for a second shop for medium- to high-price shoes. Such a shop can concentrate on carrying lines from different manufacturers from those of the competing shop, possibly provide a wider range for customers wanting less common sizes or styles, or perhaps might specialize in children's shoes.

Shops reflect the customers they serve, although it can be misleading to jump to too many conclusions. Many national chains of shops in several trades specialize in one price sector of their market so that their presence can suggest that the district contains a fair number of potential customers in the appropriate income group. The strength of the local Co-operative shops may also be some guide to the buying power of the district.

A worthwhile assessment of available trade depends on far more than simply estimating the number of customers in the area multiplied by their likely average expenditure each week or month, and dividing by the number of shops in the trade in the locality. There is likely to be wide variation between the pulling-power of one shop and another, due to the size, stock assortment, business acumen of the shopkeeper, and so on. The position will be further blurred by the extent to which local residents shop outside the district, whether custom can be built from shoppers living outside the immediate area, and the degree of competition between existing shops in the trade in the locality, which will vary from time to time and is likely to be affected by the arrival of the new or expansion-minded retailer. However, careful consideration of the information collected should provide a fairly clear picture of the trading potential.

EFFECTS OF LOCATION

Good positions for shops tend to be either in shopping centres, which naturally vary in importance, or a considerable distance away and close to the customers they serve. Those in between have a less secure trade because shopping centres attract more and more customers from increasingly large outlying areas to the detriment of these 'intermediate' shops, while bad weather may induce purchasers to use shops only very close to them or to postpone their shopping altogether until they can travel to the main shopping centre. Shops close to their customers are normally in trades selling frequently needed goods, often required at short notice; for example, confectioners, newsagents, bakers, and grocers. For any of these trades, a retailer can consider premises away from a shopping centre. Jewellers, wool shops, and similar outlets are better placed in a shopping centre – their goods are not often needed and they must depend on a clientèle from a wider area.

Some shops sell mainly 'impulse' lines, commodities bought on the spur of the moment simply because the purchaser happened to see them or an advertisement displayed in the shop window.

Cigarettes and confectionery are prime examples. Other shops, however, are rarely entered without the customer having first decided on a visit. Many trades fall into an intermediate category because they attract into the shop most passers-by on some occasions, for example, clothing stores, or a percentage of the passers-by regularly, as with ironmongers selling do-it-yourself lines. Clearly, the position of a shop may be excellent for one trade and hopeless for another, quite independently of competition.

Similarly, some trades can sell goods without delaying the purchaser: it takes only a moment to enter a shop and to ask for, or select for oneself, a newspaper, a loaf of bread, or a packet of a well-known branded food. Only an unwise shopper would purchase a bedroom suite in a hurry. Nor is it merely a matter of price: a relatively cheap pair of shoes still needs to be tried on even if the type, colour, and other details are already decided on. So some trades must expect to attract customers only when they are out shopping; others can try to sell when people happen to be passing, sometimes even if they are in a hurry.

Thus in considering the site of a shop, attention must be paid to pedestrian routes and probable purpose of passers-by. The direction or flow of pedestrian traffic can be judged by the location of residential and working districts, shopping centres, transport routes, and so on. Widths of street are not a good guide.

In most streets, one pavement collects more people than the other, possibly because that side lies on the more direct route or because it receives more sun. Naturally, the busier side is the best for a shop; displays can be seen and potential customers are not faced with the trouble of having to cross the road. Thus, shops collect on this side, these attract more shops which, in turn, bring more people.

The busiest pavement of a shopping centre often changes to the opposite side of the road at a certain point. Sometimes there are obvious reasons, such as a church or another non-trading building weakening the appeal to shoppers, but often the cause appears inexplicable. All chain stores are aware of the importance of being on the better side, so their presence is frequently the best indicator of it. But chain stores are sometimes found on the quieter side: occasionally their property specialists make mistakes, sometimes they purchase sites on both sides of a street to prepare for subsequent growth on either side, and sometimes their market research specialists decide that there is scope for a branch even on the quieter side of the street if no sites are available on the better side.

EXCEPTIONAL SITES

Good positions occur wherever potential customers are forced to wait, as at bus stops. They then have time to buy all quick-service goods and also tend to patronize other trades, for example, dry cleaners. Shoppers also tend to congregate at post offices, variety chain stores, and other good shops selling general merchandise. Proximity to stations, street markets and pedestrian crossings is also usually beneficial, but it has to be borne in mind that these and bus stops may be moved or done away with altogether over the years.

Corner shops have the advantage of tapping two streams of pedestrians, provided that the side street is used to some extent, as well as having more window display space and, frequently, larger floor area. But these advantages may not be in proportion to the extra cost in rent and upkeep. Narrow pavements outside a shop tend to be a disadvantage, as potential customers attracted by an item in the window may be thrust along by the passing crowd or may be splashed by passing traffic on wet days.

Neighbouring shops can be a guide to potential trade. Shops offering personal service and considerable advice frequently do well even close to competing shops if these use an impersonal self-service system; but a florist is unlikely to succeed next to a fish fryer's where the constant smell of fish overpowers the delicate scents of flowers; a garage may make a noisy and fume-laden associate of a high-class restaurant, yet it can be a splendid partner for a snack-bar. Clearly, much depends on circumstances.

ACCESSIBILITY

Every well-sited shop should be easily accessible for its potential customers. For the back-street shop this may mean nothing more than being on a busy pavement where people on their way to and

from work or shopping centre can conveniently make purchases.
But shops selling, for example, pets or musical instruments, and
drawing customers from a wide area, should have premises near
good transport facilities, and should be so placed that customers
will see and remember the shop for eventual purchases.

As an increasing number of customers use cars for shopping,
accessibility, therefore, also means being near convenient parking
spaces. Similarly, a one-way street may be a drawback for a site:
it makes it more difficult to reach the shop and perhaps means that
customers pass by only on their way to work in the morning because they return by another one-way street in the evening.

UNDER-EXPLOITED POTENTIAL

The potential of a shop may be under-exploited because of a
shabby exterior and dingy interior. The incoming retailer should
consider how much extra trade he may be able to attract by bright-
ening up the premises. Too much cannot be learnt from a casual
look at a shop from the street: by being in a good position, stocking
the right lines, and offering good service, a depressing shop may do
an excellent trade, even if not the maximum possible.

A very rough idea of the amount of business being done by the
shop under consideration can be obtained by comparing the number of customers who enter with the numbers entering near-by
competitors. Some multiples and similar big competitors employ
men to collect such statistics over a period of time, in bad weather
as well as good. The observers sometimes use a counting device
kept in their pockets. Far more sophisticated analyses are also possible but such methods are impractical for the small retailer: they
take time and the periods of sampling chosen by the shopkeeper
may not be comparable or representative. There are other obstacles
also: for example, the inside of a shop is not always visible from
the street so it is difficult to tell whether a customer has made a
purchase.

It may be possible, however, to get a general idea of a small
shop's custom by observing it at different periods on different
days. It can then be conjectured whether those entering are
prosperous, come out with purchases, are probably held up for

service by other customers and whether the majority are shopping or on their way to work, home, entertainment, and so on.

A single well-prepared visit to see inside a shop, whether to consider the premises for purchase or to get some idea of a competitor, can reveal a good deal. A retailer would not normally make a spying visit to a shop he is considering buying because he may be recognized when he subsequently introduces himself to the seller: his first 'official' visit replaces such a call.

On entering a shop, the buyer's first impression is what any normal customer first receives. The interior should be clean, bright, convenient for movement, and have a good range of stock on show; but a shop below this standard can still be a good investment, especially if its efficiency and appearance are improved after purchase. It is better to follow a customer entering the shop; unless more than one person is behind the counter, it gives the buyer time to observe the layout and condition of the interior and to see whether the retailer is helpful and efficient in dealing with customers.

The retailer contemplating the purchase of a shop will have a better idea of what are the signs of progressive retail management by the time he has read this book. Truly scientific market research is beyond the financial reach of individual small shopkeepers but, luckily, business accounts tell most of the story if they are properly interpreted.

TRIAL PERIOD

Even so, wherever possible, and towards the end of negotiations, an intending purchaser should ask to be allowed to stand behind the counter for a week without incurring any obligation to purchase the business. During that week, it can be seen whether total sales, verified by the intending purchaser's eyes, agree with the figures indicated by the accounts: unexplained discrepancies invite special scrutiny by the accountant. Above all, the week's free trial reveals the potential of the business. If the seller is surly to customers, frequently has to say he is out of stock or does not handle requested items, never tries to make a substitute sale, is lax in arranging attractive displays in shop and window, and so on,

Checklist 6. Market research pointers

1. General arrangement of district.
2. Town-planning changes.
3. Population changes.
4. Degree of district's prosperity.
5. Sources of district's prosperity.
6. Growth signs.
7. Merchandise to be sold.
8. Existing competition.
9. Likely competition, including from a distance.
10. Neighbouring shops.
11. Location of shop in relation to customers.
12. Accessibility.
13. A busy pavement.
14. Reasons for passers-by.
15. Special site advantages (bus stop, street corner, etc.).
16. Alterations in bus and other traffic patterns.
17. Reasons for sale of premises.
18. Under-exploited potential.
19. Trial period available?

the prospective purchaser can see that with good management he may be able to increase considerably the trade and profitability of the business. A purchase on the basis of the true value of the seller's goodwill will then be a sound investment. The trial period will also enable the prospective purchaser to confirm many of his market research findings, such as type of customer and circumstances in which they enter the shop.

VACANT PREMISES

Elementary market research may help an intending retailer to find suitable premises which do not require a payment for goodwill by buying an empty shop or changing a shop's trade. This can be an attractive way to reduce the capital required to start a business or open a branch, although it usually involves a greater risk. Although the purchaser intends to change the trade of a going concern, it may still be necessary to pay the seller a sum which he would call goodwill, but which is really a reflection of the buyer's value of the location. This is uneconomic unless there is no likelihood of obtaining other reasonable premises in the required district, and even then only if the potential profit from the new trade seems certain to cover the extra cost in purchase.

Much of what has been said concerning market research in buying a going concern applies to an empty shop. It is prudent, for example, to find out why it is empty and how often it has changed hands in recent years: the answer may indicate that the site is hopeless, and not a reflection of any retailer's efficiency.

OPENING A BRANCH

Such market research often pays off for an established retailer also: it points the way to greater exploitation of the shop's potential, while for the expansion-minded trader it can determine whether it is better to open a branch instead of extending an existing shop. By being in a different area a branch increases the number of customers, and branch overheads may be lower. Against this, there is less space for really comprehensive displays, loss of opportunities to add immediately to customers' purchases, and perhaps difficulties of supervision.

RESULTS OF RESEARCH

Important conclusions emerge from the use of market research. Foremost, the rent or freehold price of a property is not a good measure of its value to any specific retailer. Expensive premises may bring in treble the net profit of a shop costing half that rental or price. Any retailer wants to make the best use of his time, effort, and capital, so the dearer of the two premises in this example is obviously the better proposition if the finance can be raised. As previously mentioned, some trades demand main-street sites: to try to save money by opening back-street premises is folly. In other instances market research may reveal that it is unnecessary to rent or buy expensive premises, the same volume of trade being available at lower cost in a near-by location.

The second point to note is that existing trade volume is not necessarily a good guide to a shop's future trade. Existing management may be missing opportunities; stiff competition may open up; the very nature of many trades – food shops selling cosmetics, and bookshops selling gramophone records, for example – is now changing. The value of premises, and goodwill if a going concern is being considered, must be judged by present and future prospects, not the past.

Market research requires a whole district to be considered: as the intending retailer usually knows in which district he wishes to trade, there is little extra effort involved even if several near-by premises have to be considered. Comparisons may in any case be helpful in choosing the best premises, having regard to business potential; cost in rent or purchase price, and perhaps building work; size and shape of premises, and so on. A retailer gives himself the best chance of success if he carries out some market research and also pays attention to advice from his accountant, solicitor, and surveyor. The next chapter, concerning competitors, is also important when considering the true value of premises and goodwill.

5. Competitors

It is obvious that great changes are taking place in retailing. Present trends and probable future patterns must be considered if the retailer is to see where he fits in. Without this knowledge he cannot fully exploit his own investment in effort and finance.

REASONS FOR CURRENT RETAILING TRENDS

High on the list of reasons for the changing pattern is the public's increased purchasing power with an even greater potential increase. This has created and attracted heavily financed concerns who can afford to employ the best brains in the many specialist skills associated with retailing: merchandise buying, sales promotion, market research, property, and so on. Better management and changed conditions have revealed scope for improvement in methods, bringing greater efficiency, for example, by limiting the range and depth of stocks inside shops and by forming voluntary groups and chains for obtaining them.

High cost and the scarcity of sales people have speeded up the introduction of self service and self selection. This in turn has enhanced the importance of attractive and practical packaging, increased the need for pre-packaging goods formerly sold to retailers in bulk, and allowed manufacturers to take a more direct hand in promoting their products by powerful advertising in its many forms.

The changing way of life of customers also modifies retailing. More women at work increases the need for shops to be open beyond formerly accepted business hours; the greater complexity of products and higher standards of customers' education give added appeal to consumer-advice bodies; and the use of cars for shopping entails the provision of parking space, but means that more can be bought at once, and also reduces the need for the retailer to deliver.

Above all, the former major classification of shops by their trades – fruiterer, confectioner, stationer, and so on – is breaking down and, in cases where retailers' advice on products is not essential, is re-forming into retail outlets grouped, primarily, according to frequency of need. Thus the true supermarket – that is, premises over 2,000 square feet, incorporating self-service principles, with merchandise cutting across conventional trade classifications, and utilizing all modern selling methods – caters not merely for groceries, but also meat, vegetables, and most other items which housewives need on a day-to-day, or not more than a week-to-week basis: for example, cosmetics, tea-towels, kitchen utensils, cigarettes, electric lamps and toys. This trend is being intensified by reducing the need for retailers' advice about products, for example, by selling branded fruit with a guaranteed standard of quality.

Compensating for falling margins on food lines due to competition, supermarkets and other multiples perpetually widen their range of goods to capture lines with profitable mark-ups from other trades. Except for small shops in residential areas serving 'emergency' and 'convenience' needs – whose future is secure while they are run efficiently – small independent retailers are being left with the slower-moving lines and products about which customers need advice from the retailer.

FORMS OF COMPETING SHOP ORGANIZATION

All types of retail stores in the same trade and locality are competing against each other, but in addition all trades are courting the same money from each customer. If the housewife is enticed into buying an extra cake at the multiple grocer's, she may cut down on the ice-cream from the confectioner; if her husband buys a new radio he will have less to spend on a new suit. Money spent on holidays abroad may mean that carpeting the home will have to wait another year. It is therefore worth looking at methods adopted by efficient retailers in all trades: they all compete indirectly if not directly.

Multiples are often the closest rivals of small independent shops. The term is commonly used for an organization of ten or more shops selling similar goods; sometimes there are over 300 shops in a single multiple chain, occasionally over a thousand. Each shop sells a standard range of lines, shopfronts look alike and sometimes interiors also. Frequently they are no larger than small independent shops and the branch manager is usually a local man, knowing local preferences. Although occasionally hampered by a restricted range of goods, he is relieved of many or all specialist activities by the appropriate departments of the chain – buying, accounting, property, and so on – and his company has large finances, expertly administered. This includes bulk-buying on behalf of all shops in the chain, concentration on a relatively limited number of lines – all quick-moving and sometimes made by a manufacturing subsidiary of the chain – and standardization of everything from paperwork procedures to the size of doormats. Retailing has been made highly profitable by these concerns, helped by aiming their products largely at the working and lower-middle classes who have benefited most from post-war prosperity and the redistribution of incomes. There is at least one major multiple chain in almost every trade, and frequently several.

Supermarket chains are usually merely one aspect of multiple chains, though they are sometimes owned by one of the other forms of retailing organization, such as a department store or Co-operative Society. Although most accentuate cut prices, many try to cultivate an air of luxury at the same time – in their decoration, by providing coffee bars, pram parks, kennels for 'parking' dogs immediately outside the premises, and so on. Like all other kinds of shop, supermarkets grade their 'image' and the services they provide to the section of the public they seek to attract.

Variety chains are similar to multiples except that they invariably expect customers to select their own goods from display counters or racks, offer no salesmanship though sometimes a little basic advice, provide no credit or delivery, stock goods cutting across conventional trade classifications, are larger than most multiples, shop for shop, and tend to deal in the lower or moderate price ranges of the types of goods stocked. To the extent that some department stores and multiples now adopt many or all of these methods, the separate category of variety chain is largely academic, most concerns of this type being akin to some department stores aiming at the popular market, or to larger supermarkets.

Department stores, themselves often part of a department store chain, tend to be large, rather luxurious buildings on several floors, selling a wide range of merchandise grouped logically in departments, each often larger than an independent retailer's shop. Most department stores carry a fairly wide and deep range of many goods and specialize in certain merchandise, such as women's clothing and textiles. They tend to be located only in central areas of important towns. Formerly, they dealt largely in the higher-priced ranges but with their clientèle becoming relatively poorer some copied multiples in limiting merchandise ranges and lowering the price range. Some of these are partly returning to their former policy, realizing that they cannot compete on the multiples' home ground, in part because they cannot be situated conveniently in local shopping centres and partly because it is becoming increasingly recognized that there is a sizeable clientèle wanting and prepared to pay for special services: good selections of merchandise, personal attention, and delivery. To this extent department stores are becoming close competitors of small independent shops.

Co-operative shops are in fact multiples. They vary greatly in size, as do multiples, have their own wholesale organization and make many of their own products. They tend to deal in the lower price ranges of their merchandise groups and, to keep down costs, offer only a minimum of service, passing on the savings as a rebate or dividend to registered customers.

Discount stores on the U.S. pattern – where predominantly high-value items such as refrigerators can be bought at substantial discounts from what is basically a self-service warehouse, the customer providing his own transport – are still uncommon in this country, although many ordinary shops use the term to indicate that their prices are competitive or a little below average.

With the ending of resale price maintenance, this form of retailing is likely to grow, though it may sometimes take the less extreme form of purchasing through normal shops, who forewarn their supplier's warehouse that one of their customers is about to call in to collect. The retailer is then invoiced in the usual manner at the normal time, the customer paying the retailer cash at time of purchase, less a discount representing much of the retailer's usual margin.

Independent shopkeepers still account for more trade than all other forms of organization combined. The term is officially used to denote organizations of not more than nine shops, though the vast majority of independent retailers have only one shop. Although the number of independent shops has declined in recent years, the small retailer will always have a future because he has assets which his large competitors do not have and can never possess. He can thrive where turnover is too small for competing kinds of shop, he can stock more unusual lines if there is sufficient demand – which often need not be at all large – and he can offer detailed advice to individual customers, thereby gaining and keeping their custom. Unlike his larger rivals, he is in constant direct touch with his customers and his stock can be flexibly sensitive to the needs of his neighbourhood. He can offer a truly personal service, and where he employs assistants he is not too big an organization to ensure that their service is also first-rate.

While independent shopkeepers inevitably find it difficult to compete with larger retailers on their rivals' own ground, they can normally still make a reasonable living by good management and exploiting the advantages of their form of trading. They are often able to compete directly on price, but even on those occasions when this is not possible, they can usually compete very effectively through a high standard of service. Provision of services not offered by competitors also makes it more difficult for customers to compare competing prices directly.

NON-SHOP RETAILING

Street barrows vary considerably. Those with a regular site dealing fairly with customers can be real competition for shopkeepers, especially fruit, vegetable, or flower vendors. Although there is usually little choice within their ranges, individual barrows vary from poor quality merchandise to the highest. Overheads being very low, barrow owners can undercut shopkeepers' prices for truly equivalent merchandise.

Mail order has grown rapidly in recent years. The selling is performed by advertisements in the press, through people selling for a small commission to their acquaintances and neighbours, or by catalogues sent through the post. As warehouses and offices are situated in low-rent areas and there is no need of a sales staff, overheads are low. Prices, therefore, are often very keen. Credit terms are very common. Several multiple-shop and department-store organizations, seeing the growth of importance in mail-order trading, also operate their own mail-order companies.

House-to-house trading has also grown markedly in recent years. Much of this involves the 'tallyman' system, where the retailer calls weekly with a selection of lines, which are usually offered on credit and paid for in regular instalments over the following weeks.

Mobile shops are used either to trade house-to-house or to call regularly at fixed points on outlying housing estates, etc. The term is sometimes used to denote only vehicles on which goods are displayed for sale, as is common for fruit and vegetables, or where the retailer serves from inside the van, as for ice cream, or directly beside it, as for paraffin. At other times the term also covers vehicles used to make house-to-house doorstep selling more practical.

'*Party selling*' is used by some manufacturers to bypass shops, for example for some cosmetics and plastic housewares. A local agent is appointed, often a housewife, who invites friends and acquaintances to coffee parties or similar gatherings at her home, at which the range of products are introduced and sold, ostensibly as an incidental to the party. The agent receives a commission on sales. This is not very different from one method of mail-order selling, where the catalogue rather than the goods is the focus of salesmanship. It also has affinities with the practice of selling group travel, group theatre bookings, and life assurance to friends.

Club purchasing may also bypass shops if the volume of orders permits supply at trade terms directly from a wholesaler or manufacturer. Even where the purchases are made through a shop, substantial discounts are often demanded. Any sizeable group of people may band together to form the club, which usually already exists for another purpose – such as gardening, sports, or motoring. Trades unions and similar organizations often offer members a similar facility, which has its counterparts in organizations for shopkeepers, where insurance and other items are often offered to members at a discount. Some large companies arrange with retailers near their works or offices that cooperating shops will be recommended to employees, who, on production of the company's identity card, receive a special discount.

Vending machines also frequently divert trade from shops, by being placed in factory and office canteens, as well as a variety of other locations. A few are placed by retailers outside their own shops to offer a round-the-clock service to customers, and this facility is their greatest advantage to the shopkeeper. The reduction in staff costs is normally more than offset by the cost of the machine and prevalent vandalism, while problems of pricing for coins, multiplicity of pack sizes, and their generally inhuman air has stopped them being of much help to retailers.

RETAILING ON THE MOVE

The former distinction between multiples, department stores, and variety chains is tending to be blurred as each adopts similar retailing techniques and traditional trade-group barriers are broken down. Supermarkets and some other multiples are in many ways similar to variety chains, even in the type of merchandise they sell. Department stores, however, while often including a supermarket, still keep most merchandise grouped in watertight compartments, even if they are all under the same roof. But all types of large-scale retailers have in common board-room tacticians to plan out retailing battles. They constantly strive for more efficient methods, supported by highly paid, highly trained, skilful specialists.

Retailing is becoming more and more a matter of property, not only in deciding where a shop shall be located but also in the use of space inside. Some department stores rent out whole departments to multiples who provide their own merchandise as well as staff, because the store does not wish to deal in such products though it feels that such a department helps to attract customers to other sections. Often there is nothing to indicate to customers that the particular department is not operated by the store itself. On a smaller scale, the same occurs in supermarkets and smaller shops where 'rack jobbers' rent shelves.

Shelf space is apportioned in many large shops in ratio to sales volume. Target turnover per square foot of shop floor is calculated; lines not reaching the target after a trial are discarded for something better. Profitability is increased by raising turn-over targets or widening profit margins through suppliers' special discounts – often both. Symptomatic of this continued effort to move ever larger volumes of profitable goods through a limited shop area are the increasing number of special promotions and cutting selected prices as loss leaders – that is, lines sold temporarily below normal retail prices to attract customers, margins on other lines being adjusted upwards to compensate.

Other changes taking place include experiments in operating out-of-town shopping centres, where rents and rates are cheap, and there is sufficient space to offer customers good parking facilities. Also, some Co-operative shops offer 'dividend stamps', a more flexible and administratively easier system than the traditional year-end dividend payment. Use of trading stamps has grown. As stamp schemes usually cost the retailer about $2\frac{1}{4}$ per cent on his total turnover they need to raise sales considerably if they are to be profitable. The necessary increase in business to cover the cost of stamps depends also on each shop's gross margin and whether further costs arise in handling the extra trading and the stamps themselves. Selective and special promotions usually bring better results at lower cost and are easily adjusted to daily conditions.

Large retailers and voluntary chains of small shopkeepers are increasingly selling goods under their own brand names, often products made by manufacturers who distribute identical lines in large quantities under the manufacturer's name. These 'private label' brands of retailers are usually fast-selling lines where the large retailing organization or voluntary chain can promote sales at negligible cost. This makes available what is normally required to cover the manufacturer's marketing costs to provide an extra margin for the retailer while still offering big price reductions – sometimes over 20 per cent – for the shopper. Sales promotion for 'own brands' often publicizes the retailing chain as a whole rather than specific lines. The success of this policy is demonstrated by some lines sold under private-label brands having a bigger national sale than any other, including manufacturers', brands. The practice of some large retailing chains having products made to their own specification is also continuing.

The major retailers of the country are becoming increasingly concerned with functions other than pure retailing, such as wholesaling, property, and hire-purchase finance. Some retail chains have important lines made by their own manufacturing subsidiaries, to reduce costs and guarantee supplies. In addition, some manufacturers are obtaining control of retailing establishments to guarantee their sales outlets and fully integrate all processes from initial stages of production to purchase by the consumer.

PROBABLE FUTURE CHANGES

It seems logical to expect the strengthening of certain developments in the coming years. For example, display and special promotion in shops are taking on a greater importance and many manufacturers use mobile teams of merchandisers, sometimes quite distinct from their normal sales force, to promote their products in this way. This trend, together with the retailing practice of placing associated lines near each other – the breakdown of conventional trade-group barriers brings many extra opportunities – points to the increasing use of joint promotions by manufacturers of complementary products, or by retailer and manufacturer, or by retailer and wholesaler. The emphasis on the importance of display is leading to a wider range of display fittings, some available on hire.

Elimination of double handling of goods in factories is not new yet scope still exists in retailing for greater efficiency in this respect. Instead of larger products such as furniture being delivered to a shop and subsequently rehandled for delivery to the customer, it is becoming a common practice to make deliveries direct to the customer from the warehouse, the products in shops being merely samples for display and customer selection.

Another form of selling by sample that has evoked experiments is fitting out a self-service grocery shop with only one pack of each line available on show, beneath which is a code-punched stack of tabulator cards. Taking one card for each pack required, the customer presents her selection to the tabulator operator at the check-out, whose machine produces an itemized printed bill almost at once. This is passed to the adjoining warehouse where the goods are mechanically selected from store and quickly packed with the bill, while the bill's total is being paid to the tabulator operator. For the retailer, this system offers big savings in floor space, handling of goods, staff, and pilfering, while stocks can also be smaller and there is less paper work. However, early experiments have not been an unqualified success.

It may become economic to retail smaller items without shops if they are required frequently enough or in sufficient quantities – as is likely for many lines of pre-packed branded food and certain other articles. It seems pointless to incur all the expenses of normal retailing, including the extra handling, when merchandise can be delivered directly from the warehouse to the customer, who telephones the order. Free delivery is a big incentive to customers; the cost to the retailer may be offset by the difference in overheads between an out-of-town warehouse and an elaborate main-street shop. Success of such a system depends on being able to operate on a sufficiently large scale within a fairly compact area, which implies customers being city dwellers, with a high proportion of telephones.

Retailing is becoming more mechanized to reduce running costs, though this involves higher initial capital investment. One example of mechanization is use of computers, used by larger retailing organizations for stock control and re-ordering calculations, sales forecasting, stock rationalization and payroll calculations. Computers have the advantage over humans in such work because they calculate so rapidly. Their benefits are likely to be reaped in time by smaller retailers banding together – for example through trade associations or voluntary buying chains – to hire the services of computer bureaux.

Over recent years the increase in the amount of money people have been able to spend on non-essentials has often been used for improving the home: purchasing television sets, furniture, fabrics, and decorating materials. With several domestic electrical appliances now in most homes, repair and regular maintenance of all by the same firm of servicing engineers working on long-term contracts seems likely. Shorter working hours will allow more time, and therefore money, for leisure activities such as travel and cultural and sporting pursuits. This suggests not only the prospect of relatively more rapid growth in trades catering for pastimes, even indirectly as in the provision of sports and casual clothes, but also that centres for leisure-time activities are likely to attract shops catering for the associated products and services, such as cafés, sports equipment, and, possibly, automatic laundries.

Because good shops are complementary, comprehensive shopping centres in varying scale tend to develop. Just as the main shopping streets today draw away trade from shops in less prosperous locations, so customers may come to expect complete shopping centres under cover, at controlled temperature, with adequate car-parking facilities, and children's supervised playgrounds adjoining the shopping area. Such facilities seem likely to be produced by carefully planned, often multi-storeyed, shopping centres that are free from road traffic. The small independent retailer is at a disadvantage in competing for such good positions: rents are high, requiring large trading volume, considerable financial backing, and efficiencies associated with large-scale enterprise to make them profitable.

CAR PARKING

Car parking, usually difficult in main shopping centres where so many large shops are located, provides the small retailer with a

Checklist 7. Advantages of the independent retailer

1. Can thrive on smaller potential than most chain stores.
2. Flexible range of merchandise through direct contact with customers and knowledge of the locality.
3. Wider range of products on offer.
4. Smooth-running enterprise: business not too big for single man to control.
5. Sound advice freely available to customers.
6. Personal touch throughout.
7. Can ensure above-average-quality assistants.
8. Extra facilities for customers possible, including flexible hours.
9. Customer usually feels more welcome, thus more important.
10. Most customers like being served, known, or acknowledged by 'the boss' and feel more secure in their purchases because he will not be moved to another shop by an impersonal head office.

valuable opportunity. There may be space outside his shop for customers' cars, in which case it is worth mentioning this in any advertising or by proclaiming it on a notice in the window along the general lines of 'Why give yourself all the trouble of traffic jams and finding parking space in the High Street when you get the same goods and better service here with complete convenience?' If there is no space for cars outside the shop it may be possible to arrange to use some near by, for example in a forecourt. If so, a large notice should be put up outside the shop and by the car park saying that these facilities are available and free to customers.

It is worth encouraging customers with cars because they tend to buy more at a time, purchasing their second-choice brands if first choices are not available, for example, rather than make an extra stop at another shop. Time is becoming increasingly important to shoppers; those with cars and able to carry away goods easily tend to shop less often and to buy for a longer period, especially if they have storage space, refrigerator, etc., at home. This promotes marginally greater consumption, while their running a car may present the retailer with opportunities to sell additional lines associated with motoring. The number of women shopping by car increases every year; more and more are coming to expect the amenity of convenient parking facilities.

OPENING HOURS

It is common sense to open the shop at the most beneficial times. Big shops are inflexible and have staff problems: the small man can do almost as he pleases. Most shops have an early closing day and in districts where the same day applies to the majority of shops it may be a bad time to open, because few customers go shopping when almost all shops are closed. On the other hand, such an occasion may be an excellent time to open, especially if goods sold have an 'emergency' value such as bread. The local authority formerly fixed the early closing day and either applied it to all shops or allocated various days to different shops according to their trade. Now, under the Shops (Early Closing Day) Act, the retailer can choose his own half day. Some retailers have applied to their local authority to remain open six days a week: if the majority of retailers of that class of shop in the area wish to stay open the local authority is forced to permit it.

Flexibility in opening hours also exists for evening trading: shops may stay open until 8 p.m. on normal evenings and 9 p.m. on one late night each week. Sunday trading is also permitted for a considerable range of products, while retailers of certain other articles at holiday resorts have further exemption from the general no-Sunday-trading rule.

Lengthy permitted opening hours are not necessarily long working hours. They enable a retailer to choose the most advantageous times to receive customers, without necessarily increasing the total number of hours. If it is preferred to keep open longer, it may be possible to do so without increasing the working hours but by staggering slightly the working periods of assistants or the retailer himself. Through the value of its site, premises, and stock, a shop represents a considerable capital investment: it is bad business management to refrain from using this investment purely because of convention. Not that conventional hours are necessarily bad, but each retailer should consider when would be his best opening hours and whether he can arrange to trade in them. Current permitted hours for any particular shop can be ascertained from the local authority.

Considerable scope exists for special sales promotion on the quieter trading days of the week to help spread the rush of peak periods. This may directly save a little in part-time staff costs, but, more important, it enables more personal service to be given, increasing the likelihood of subsequent sales, and will normally attract new custom also. Examples of what can be done include selective but really big price cuts on quiet days, reduced prices for pensioners, and use of such sales incentives as extra trading stamps, where these are already given, or similar purchasing incentives. The late opening one night a week now common also helps to spread peak period rushes, as well as attract extra sales.

SMALLER RETAILER'S APPROACH

The basic approach for the smaller retailer should be to consider his assets: his trade and sales knowledge, enthusiasm, and finance. He should be circumspect in setting up a business, making full use of professional services and appropriate market research. He should decide what major lines and class of goods would sell best in the circumstances and provide customers with a fair choice within the chosen ranges, and advertise that the shop specializes in certain lines. He should keep note of stockturn rates and continually experiment in a small way with a few lines so that when profitability of existing lines can be improved upon, the new lines can be substituted. He should compare continually net profit with capital invested in the business and constantly seek to be more efficient.

Success breeds success: if a retailer can overcome a difficult patch by good management he is likely to thrive at all times. Within the national economy as a whole there is plenty of scope for the smaller trader as the population and its spending power grow. But just as success breeds success so failure breeds failure in today's increasingly competitive situation. There tends to be less and less room for the comfortable jogging along formerly often found in retailing. The independent retailer needs to keep alert, face problems squarely, and constantly seek to improve: that is his way to success.

6. Buying Merchandise

Shrewd merchandise buying is vital. To have too much in stock of certain lines is to have capital tied up unnecessarily and to be making bad use of it; to be out of stock is to lose opportunities to make profitable sales and build goodwill while actually driving would-be customers into the arms of competitors. But the problem is not so clear-cut: to have capital tied up unnecessarily in slower-moving or less profitable lines is to be equally inefficient. Furthermore, mistakes are costly: badly bought lines have to be sold off at a reduced profit, perhaps at a loss, or else lock up capital unproductively. Either is a drag on the profit-earning capacity of a shop.

In many ways, buying is the most important part of retailing; an accountant can help with financial matters, advice is available about advertising, display can be carried out by a specialist – but only the retailer himself can successfully do his buying. This emphasizes the need for a retailer to know thoroughly the goods dealt in and to be enthusiastic enough about them so that the considerable effort to keep up-to-date with competitive products and prices does not seem a chore.

DISCOVERING CUSTOMERS' WANTS

Good buying consists of stocking what customers want. Luckily there are several ways to discover this. Analysis of orders over the previous year or two indicates roughly what quantities were sold over given periods; the retailer's own market research should confirm these results and also suggest a large number of other lines which would probably sell with a fair degree of success. Experiments should be made constantly by ordering small quantities of lines which seem likely to sell reasonably: if they sell well, they should be retained and perhaps the lines built up by special promotion; if they are not successful, they should be replaced by the next trial line.

Customers themselves are the best source of information about their wants. Whenever the retailer is asked for an article he does not have he should note it in a 'wants' book, which can be any notepad or exercise book kept handy by the counter. If this is maintained conscientiously, occasional analysis of the 'wants' shows accurately what lines can be sold in sufficient and steady quantities to make it worth while, bearing in mind that entries in the 'wants' book have arrived without any promotion of the line by the retailer so would certainly sell better if displayed in the shop. Any wants recorded for lines already handled indicate that the article was out of stock: if this occurs frequently it suggests that attention to the ordering system is required, either in timing or size of re-orders, or in obtaining speedier service from the supplier. A 'wants' book should not be used, however, for merchandise requested only on special occasions unlikely to recur: this embraces many items of fashion in its widest sense.

Some goods are bought by customers because they are the nearest stocked to the required article. By discreet questioning the retailer may sometimes be able to find out in what ways his stocked products differ from the ideal. If the same replies occur often he may be able to modify his ordering appropriately.

Direct mail can also be of use to discover customers' wants if a fair number of existing customers' addresses are known. A carefully worded letter, enclosing a stamped addressed envelope, usually gets a good response. People like to be asked their opinion even when they are not directly concerned; they are all the more keen to help if it means better facilities for themselves. A typical letter beginning at the top of a foolscap sheet and allowing plenty of space below each question for replies, might read:

Dear Mrs Brown,

You are good enough to buy from me and your support is greatly valued. But good management never allows a retailer to stand still, so I am wondering in what ways my service to you could be improved. Could you please let me know your feelings by jotting them down below? An envelope addressed to me and already stamped is enclosed.

Your help is very much appreciated and I trust it will make my shop of increased use to you.

Yours sincerely,
John Smith

1. Are the products I stock those which suit you best? If not, are they the wrong brand, colour, or size, or is quality too poor or unnecessarily good?
2. Have you sufficient choice when you buy here? If not, how would you like to see it improved, and for which products in particular?
3. What additional products would you like me to stock?
4. How can my shop service to you be improved?
5. Would you welcome an optional delivery service, separately charged for?
6. Please add any comments you wish.

Such a letter stresses the benefits the customer obtains by filling in a form, which is itself made to seem as easy and brief as possible. Reference to good management wins admiration and cooperation. The letter should be addressed to each customer individually. By having the questionnaire on the same sheet as the letter the retailer can tell who troubled to reply by seeing to whom he addressed it. He can thank the customers when they next enter the shop and some of their suggestions can also be elaborated with them then.

A competition can be run occasionally to find out customers' needs. On two forms, list ten or so major lines, noting against each three prices, styles, and colours, or whatever is appropriate. Competitors – that is, customers who trouble to pick up the forms, which are on the counter or are handed over with goods, and return them filled in – are asked to tick on one copy which price, style, and colour for each product they prefer and on the other, the competition entry form, to tick which they think likely to be the most popular. Analysis of the first form provides the retailer with his information, while the second form enables him to nominate competition winners.

Prizes, perhaps three of varying amounts, can be vouchers to spend in the shop. Judging can be by someone impartial, perhaps even a local councillor's wife. The event can be used for considerable local publicity, itself worth the small cost of prizes, once the competition is completed. The competition should be well advertised within the shop, but not outside, so as to confine entries, largely at least, to existing customers. Information from others may not be a good guide to probable sales if subsequent buying by the retailer reflects the competition results.

A further means of finding out what customers want is to ask them directly over the counter, but this can be done only with regular and friendly customers who must also be typical in their wants.

STOCKING FOR PROFIT

No shop can stock everything; therefore what is stocked must bring in maximum profit. The general type of goods is largely predetermined by the retailer's own knowledge of and preference for a trade, although associated lines cutting across conventional trades may well be handled. It must then be decided whether to stock in breadth: for example, a shop selling ladies' coats for all age groups at popular price levels in the more usual sizes and colours; or in depth: in which case the extent of the range may be restricted to fashionable coats for younger women but available in a wide choice of materials, styles, colours, and price levels. The latter may be necessary if a near-by competitor stocks similar goods but in breadth.

Stocking in depth invariably leads to slower stockturn. Luckily a higher mark-up can be obtained because customers for such products are more discriminating and are prepared to pay a little extra. Stocking in depth makes knowledge of the trade all the more important and also increases the need for good salesmanship and display. Mistakes in buying such merchandise can be costly to rectify.

Even when stocking in considerable depth there must be limitation of the number of different articles offered. Shops stocking in breadth have exactly the same problem in relation to ranges of goods at different price levels and overlapping of similar articles having different brand names.

The selection in relation to price levels for many shops, whether stocking in breadth or depth, shows the way to deal with

Checklist 8. What to stock

1. Which trade?
2. Who are potential customers?
3. Specialize in what?
4. How wide?
5. How deep?
6. What price levels?
7. Which competing brands?
8. What else can be tried?
9. Local agencies available?
10. Can stockturn rates be raised?
11. Can slower moving lines be eliminated?

the other variables also: establish the most popular price level, stock mainly this, but have one range of comparable articles more expensive and another at a lower level. Although none of the three comparable choices may be exactly what a particular customer wants, one is certain to be close to it and most customers will be content to buy. Thus very few sales opportunities are lost yet stock variety is kept to a minimum. Depending on the trade, it may be necessary to have more than three alternative price levels for a line, but the number should always be kept to a minimum consistent with meeting the wishes of most customers.

OBTAINING SUPPLIES

Having decided in some detail what stock seems likely to sell best, the retailer can consider what manufacturers and wholesalers can offer to suit him. The process of stock selection should always be in this order, rather than consideration of what is available to suit the shop. Theoretically, this should give the same result: in practice it never does because gaps in a shop's stock are not so apparent and criteria for an ideal range of stock are continually modified to accord with suppliers' catalogues. Shopkeepers also tend to restrict their search for the required lines and varieties unless they buy to a predetermined plan.

It is usually risky to obtain all supplies from a single source as the retailer then is too dependent on one firm. On the other hand, it pays to be a good customer of a supplier because the retailer may then receive quantity discounts, preferential treatment at times of shortage or difficulty in delivery, first opportunity with special offers, and longer credit, so a compromise is needed. Most retailers find it best to obtain most of their stock from three or four sources, the remaining lines coming from a few less important firms, each supplying goods for gaps in the retailer's planned stock which cannot be filled by the main suppliers.

Although buying to take advantage of quantity discounts is attractive, care must be taken to see whether a bargain is really being obtained. Because buying a quantity means tying up capital beyond the minimum otherwise necessary, it can lead to lower net profit: it sometimes pays to reject the quantity discount, buy in small amounts and spread available capital over a wider range of stock. There are sometimes the added risks in quantity buying that fashion may change, or that a competing or new product may be powerfully promoted soon after purchase of the existing line. The articles may also deteriorate or be damaged while in stock. So quantity discounts, while often beneficial, are not always an unqualified blessing.

Cash discounts are usually worth having, but to decide, it is necessary to compare the cash-discount offer with the source of finance, such as bank overdraft, on the same basis of time. A bank overdraft at, say, six per cent per annum for one month is effectively a half per cent, which is the rate to compare with the supplier's offer of, perhaps, two and a half per cent cash discount for immediate settlement.

Ordering well in advance, particularly for seasonal lines, sometimes gains an extra discount. However, in attempting to gain this discount the retailer needs to ensure he does not lose to any serious extent his flexibility in choosing sources of supply or range of stock, nor should he risk overstocking, perhaps through introduction by another manufacturer of a competing line immediately before the season begins. With rising transport costs, some suppliers stipulate a minimum value for any delivery. Others try to achieve the same result either by offering an extra discount on deliveries over a given value, irrespective of quantities within individual lines, or by making a charge for delivery, representing only part of the considerable actual cost, for smaller orders.

In deciding sources of supply, first consider what is wanted so that alternative sources can be compared. Most retailers want an adequate range of goods of the class required for the shop's customers – merchandise that is value for money and often includes well-known branded lines. The frequency of delivery and speed of delivery in emergencies are important considerations: capital and space tied up in reserve stock can be smaller if deliveries are frequent. Fair profit margins and discounts, a sprinkling of worthwhile special offers and, perhaps, a certain amount of credit are further criteria. The function of wholesaling evolved to satisfy these requirements. Even in these days when more manufacturers sell directly to retailers, the function is still present, even if performed by the manufacturer.

Smaller retailers in some trades obtain many of their supplies from manufacturers directly, but in others, not at all. Supplies coming direct from manufacturers usually mean a slightly lower price, less frequent delivery, and no opportunity to compare competing products under one roof or to obtain them within one order. Retailers usually need wholesalers in some degree because manufacturers are normally unwilling to supply very small quantities. So a retailer's sources of supply are usually wholesalers serving his district and possibly some manufacturers selling directly. Appendix 4 gives further information on finding suppliers.

Sometimes it is also possible to buy from a cash-and-carry warehouse: a largely self-service warehouse where the retailer provides his own transport and pays in cash or by cheque in return for greater discounts, often substantial. If the warehouse is conveniently located, the retailer may also gain by using it as an extension of his stockroom, which then needs to hold a much smaller stock, saving him capital and space. It may also be helpful in reducing the need to deal with representatives and to accept and check deliveries at awkward times. The wholesaler's full range of stock, the latest special offers, new sales-promotion aids, and, if required, the wholesaler's representative, can be seen during the visit also.

Against this, the retailer must consider the cost of his transport and the value of his time. Cash-and-carry warehouses are usually open at least one evening a week as well as during the day.

DEALING WITH REPRESENTATIVES

Merchandise for stock can be selected from suppliers' catalogues, advertisements in trade magazines, visits to warehouses – where the complete range of goods rather than illustrations can be viewed – and information from representatives, who usually try to help retailers by suggesting additional lines they genuinely believe will sell. But their job is to sell, and they may earn a commission on sales, so they are always biased to some extent. And although they wish to remain friendly for future calls, they may try to overstock a retailer to help themselves win a competition of the type often organized between representatives by the manufacturer. Thus, although every suggestion should be carefully considered, any refusal should be firm.

But all representatives should be dealt with courteously: often they can be very helpful in pushing through orders quickly, in giving favouritism with special offers, in offering sound information on products, and in advising on retailing. Sometimes they can solve problems concerning their products if the retailer will only mention the difficulties; also, part of their job is to channel information from the retailer to the manufacturer. There is now a strong trend for manufacturers and distributors to take a greater interest in moving their goods off the retailer's shelf in addition to placing them there: the economics of competition and the need for rapid stockturn affects them as well as retailers. Consequently they frequently provide point-of-sale material and offer to organize special shop and window displays. These are usually advantageous to the shop's trade but it is the efficient retailer, not the representative, who is in the best position to judge their real value to the shop.

Representatives sometimes offer articles on sale or return. With nothing to lose except a small amount of display space, such offers should be welcomed as a means of trying out the market for new lines. It also helps to develop trade in all lines stocked if two or three local agencies for well-known brands are handled; often these are exclusive for the retailer's area and thus, if chosen so that they are well suited to the people in the district, provide big scope for go-ahead shopkeepers. When a retailer stocks a line

Checklist 9. Required from suppliers

---

 1. Suitable merchandise.
 2. Sufficient range.
 3. Value-for-money products.
 4. Frequency of delivery.
 5. Speed of emergency delivery.
 6. Fair profit margins.
 7. Reasonable discounts.
 8. Occasional worthwhile special offers.
 9. Sufficient credit.
10. Minimum orders not too large.
11. General advice on sales promotion, forthcoming new lines, etc.
12. Reliable service.

---

which is exclusive to him in the district he should see that the products are fair value for money and of good quality, to avoid frequent complaints and getting his shop a bad name for other merchandise also.

VOLUNTARY GROUPS AND CHAINS

Many small retailers are today benefiting from bulk-buying terms by joining together and combining orders through a buying group. Such organizations are not at all new, but it is in food retailing that this form of buying has made most headway. In the grocery trade, the concept of a few small retailers banding together to buy a small proportion of their stocks to win the extra discount soon led to similiar operations on a larger scale: one hundred, sometimes two hundred retailers combining. This level is sufficient to support an independent organization comprising warehouse, manager, clerks, and drivers, instead of retailers themselves having to do the necessary wholesaling work.

These retailer-sponsored buying groups constitute a threat to the livelihood of wholesalers who, to ensure their own survival, have taken parallel measures to help retailers. Some of the large wholesalers have formed wholesaler-sponsored voluntary buying groups among their customers, arranging that retailers obtain extra discounts and sometimes other advantages in return for agreement to purchase a specified proportion of their merchandise from the wholesaler – a minimum weekly delivery is often stipulated – and compliance with the voluntary group's other regulations, which vary a little from group to group.

The next step was a combination of two or more of these wholesaler-sponsored voluntary buying groups into a so-called voluntary chain. This volume of trade enables a voluntary chain to offer members more than mere discounts: advice on aspects of shop management, such as ways to increase stockturn and how best to use a shop's floor area; chain-organized special promotions and publicity; shop equipment at a discount; loans for stock, and other useful benefits are now available. Members usually display the insignia of their chain on their shopfront and some chains accept only one retailer in each locality. Most chains also promote their own brands of products.

Voluntary groups do exist outside the food trade, for chemists, hardware, clothing and footwear shops, for example, but are not so common, apparently because competition is on the whole not yet so severe as in food. Retailers in any trade may think it worth investigating from trade associations or similar sources whether any group-buying schemes exist to suit their own business.

NEW PRODUCTS

New products constantly arrive on the market. Some make little headway, but others grow to become money-spinners. Every retailer should keep up-to-date with new lines in his trade. If new lines are handled by existing suppliers, either wholesalers or manufacturers, representatives will automatically mention them, leave literature about them, and possibly demonstrate them. But many new lines are introduced by other companies so a retailer cannot expect all to be brought to his special notice. Instead he must be prepared to look for them from time to time.

There are many opportunities. Exhibitions, specially those solely for the trade, make a useful hunting ground. Visits to suppliers' warehouses, and those of their competitors, may give ideas on display as well as bring to light interesting lines, old and new. Manufacturers selling directly to retailers also welcome visits to their showrooms and usually offer to place any retailer on their mailing list for new products. The trade press, both editorially and in advertisements, invariably draws readers' attention to new lines. Helpful information on exhibitions will be found in Appendix 5, and on the trade press, in Appendix 6.

7. Stock Management

It is common to think of stock in the wrong perspective: as something static and solid, perhaps because most retailers consistently have a substantial capital sum tied up in stock. The successful shopkeeper, however, regards it in terms of movement. It may help to remember that stock is cash in another form, though as it does not attain its full value until it has been sold, stock valuations should always be at cost price, or at probable selling price where this is likely to be below cost.

CONTROL SYSTEMS

Stock control is necessary if the retailer is to know what he has in stock, where it is, its value, when he should re-order and how quickly each line turns over. There is no single 'best' system; much depends on the type of goods being sold, value of each item, speed of stockturn and the frequency of stocktaking and deliveries.

Stock control systems may be time-consuming and intricate and therefore cost the smaller retailer money instead of saving him worry and expense. It is pointless installing a system unless it is really useful and can be easily kept going. Normally it is sufficient to know when further supplies must be ordered, to be able to calculate stockturn rates, and to see that stock is kept free from damage and theft.

Some systems of re-ordering are based on measuring sales of the line concerned; others on measuring what remains in stock. Sometimes the easiest method for stock re-ordering is to use a sufficiently detailed ticket removed from each item as it is sold. This can be placed in an ordinary cardboard box to indicate that a replacement is needed to maintain the planned stock and dealt with when making up the regular order. Another method sometimes adopted, again based on sales analysis, is the use of a simple counting device, the lever of which is depressed each time a sale is made of the line to which it is allocated.

In many shops a sales bill is written for each sale, primarily to form the basis of the stock control system. It can record details of the article or its re-ordering code reference, indicate the number of articles and value of each transaction, be analysed if required according to department or assistant, and act as a check on cash received. In addition, it can record credit sales, give delivery instructions and provide a mailing list of customers. Customers often welcome a sales bill, although in law it is not an official receipt, and it can save much time in the event of a query or complaint. For some small shops, a sales bill may not be worth the trouble involved in its completion, but its use is often worth consideration, at least for certain classes of goods.

Cash registers issuing a printed slip and recording item and value totals, perhaps dissected by assistant or department, may be a suitable alternative to the written sales bill. Representatives of the many cash-register firms are always pleased to explain how their products can be used for more than simply a receptacle for cash, though the retailer will need to consider the real usefulness of such equipment for his particular business in relation to the price.

In a number of trades it is more convenient to have the stock-control system based on quantities remaining in stock. For small retailers this often depends on merely a visual check: when supplies on the shelf, rack, or in other storage space are getting low, more are ordered, the time for ordering being judged by the level and taking into account likely sales in the immediate future before goods are delivered. Storage bins and similar receptacles can be marked to indicate the level at which it is normally necessary to re-order.

Where individual items are of considerable value, it may be desirable to institute a system of unit stock control, by which a ticket kept with the stock of each line indicates at any time the quantity held. This is achieved by booking the numbers received, adding them to the existing stock, and noting both the numbers taken away for sale and the resulting balance.

Keeping valuable items under lock, perhaps in a separate small room or caged portion of the general stockroom, theoretically stops pilfering, but this is often not practical. If a unit stock control system is maintained for valuable items it is possible to hold spot checks from time to time, letting staff know that this is policy. If no special stock records are kept, probably the best policy is to remove temptation wherever possible and to accept small losses philosophically: they may be smaller in value than the cost in time and worry of maintaining an elaborate stock control system.

Sometimes the 'cost and selling' method of stock control, by which stock records are maintained at selling price as well as at cost price, is preferred. This method, also called the 'retail system', gives a fairly accurate value for book stock, enabling gross profit to date to be estimated at frequent intervals without the need to take physical stock each time. But because considerable paperwork is involved it tends to be used only by larger shops. The system is also open to manipulation by a dishonest or incompetent employee: it is necessary to check that the figures reflect what is actually happening in the shop, for example that selling prices are what they are said to be, and that items in stock are of the correct quantity, kind and value.

There is an infinite variety of stock-control and re-order systems. The retailer's accountant should be able to advise on a suitable system for any particular shop. In addition, there are books devoted entirely to this subject, as indicated in Appendix 14, while trade associations and occasionally manufacturers supplying the retailer with goods for resale may be able to help by suggesting systems especially suitable to the particular trade or certain classes of its products.

ACCEPTING DELIVERIES

Some retailers keep a book in which they enter all suppliers' orders so that they can check that deliveries contain exactly what was requested, as a safeguard against duplicate ordering while still awaiting delivery, and as a record for future ordering. Such additional records are unnecessary if the system suggested on page

123, using slips of paper in conjunction with the stock plan, is employed; if the slips are dated and clipped together they automatically form a record of purchases.

Goods should of course be checked on receipt for correct quantity and condition. If they, or their cases if these are used for display, are not as they should be, the delivery sheet should be marked accordingly, returning damaged items, and the supplier's representative told when re-ordering.

STOCKROOM PROCEDURE

Knowing where on the premises stock is located is a simple matter of having a regular place for each line and keeping stock where it ought to be. It is important to store goods neatly, especially where the only control on quantity and time to re-order is visual. All goods should be used in rotation, and it is usual to mark outer wrappings with the delivery date or to indicate this in some other way, for example, by stacking them separately.

If individual items are price-marked when on display in the shop, it is better to mark them just before transferring them from the stockroom rather than soon after delivery, to allow for any price changes notified by the supplier or due to a special promotion by the retailer. Pricing each article is expensive in time and may only be worthwhile for a fairly small number of items where each sells for a substantial amount, though it will be necessary to price-mark everything if self service is adopted. A variety of machines is available to avoid the drudgery of marking and ticketing by hand. Pricing of each article does reassure customers that they are not being overcharged, may save staff being interrupted in a sale to tell another customer the price of an article, and does enable a coded date to be put on everything as a check that older merchandise is sold before newer stock.

It is preferable for stock to be transferred from stockroom to shop a whole case, outer pack, etc., at a time. This reduces effort, as it is easier and quicker to move than a number of loose individual items, it avoids odd quantities in the stockroom, and may reduce pilfering by staff, especially if outer packs are not opened until being taken into the shop.

Stock of all types should be examined from time to time, frequently if perishable, as a safeguard against deterioration. Possible causes of damage include bad packing and stacking, poor ventilation and, sometimes, sunlight. Any items beginning to deteriorate should be sold at a reduced price, if saleable, or discarded. A wise retailer dealing with fashionable goods of any description naturally errs on the side of taking slightly less than he hopes to sell, making arrangements where possible for quick deliveries should he run short. Where this is not possible, he can stock articles in the season's fashion, but that are not too extreme, so that if he is left with these on his hands there remains a chance of selling them subsequently, if at a reduced price. After highly fashionable merchandise – a term applying to much more than merely fashion clothes – has gone out of fashion even big reductions may not evoke a buyer.

Keeping stock neatly reduces the risk of damage and accidents when working in the storage area, and may help to reduce the possibility of fire. Exact storage methods depend on the type of goods and available space, but points to consider are size, weight, frequency of withdrawal, need for rotation, largest quantity normally carried and whether fragile, inflammable, or exceptionally valuable. Some products may need to be kept at a particular temperature or humidity, or may be liable to attack by pests. Others may absorb near-by strong odours.

To reduce the floor area that stock requires, it is better to store in height, but items must still be easily accessible for withdrawal as well as stocktaking when considering re-orders. Stock required most frequently should be the easiest to get at. It is a considerable advantage to be able to clean the floor of the stock area thoroughly from time to time. A vacuum cleaner is usually more efficient than a broom. A fire extinguisher, kept handy for both stockroom and shop, is a good investment of only a few pounds, particularly if it is one of the effective versions of the 'direct powder' type. This deals with all kinds of fires except deep-seated and electrical blazes, requires no maintenance, its contents are easily swept up after use, and can be very simply replaced by a cartridge refill should a fire occur. It is best not to smoke in the stockroom, where there is much inflammable packing and other material.

ANNUAL STOCKTAKING

It is important to have an annual stocktaking, when everything in stock is listed and valued so that a correct figure can be inserted for 'Stock' in the retailer's annual accounts. Other than on this occasion, it is unnecessary in many shops to know the precise value of stock.

The annual stocktaking is ideally carried out when the shop is closed, when stock is at a fairly low level, and if many items are expected to be price-reduced as a result of the stocktaking, shortly before a suitable time for a clearance sale. But as this annual event is closely linked with the end of the financial year and preparation of the annual accounts, where other factors such as delaying tax liability through choice of year-end date may be more important, the date of stocktaking needs to be agreed with the accountant, who in any case may supervise, aid, or sample-check on this important occasion.

As the physical counting takes a long time, preparations for stocktaking should be made as much in advance as possible, for example by not breaking open bulk packets unless essential, which avoids counting numerous smaller packets. It also helps if the locations of all goods – including fixtures, shelving units and drawers, and not forgetting window and interior displays, emergency stocks, charged-for empty containers, items being returned to suppliers, and so on – are listed for checking off as counted. As many outstanding claims as possible with suppliers and customers should be settled up beforehand and all stock, marked with correct prices, tidied up to make counting easier.

The most common errors include double counting sections of stock or missing out sections altogether; mistakes in counting and recording; mistaking the number of items in unopened packages, such as dozens for tens; misreading figures booked, and miscalculating price extensions and totals. If the shop is to be open during stocktaking, arrangements must be made to allow for sales and deliveries while it is going on, as well as to minimize inconvenience to customers.

STOCK DEFICIENCIES

Annual stocktaking is a particularly good time to weed out slow moving and damaged stock physically – though an efficient retailer will be watching to do this throughout the year – and to calculate the stock deficiency percentage. This is the amount by which actual takings have fallen short of theoretical takings, expressed as a percentage of actual sales. This deficiency percentage reflects loss of stock through short delivery, customer or staff pilfering, breakage, and natural shrinkage; discounts and price reductions granted to customers for any reason; inadvertent undercharging or giving too much change. It also covers inaccurate measuring when selling goods and a large number of possible clerical errors in stock-keeping and price-marking.

After adjusting from the record of price reductions made during the year and for other known factors, the deficiency percentage may be some indication of the accuracy of the annual stocktaking, as big changes not accounted for by trading conditions may suggest that on one occasion important items of stock were either missed or counted twice.

CLEARANCE SALES

Inevitably some items will have to be sold below the price estimated at the time of purchase, perhaps even at a loss, because special promotion does not move them. The best policy is to turn even a loss to some good account: make the reduction sufficiently drastic to arouse thoroughly the attention of customers and passers-by. This can bring in extra sales, as well as create goodwill through customers finding subsequently that they have a real bargain. The great advantage to the retailer is that when the goods are eventually sold, capital is freed for something more profitable. In addition some experience of the shop's market has been gained. A record should be kept of all price reductions as a check on takings and as a guide for future buying.

If attention is drawn to reduced prices by window stickers or other forms of advertising, be specific. Phrases such as 'Amazing reductions' and 'Terrific bargains' evoke cynicism and apathy;

'25p in the £ off all sale lines' is much better, and 'Handbags in perfect condition at three-quarters normal price' is better still.

It may be possible to clear a slow-selling line more advantageously than by a substantial price reduction, for example by offering it at the lower price if bought in conjunction with a normally-priced associated product in stock. It may even be practical to link two poor-selling lines so that the price reduction on the pair looks such an exceptional bargain that buyers are quickly found.

Bargains can be placed in a window, but it is usually better to make a bargain corner inside the shop, well lighted and attractively laid out, so that it can be seen from the doorway. Potential customers are then enticed inside and even if they do not buy one of the sale items they may purchase some other article. It should of course be made clear that there is no obligation involved in coming in to look at bargains. Two further advantages of keeping all sale lines together are that the retailer can better judge the amount of interest they provoke, using this knowledge for future trading, and it provides an opportunity for those shoppers who like to rummage, which cannot be done if half the bargain items are in the window and only half inside the shop.

Clearance sale periods should be as short and as infrequent as possible to avoid the appearance of running faked sales for which inferior merchandise has been specially bought. Selling price-reduced items as soon as possible after the decision to cut the price is usually better than saving them for a big clearance sale. It frees more quickly the capital tied up and makes it more likely that a buyer will be found, especially if the line is seasonal, while there is also less chance of the goods becoming soiled or damaged.

8. Profitability

The retailer has decided roughly what ranges of goods to sell and which require a certain amount of depth of stock. He also knows what capital he can spare to tie up in stock. The problem is to allocate the capital over the desired stock to ensure that supplies never run out, that items stay on the premises no longer than is necessary, and that the maximum net profit is earned. These three aims are an ideal rarely achieved, but they must remain the target. A modified stock plan can be a great help: it takes the guesswork out of buying and selling and enables retailing to become more scientific – and profitable.

MEASURING PROFITABILITY

Some stock plans merely list items and show the ideal quantity to stock of each. The following suggested system does a great deal more. It lists all the stocked items and has headings as indicated in Table 10.

This example assumes the normal delivery cycle is one month, that the period taken is one year and that it has now ended. It shows how capital can best be used, offers a factual indication of the success or failure of every line in relation to others, and a pointer towards increased profitability through possible reduction of lines in depth or breadth. It makes known the lines most likely to benefit from sales promotion, and provides a guide to future trading. It also shows the measure of success achieved, compared against a sensible estimate. It gives interim notification of the progress of the business between annual accounts, and is a help in stocktaking and re-ordering. A profitability table is perhaps a more appropriate name than a stock plan.

Stock plans are made weekly by some chain stores. Small retailers should make them at least annually, and possibly half-yearly if mainly seasonal lines are dealt in. It will be seen that the more frequently they are prepared the easier it will be to upgrade planned minimum profitability and also to keep a check on changing trends, but because their preparation takes considerable time it is often sufficient to prepare them annually while maintaining monthly or weekly analysed sales figures. If the retailer cannot

Table 10. Assessing profitability

| Article | Quantity | Capital (£) | G.P. (per cent) | Stockturn rates in period | | Index of profitability (G.P. per cent × actual stockturn rate) |
				esti-mated	actual	
Toothpaste Brand A: Small	3 doz.	4	20	12	13	260
Ditto ditto: Large	5 doz.	9	20	13	15	300
Ditto Brand B: Small	2 doz.	2	20	12	8	160
Ditto ditto: Large	4 doz.	7	20	12	9	180

bear to involve himself in these details his accountant will do the job for him for a fee. As a profitability table rather than a re-order stock list, the method can also be used selectively only, where appropriate, concentrating on the slowest-moving lines or comparing the profitability of certain lines. It may also be used for groups of lines instead of individual products, though this risks blurring the vital facts the author has designed it to uncover. Even its selective use, without need for detailed calculation for each line, helps the retailer think constantly in terms of the profitability of each line and the capital necessarily, or unnecessarily, tied up.

It is not claimed that this is the best system for all shops: there is no single 'best' system to suit all circumstances. But the results are essential to good management and similar results must be obtained, whatever system is used.

The 'Quantity' column contains the retailer's assessment of his minimum requirements for each line to ensure that he does not run short before his next normal delivery. This quantity of course increases as stockturn rate is speeded up.

Used in conjunction with a stocktaking list, the column shows what amount should be ordered. If the list is completed in an exercise book ruled up by the retailer, he can do stocktaking on separate sheets of paper having horizontal lines printed the same distance apart. Placing the stocktaking sheet on top of the relevant page of the exercise book with the left-hand edge of the sheet against the right-hand vertical column of 'Article' and with horizontal lines meeting – the stocktaking sheet can be held in position by paper clips at top and bottom while being used in this way – stocktaking becomes a simple matter of entering the quantities in stock. It is unnecessary to write the names of articles as they are already listed in the stock-plan book; however, it is important to number the stocktaking sheets to correspond with the page number on the stock-plan book. After use, stocktaking sheets should be clipped together and retained for subsequently calculating stockturn rates, the date of the stocktaking being entered on the top sheet.

Amounts to be ordered are roughly the difference between the quantity in the stock plan and that on the stocktaking list. They will not always be exactly this: depending on the type of goods concerned, they may be rounded off to the next quantity – tens, hundreds, etc. – in which the goods are supplied. There may sometimes be a further addition if the retailer considers he can sell a larger quantity through a special offer to his customers and so take advantage of a supplier's special offer or extra quantity discount. The order figures can be entered in a column to the right of the stocktaking quantities.

Capital normally tied up in each line is inserted in the next column of the profitability table. This serves two purposes: it enables the retailer to plan his stock to give a balanced range of goods, and it forcibly reminds him how much capital is locked up in any particular line.

Against each article in the profitability table should be inserted the gross profit percentage, found from invoices.

Sales forecasting. The 'Estimated stockturn rate' column is a forecast of likely sales over the coming period. The previous year's figures, or the comparable period of the previous year if the plan is being prepared more frequently than once a year, can be taken as a basis to start with. Experience over subsequent years will enable the retailer to pay less and less attention to previous figures, as he should do. The future is not dependent on the past in the present changing state of retailing. It is far more important to consider what changes are taking place in the sales potential, what competitors are doing, and the likely effects of the retailer's ability to increase his share of local trade by salesmanship, wise buying, sales promotion and the building up of goodwill.

But taking the previous year as a basis when first preparing a buying plan, the figures for each line should be adjusted to take into account all probable trends, such as whether the area is becoming more populous; whether customers have more money to spend; whether the goods or services are becoming more popular or fashionable; whether local employment is likely to continue at existing levels; what may be the government's likely attitude, during the period, in financial policy as reflected by bank rate, hire purchase controls, and taxation; and what the prospects are for general business activity, reflecting the national economy and international situation. The retailer's accountant will be able to advise on these matters. These factors influencing estimated stockturn rates during the coming period should be noted down separately and kept with the profitability table so that the forecast can be compared with actual results at the end of the period and reasons for error located, assisting in more accurate subsequent forecasting.

Measuring stockturn. Actual stockturn rates should be inserted in the next column of the profitability table but these figures are prepared, as are those in the 'Index of profitability' column, at the end of the covered period, whereas all the other columns are completed at the beginning. As it is necessary to take stock at the end of each stock-plan period it is easier if the occasion can be made to coincide with the re-ordering date of the major supplier, as stock has to be taken then in any case for that supplier's lines. This usually cannot be done if it is an annual stock plan, but if stock plans are made more frequently, they give greater flexibility. Unlike annual accounts, because results are not required for a specific day, a day or two's variation in length of period is not important.

Stockturn rates can be measured by dividing the quantity sold in the period by the average quantity in stock. This saves calculating in money terms, avoiding awkward division sums and possible confusion between valuation at cost or selling prices. If a high proportion of a line has been sold at reduced price, two different items can be entered in the profitability table, one at the normal gross profit percentage and one at the usual reduced percentage.

The quantity sold can be found by adding all orders for the line during the period to existing stock at the beginning of the period, as shown by the previous stocktaking list, and deducting the quantity remaining at the time of stockturn rate calculation. The average quantity of stock for practical purposes is the mid-way point between maximum and minimum stocks normally held, making allowance for any major seasonal fluctuations. When the profitability-table period does not coincide with re-ordering times, the quantity last ordered in the previous profitability-table period should be counted as being in the current period: the overlapping period at one end of the profitability-table term roughly equals the gap at the other.

A comparison of figures in this column with the forecast stockturn rate reveals to what extent the forecast was wrong, while comparison between the list of factors on which the forecast was made and actual conditions shows why the estimated target was incorrectly set. This information enables a more sound estimate to be made for the next period. Completed profitability tables should be kept for several years: comparing each with the others shows the development of the business and of accuracy in forecasting. The latter should be constantly improving, while trends of lines handled and their profitability may provide ideas for further experimental lines.

Figures in the 'Index of profitability' column are the result of multiplying the gross profit percentage by the actual stockturns in the period. It is emphasized that this table is only a rough guide. Large organizations use much greater refinements, but they are able to employ staff who do nothing but compile such statistics; smaller retailers need short-cut methods which give answers that are accurate enough for their own purposes.

Thus, the gross profit percentage on each line is used as this figure is easier to obtain, and not the net profit percentage which theoretically would be more accurate. The difference between the two reflects overheads of the business, but to calculate net profit on each line involves much work and is frequently inaccurate even then because some overhead costs cannot be apportioned with any precision to particular lines. In any case, the stockturn rate figures are not an exact result; with such approximations it is pointless to try to be precise elsewhere in the calculation producing the 'Index of profitability' figure. The first table prepared for a shop may not be very accurate: estimated stockturn rates, for example, may be largely guesswork. But a start has to be made somewhere and subsequent tables become more accurate and easier to prepare.

Index of profitability. Important facts in the completed table stand out immediately. A glance down the 'Index of profitability' column shows at once which lines are earning good profits and which are not; furthermore, lines can be placed in an approximate order of profitability, although those with almost similar figures may be slightly out of true order due to the inaccurate calculation of actual stockturn. Most retailers know some of their most profitable and least profitable lines without this table, but without it they cannot be as precise, nor can they be certain of the profitability of each line in relation to others. This is necessary so that sales of the most profitable lines can be boosted even more and action taken with the least profitable lines. The aim should be to increase the profitability index figure of each line, by increasing stockturn rate and perhaps by buying more advantageously, every time the table is prepared, and to substitute new lines for a few of the least profitable lines. The profitability of the new lines, bought initially in small quantities to avoid major mistakes, can be found out after a trial period.

After this period, unsuccessful new lines should be dropped and others tested, while successful new lines should lead to larger purchases on a permanent basis and so become an item in the next profitability table to be prepated. Care has to be taken to compare experimental with established lines over an equivalent period: if this differs from the period covered by the profitability table for established lines, a separate table should be used, similar but noting the starting and finishing dates of each experimental line.

Turnover in some shops fluctuates widely according to seasonal and other factors. When planning stocks it is important to include some lines which do not fluctuate and others which are a direct counterbalance. An outfitter selling swimwear in the summer and scarves in winter is an obvious example. In this way, capital – employed in all overheads, not merely stock – is kept fully used.

It is usually revealing for a retailer to do two or three quick calculations from the profitability table: three quarters of the shop's profits may be coming from much fewer than one quarter of its lines, while a few may produce such low gross profits that they incur losses after allowance has been made for overheads.

A few basic lines have to be carried irrespective of profitability because they attract customers for better-paying items, but such lines are very much fewer than is often supposed. Other than these, all lines stocked should be earning the most profit possible, which means all figures in the 'Index of profitability' column should be as high as possible.

It pays best to promote fast-selling lines. Naturally, advertising and good salesmanship have to be used to move slower-moving lines once they are in stock for too long a period, but emphasis should be on the quick-sellers. A glance down the 'Actual stockturn rate' column shows which they are, so the retailer can see at once which lines to use in display and advertising, and which to suggest when making additional sales.

SPECIALIZATION

Mention has been made of dropping lines which do not produce a good profit. Two associated principles are involved here: variety reduction and stock specialization. One reason for the inadequate turnover of a line may be that other items stocked are too similar; reducing the variety of articles offered by cutting out one or more similar brands and sizes loses comparatively few customers because most can be persuaded to take willingly the remaining alternative.

Stock specialization means concentrating stocks and selling effort on a still more limited range of products. The degree of limitation varies with each business; it will rarely be as great for the smaller retailer as that adopted by chain stores but the profitability table helps by indicating lines dragging down his average profitability. On dropping a product he has the choice of investing the freed capital in a new line likely to give better results, or increasing his stock of an existing article; in the latter case sales promotion must increase if the stockturn and thus 'Index of profitability' is not to decline.

The fact that stock specialization is one of the major factors in the success of chain stores is a good reason for a smaller retailer to adopt it to a degree suitable for his own purposes. It leads to a higher return on capital invested in the business both because effort is concentrated on the most profitable lines and because unprofitable lines have been dropped. The potential trade is increased because specialized lines can be widely promoted, drawing customers from a wider area through good selection of the specialized ranges. In this way a niche in the market may be created against which even chain stores find it difficult to compete.

Specialization also makes better salesmanship possible, because assistants have less to learn in the first place and less to remember, enabling their knowledge of the product to be all the greater. Less storage space is required and a smaller investment in minimum stock necessary, while more frequent deliveries of faster-moving lines is often possible. Bigger discounts may become available through needing to order larger quantities, which at the same time increases the importance of the retailer to the supplier, possibly bringing further benefits. Keener buying may also be possible as job-lots come within the range of the small shopkeeper, although he should consider whether the reason for their being jobbed off is likely to affect their sale from his shop.

Perhaps one of the greatest benefits is that average margins tend to increase with specialization. Mark-up normally rises as the difficulty of sale, taken on a national average, increases. Because many lines specialized in are, for many other retailers, relatively slow-moving, extra profit on specialized lines results from both faster stockturn and wider profit margin.

But specialized lines must be well and widely promoted. Once a shop is noted for a certain range, customers are drawn in and near-by competitors find that they cannot sell the line in sufficient volume so they are forced to drop it. Thus the policy for today's successful shopkeeper must be 'Specialize and advertise', or more accurately 'Find your corner of the market, concentrate on these lines and make the fact that you are doing so as widely known as possible by all practicable means.'

Two arguments are sometimes raised against specialization. Both are fallacious. The charge that 'Specialization means reduction in turnover' is doubly false: specialization leads to increased profit because only the most profitable lines, after considering both margin and stockturn, are specialized in, and furthermore reduction in turnover would not be necessarily a drawback as turnover is no guide to net profit, which is the only sound criterion.

The other argument, that 'Customers will go elsewhere and goodwill will be lost' is even less likely after adopting specialization. Occasionally customers may have to be told that the item requested is not stocked, but normally either a substitute sale can be made or, sometimes, a special order can be placed. Even if the retailer has to suggest that the customer tries another shop it can be turned to advantage: most customers respect a retailer who proves he genuinely wants to help to such an extent that he names a competitor, while the point can be made that the line was dropped because it did not pay and that it is only by giving attention to such ideas of good business management as profitability that the smaller retailer can today survive at all.

In any case such instances will be comparatively rare: had there been frequent call for the line, it would not have been dropped. It must also be remembered that the retailer will profit in just the same way on the odd occasion when his competitors are asked for a line they do not stock and when they cannot make a substitute sale or obtain a special order. They too must specialize in today's conditions. If they do not, they are working for a much lower return on their capital and labour, and may well be heading for bankruptcy.

Although near-by competing shops may stock many lines in common, it is rare that sufficient trade exists in one district for them both to make similar ranges their specialities. Thus the retailer who first foresees the potential and who builds up that aspect of the trade comes to dominate his district. The three keys to this success, dealt with at some length in this book, are market research, a stock list disclosing profitability, and sales promotion.

Special orders. Personal service is one of the great advantages the small shop has over chain stores, so the wise trader will set aside a small amount of capital for special orders to customers' requirements. Although involving some extra bother, these occasions provide excellent extra opportunities for building goodwill: customers can see their wants are being specially attended to, a service not available in an increasingly large number of shops today. All the time, the retailer is really helping himself by not tying up his capital in a wide range of items rarely requested.

Most retailers are able to combine this financial efficiency with the appearance of a comprehensive service to customers by making widely known that special orders are welcome. Suppliers' catalogues, kept up to date, can be neatly arranged in a suitable position in the shop where customers can browse without obligation and without disturbing the serving of other customers. A would-be browser should not have to ask for a catalogue: many would be deterred. Each time this happens a good sales opportunity is lost: browsers only browse because they are interested, so they are highly potential customers, even if not always at that particular time. Manufacturers spend a lot on making their catalogues attractive: the 'catalogue corner' can be an extra sales assistant, and the additional sales won without tying up capital. A practical point to remember is that some browsers are so interested and some catalogues so attractive that the latter should be secured to the wall or counter, although remaining easy to manipulate.

Ruthless efficiency by retailing chains has forced small shopkeepers to be even more efficient if they are to stay in business. They cannot afford to be lax: they will fail if their shop is inefficient, gives bad service, or stocks the wrong products for the district. Chain stores can get away with similar errors because, if the faults cannot be corrected after highly skilled specialists from chain headquarters have taken their best remedial action, the branch can be closed down. A dozen other branches of the same organization are making sufficient profits to cover the losses.

Thus maximum efficiency is vital for a small shop and the best use of capital is one of the major paths to success. It no longer pays to stock everything; only those lines which give a reasonably quick stockturn in worthwhile quantities can be handled if the small man is to get a fair return for his labour, investment, and risk. 'We haven't any in stock but we'll gladly put an order through for you today' is the sign of a changing basic principle in retailing; customers are coming to recognize that this is more likely to indicate the retailer's efficiency rather than show that he he does not stock what is in demand.

RAISING STOCKTURN RATES

No retailer can be fully efficient without a thorough understanding of stockturn. The advantages of raising stockturn rates include larger gross profit than would otherwise be received and increased net profit in proportion to the capital employed. As shortage of capital is the most usual limiting factor to business expansion, it is clear that any method which frees capital for profitable lines instead of being tied up in slow-moving stock is worth close study. There are also the smaller advantages that goods passing through the shop quickly have fewer opportunities to become out of date or shop-soiled.

As mentioned briefly near the beginning of Chapter 2, a shop's stockturn rate is determined to some extent by the nature of the trade carried on. The average percentage mark-up in the trade reflects this: thus grocery shops, turning most goods over rapidly throughout the year, have a lower average mark-up than milliners, electrical goods shops, and many others. So the way to higher profits is to have a stockturn rate above average for the trade: stockturn rates between trades cannot normally be compared.

Factors affecting stockturn include the type of product being sold, for example, whether it is perishable; whether it is a standard product often wanted, less frequently required, or a product that is purpose-made for clients; whether pre-sold by branding and heavy advertising by the manufacturer; the extent of the varieties of the product in sizes, colours, and shapes, and whether it is suited to customers of the particular shop. Other factors are the proximity of directly competing shops, and the degree of substitution by other products, possibly from other types of shop. But these are by no means all: almost every aspect of a shop's activity – especially salesmanship, site location, and sales promotion – affects stockturn rates.

It can be seen that much can be done to speed stockturn. Some methods have already been dealt with, such as keeping stock variety in depth and breadth to the most profitable minimum; market research; and good product knowledge for sound buying. But others are so untechnical that they are sometimes overlooked. The effective demand for a retailer's goods is limited to the extent to which his potential customers know the products are available at the shop: they need to be constantly informed by window display, advertising in various forms, display inside the shop, and by word of mouth over the counter, suggesting additional sales or substitute sales. Customers must also be able to buy easily, which implies that the shop should be open at the most profitable hours, that the geographical position is suitable and that orders can be given over the telephone. Potential consumers must also be given good reasons for buying from that particular shop instead of elsewhere; pleasant, quick, and helpful service, the choice of stock, a reputation for good value for money, a bonus on large purchases, credit facilities, free delivery – all help in the drive for faster stockturn.

DECIDING MARK-UP

In addition to stockturn rates, profitability of a business is closely
geared to mark-up. Except where goods are still price-maintained,
there is considerable scope for enterprising retailers to vary their
selling prices upwards and downwards to obtain maximum profit.
Greatest profit for an article does not arise from charging the highest price some customers will pay, nor from lowering the price so
that stock turns over at the fastest possible speed: it results from
choosing the best combination of mark-up and stockturn.

The demand for many products varies with the price: the
cheaper they are, the greater the number of people attracted to
buy, while those customers who would have bought even at a
higher price may buy in larger quantities. Theoretically, the
retailer sets his price at the point where the profit for the line, not
on each article, is the greatest; in practice, he may be deterred
from reducing a price below that ruling in his district for fear of
starting a price-cutting war.

A retailer may well be able to charge a little above the usual
price for some articles. It may be that he is known for stocking only
best quality merchandise and customers are prepared to pay extra
to be sure of getting first-rate goods; possibly his shop has no
near-by competition, gives particularly helpful service, offers free
delivery, or has some other advantage over the theoretically average shop. One result of building up goodwill and a value-for-
money reputation is that customers are usually more ready to
accept stated prices without comparing them with other shops.
Certain prices have greater appeal than others. An article offered
at, for example, 99p would possibly sell better than if priced five
pence cheaper at 94p.

Some lines incur extra overheads, cause extra trouble in selling,
or take longer than most to serve. An example may be a hardware
shop that stocks paraffin. It requires a storage tank or special shed
for drums, extra fire insurance, perhaps a delivery pump, and
risks the smell and mess while serving. Profit on such lines should
reflect as far as possible the additional overheads when the relative
profitability of a line is being considered: a retailer would be
misleading himself considerably if, after averaging out all the

shop's overheads over the whole range of stock and finding that his apparent net profit on such lines was average, he considered the line paid as well as most others. Big-shop competitors can afford to employ trained staff to apportion overheads to various lines so that the true position is known: the small trader cannot, but provided he takes such factors into account when the additional overheads are substantial, he will not be far wrong.

It is worth remembering that although most well-known branded lines offer a smaller margin than lesser-known competing lines, the big manufacturers usually provide the retailer free with the goodwill attaching to the brand name, extensive advertising of the product and brand name, shop display material, special promotion schemes, and so on. Such lines may offer a better net profit than at first appears, because items normally chargeable to the retailer's general overheads or sales promotion have in effect been paid by the manufacturer.

Although the retailer should constantly aim to substitute better-paying lines for those showing the lowest 'Index of profitability' in the profitability table, the profitability of a line can be improved sometimes, avoiding the need to drop it. Extra promotion is one method, although it is no panacea. It normally pays best to promote quick-moving lines, to make them move even faster, rather than spend time and effort on products customers clearly do not want. Clearance sales were dealt with in the previous chapter. However, awkward placing on shelves or avoidable fuss in serving the line may be factors contributing to slow stockturn; there are obvious remedies.

Raising the price may be another possible solution: increased profit may result from the higher mark-up if the frequency of sale is not greatly retarded. Occasionally a product appears too cheap to customers; raising the price has been known actually to increase the frequency of sale. A further method is to charge for any extra overheads, such as cost of delivery on bulky items, directly associated.

MEASURING EFFICIENCY

Although the test of good retail management lies in its profitable trading it is not always easy to measure just how well a retailer is running his business. Annual accounts are not an accurate guide to business efficiency. A retailer may be making comfortable profits yet still be inefficient, for example, because higher sales attributable to lack of competition hide losses due to wasteful methods. Conversely a retailer struggling to make a bare living may in fact be highly efficient, his profit being kept down through trading conditions beyond his control.

There are four ways in which a retailer can obtain some measure of his own efficiency: he can see that his net profit before tax rises from year to year; he can seek the advice of his accountant; he may be able to join an 'inter-shop comparison' scheme, or he may be able to compare certain key statistics and ratios of his business with the national average for broadly similar businesses through details published in the latest government-run census of distribution or in other reliable publications.

Small annual increases in net profit may in fact indicate retrogression: the value of money tends to fall over a period of years, and quite sharply in periods of inflation. If it falls, say, three per cent in a given year and net profit has risen by only one per cent, there has been a decline in the value of the trading in real terms to the retailer. Appendix 9 elaborates on this matter.

Similarly, if the purchasing power of his customers increases from year to year while a shopkeeper's net profit remains static after allowing for any decline in the value of money, he is losing ground to competing retailers, who are not necessarily in the same trade. Net profit, it will be noted, not turnover, is taken as the criterion. Turnover can soar upwards while net profits plunge downwards if profit margins are too slim or overheads too high. Trends of costs should be recorded as well as trends of net profit.

The second possible check on efficiency is the advice of the retailer's accountant. He can calculate the rate of net profit earned on capital invested in the business and see whether this is a reasonable return compared with other forms of investment. If he has experience of the accounts of other retailers in the same trade

Checklist 10. How to increase stockturn

---

1. Conduct market research to determine best lines to sell.
2. Plan balanced stocks.
3. Maintain a profitability table to disclose weaknesses and strong points.
4. Consider reduction in variety of stock, in both depth and width.
5. Test new lines and price levels.
6. Select value-for-money merchandise from suppliers.
7. Avoid overstocking, thereby freeing capital for additional lines.
8. Keep merchandise easily accessible and in good condition.
9. Improve salesmanship of all who serve.
10. Introduce additional sales and substitute sales where appropriate.
11. Offer above average facilities (special orders, delivery, quick service, etc.).
12. Give sound advice freely and cheerfully.
13. Make display in window and shop more effective.
14. Inform customers of the shop's merchandise and services through various low-cost but effective sales promotion methods (see Chapter 14).
15. Make it easy for customers to buy and order, e.g. open at profitable hours, publicize acceptance of telephone orders, etc.
16. Clear slow-moving stock by special promotions or price reductions.

---

he can say, without disclosing any confidential matters whatever, how the retailer's return on capital compares. Calculation of return on capital needs to be made with care: freehold property, for example, may be worth far more than was originally paid for it. To arrive at a true figure for return on capital, the current value must be assessed even though the retailer's accountant may decide it is better for the revised value not to be included in the balance sheet but treated as a hidden reserve.

Properly run inter-shop comparison schemes, the third possible measure of efficiency, involve cooperation with other retailers and an impartial organizing body such as a trade association or independent management consultants. Retailers in the scheme analyse their costs in an agreed way and supply the information to the organizing body under a code number so that the retailer remains anonymous. The organizers compute average figures, together with maximum and minimum, for each analysed item so that retailers can see how well their costs compare with those of competitors. Thus, if a shop spends too much on wages in relation to sales, it is a warning that the employer is drawing out too much in the form of wages, or that the staff is inefficient or badly organized. Sponsors of these schemes always see that shops compared with each other are of similar size and class of trade.

The fourth possible method of measuring efficiency needs to be handled with care as on many occasions it is so difficult to determine whether the published statistics with which the retailer hopes to compare his key figures relate to truly comparable businesses. The accuracy of published statistics, other than in the census of distribution and similar sources, is also sometimes open to doubt.

Some of the most usually adopted measurements include the value of sales per square foot of selling space, or in some trades, per linear foot of shelving; value of sales per assistant, or per employee-hour; number of sales per assistant; the average value of each sale, and the extent of complaints or need to reduce prices through outdated or shopsoiled stock. Sometimes the value of sales per square foot is based on total area – that is, including storage and office space – while occasionally the value of sales per linear foot of counter is adopted.

Other common financial measures of efficiency include the ratio of current assets to current liabilities; gross profit per square foot; and the ratios of the major expenses, such as staff, sales promotion, and occupancy costs, to gross profit. Larger firms sometimes compare the ratio of sales staff to non-selling staff by wage cost. The average rate of stockturn is of course a key statistic for retailers of all sizes of business, while every retailer needs to be constantly aware of his turnover performance, gross and net profit margins, and the return on his investment in the business.

Such figures can be used to compare progress in the same shop from year to year, or whatever other period is chosen, but special care is needed in interpretation when comparing with published national and similar averages. For example, assistants selling a substantial volume of fairly high-value goods involving negligible effort or time – for example, cigarettes – may appear to be far more efficient than others, though the profit they contribute, because of the low margin common on such goods, may be no better than that of assistants in other trades. The position is also distorted if the goods carry a high rate of tax on which no profit is earned. Similarly, a shop serving many customers, each buying in fairly large quantities, may appear to be far more efficient than another in the same trade where customers buy smaller sizes of the same goods. To the extent that the retailer aims to sell in larger quantities the first may be considered more efficient, but this is no accurate measure, as he may be able to do so only through the relative prosperity of his district, the lack of local competition, the distance customers have to travel to the shop, and so on.

Whichever system of checking efficiency is used, it is essential to keep sufficient records so that the information can be found easily. More than ever before it is vital for smaller retailers to be able to see frequently where they are going and how their trading can be improved. This does not mean wasting time on elaborate paperwork systems of control simply because they are theoretically perfect; it does mean that certain records must be kept.

9. Accounts and Credit Trading

Rudimentary accounts have to be kept by every business so that the proprietor can know how his affairs stand. Proper, even though elementary, accounts are also required to satisfy the inspector of taxes, who always has the power to raise an excessive assessment, forcing the retailer to produce the necessary figures to support his case for reduction in the tax assessment. Preparation of accounts is usually stipulated in partnership agreements and is also necessary once a limited liability company is formed.

But the shopkeeper does not need to master accountancy: most small retailers arrange with an accountant to prepare their annual accounts, act as auditor and also sometimes to give advice on financial and general management throughout the year, possibly during monthly or quarterly visits. How to find a suitable accountant is explained in Appendix 1.

There is a great variety of accounting systems and it is best to let the accountant decide which is the most suitable for any particular business. The retailer should discuss with him what kind of information needs to be kept, and in what manner, so that the accountant can prepare the accounts and also so that the retailer is able largely to manage his own financial affairs and check his progress at any time.

SHORT-CUT ACCOUNTING

For many retailers the simplest system is to use an analysed cash book, which is easy to maintain and from which accountant and retailer can get quickly most of the financial information they ever need. An example of an analysed cash book is on pages 140–41.

Items in the 'Bank in' column represent amounts paid into the bank account; items in the 'Cash in' column represent amounts

Table 11. Specimen pages of an analysed cash book suitable for a small shop

Date	Details	Bank in £	Cash in £	Bank out £	Cash out £	Purchases £
Mar 25	Balances	356·41	19·51			
	Takings banked	135·86				
	Petty cash drawn		10·00	10·00		
	Window cleaning				1·50	
	Business insurances			30·72		
	Trade subscription			8·00		
	New display fitting			52·50		
26	Takings	58·37				
	Cleaning materials			0·56		
	Postage on sales				0·22	
	Floor repair				4·75	
	Tips				0·20	
27	Takings	57·74				
	Purchases (Smith)			84·93		84·93
	Window display material			4·28		
28	Takings	46·98				
	Purchases (Brown)			159·44		159·44
	Purchases (Carter)			82·67		82·67
	Direct mail postage				2·50	
	Stamps for business letters				0·50	
	Phone account			28·19		
	Wrapping materials				6·75	
29	Takings	67·79				
	Rent, inc. rates			92·34		
	Printer			16·45		
	Petty cash		90·00	90·00		
	Stationery			4·34		
	Fares			0·15		
	Electricity			43·81		
	Wages				34·85	
30	Takings	116·14				
	Delivery boy			1·50		
	Drawings				30·00	
	Closing balances			129·41	38·24	
		839·29	119·51	839·29	119·51	327·04
Apr. 1	Balances	129·41	38·24			

Wages £	Deliveries £	Advertising & display £	Occupancy £	Office £	Repairs & capital expenditure £	Drawings £	Sundries £
			1·50				
			30·72	8·00			
					52·50		
	0·22		0·56				
					4·75		0·20
		4·28					
		2·50					
		2·14	26·05	0·50			
		6·75					
		12·00	92·34	4·45			
				4·34			
			43·81				0·15
34·85							
	1·50						
						30·00	
34·85	1·72	27·67	194·98	17·29	57·25	30·00	0·35

withdrawn from the bank in cash to pay those expenses not paid by cheque. All money received from sales should be banked and cash withdrawn in this way when necessary. Takings should never be used as cash or petty cash. Each time an entry is made in either the 'Bank out' or 'Cash out' column the same amount should appear in one of the other columns to show what type of payment it is.

At the regular intervals suggested by the accountant the bank balance should be calculated by deducting total 'Bank out' from total 'Bank in', and compared with the statement of balance issued by the bank; the cash balance should be compared similarly with cash in hand. The sum of all other column totals should be the same as the sum of the totals of the 'Bank out' and 'Cash out' columns before the closing balances, less amounts transferred to the 'Cash in' column during the period.

The aim is to keep the number of columns to a minimum consistent with being able to arrive quickly at certain totals, such as drawings and capital expenditure, and to see how expenses vary with the volume of trade and which are fixed overheads. Items should never be placed in columns headed 'Miscellaneous' or 'Sundries' unless it cannot be helped and unless the amounts are infrequent and small. Otherwise, the whole system is pointless because it is not a true analysis. Entries should be made as they occur: where this is not convenient, a note of details should be made and entries made later the same day. Private affairs should be kept completely separate from those of the business.

The example illustrates several points which apply to many retailers. Costs are analysed according to purpose rather than source: thus the total phone bill may be divided into telephone-selling calls (a few regular calls each week have been assumed) classified under 'Advertising' and the remainder allocated to 'Occupancy' and attributed to 'Phone' – the retailer's accountant will apportion the latter between business and private calls. Similarly, a printer's bill for circulars, showcards, and price tickets, etc., would be classified as 'Advertising and display', and only letter-headed notepaper or receipt forms charged within the 'Office' column and attributed to 'Printing'. Postage and stationery would be treated in the same way.

The 'Wages' column includes national insurance and any similar payments as well as employees' income tax. It might be useful to add an extra column for commission if this is paid to staff so that the total can be found quickly. Wages of delivery boy are classified under delivery because it may be more important to arrive at total delivery costs than total wage costs, which can still be found easily. Postage on an article mailed to a customer is in effect delivery cost. 'Purchases' include carriage inwards but discounts won are subtracted: that is, entries are the amounts actually paid to suppliers.

Charges for wrapping materials might form a separate column if the retailer particularly wanted to check easily on their total cost, but usually they can be added to 'Advertising' because in addition to carrying advertising frequently, their total varies in some relationship to total sales, as should all advertising outlays. Capital expenditure and repairs may well share a column if both items are infrequent, as they can be separated easily if required; on the other hand 'Advertising and display' may be better as two or more columns if the retailer is particularly watching expenditure on, say, window dressing or direct mail.

'Occupancy' may cover rent, rates, insurance, lighting, heating, cleaning, and phone. 'Office' might include stationery, printing and postage, bank charges, accountant's fees, and trade subscriptions. It may be better to keep drawings – cash taken from the business by the retailer as an advance payment of end-of-year profit – separately from wages even though they are, largely at least, the retailer's own wages. Decisions on column headings are best taken in consultation with the accountant.

Unusual fluctuations in a day's takings, like those caused by deep snow or a bus strike, should be mentioned in brackets in the details column after the word 'Takings'. A steady fall in takings or available cash may or may not be a sign of impending failure: the only real test is whether net profit is declining. Such an occurrence should not be ignored as it is more likely to worsen rapidly than to improve. The reasons are usually obvious, but if not, the accountant should be consulted.

Some retailers find it useful to maintain a 'payments' book, a simple notebook ruled for pounds, and possibly, pence in which each page represents one month and each line a working day. As soon as they are known, all commitments, such as rate demands as well as invoices, are entered against the last possible date for payment, consistent with claiming any discounts and the general policy of paying all bills within a reasonable time. The total of any page indicates the amount owed to date in that month and acts as a guide to the commitments the retailer must meet.

The accountant will advise, if necessary, about pay-as-you-earn tax procedure and arrange what other records need to be kept. Often these are only invoices, statements, and receipts, and a profitability table with associated stocktaking and re-ordering sheets, or whatever alternative system is used. This comparatively small amount of paperwork is usually all that is necessary, but retailers wishing to study bookkeeping in more detail can find recommended books in Appendix 11.

The annual accounts which the accountant prepares are the trading account, profit and loss account, and balance sheet. He will explain the implications of the results, although any retailer can tell unaided a certain amount from the balance sheet: whether the business is solvent, that is, whether at the date of the balance sheet the assets were greater than the liabilities; and the type and value of all assets and liabilities, in particular whether liquid assets (cash in hand and at bank together with total debts outstanding to the business) were sufficient to pay outstanding creditors. The importance of not tying up too great a proportion of capital in property, equipment, and other fixed assets can be realized: they cannot be used by a going concern to pay creditors.

SETTING TARGET PROFITS

Most people achieve better results when aiming at a target rather than taking things as they come. It is, therefore, beneficial for a retailer to aim to achieve at least a targeted increase in net profit each year. The target should be high enough to make it difficult to attain but low enough to make reaching it practicable. There is little thrill in having accomplished a target set too low, nor much encouragement if one consistently falls short of a target deliberately set too high.

The targeted profit increase will vary from shop to shop and may vary from year to year, depending on trading conditions and local circumstances, but it might well be practicable to aim to increase net profit before tax by ten per cent annually over each previous year's figure. The practical result of such targets will be reflected in the 'Estimated stockturn' column of the profitability table but the measure of financial success will best show up in the accounts. The retailer's accountant will advise to what extent it might be worth preparing monthly or weekly analysed sales figures so that the retailer can have a frequent and accurate check on his trading progress and, whenever necessary, take remedial action in time.

The accountant may also be able to save the retailer paying tax unnecessarily. For example, it is nearly always an advantage to have the retailer's wife paid a regular wage so long as she does in fact work in the business. The money she earns as wages qualifies for wife's earned income relief; if she worked ostensibly for nothing the money would appear as net profit at the end of the year and would probably carry a great deal more tax.

Even if her rewards were drawn weekly in the retailer's name, the amount being added to the retailer's own drawings and subsequently handed over to her, tax is likely to be paid unnecessarily. The first few pounds earned by anyone attracts much less tax than if the same sum is added to existing wages. Similarly, it may be an advantage to pay regular wages to a son employed in the shop or for deliveries. If the wife is a partner in substance and not merely in name, her share of the profits under the partnership agreement attracts earned income and reduced rate reliefs whether or not she actually works in the business.

An accountant can also advise on many other matters which may save the retailer money, regarding death duties, for example, and whether or not formation of a partnership or limited liability company will save tax being paid unnecessarily. Should it ever be necessary to dispose of a business, the accountant can advise whether it would be more advantageous to try to sell as a going concern, to sell the company, if there is one and if this is possible, or to realize on individual assets separately.

BRANCH SHOP ACCOUNTING

It is best to consider any branch premises as an entirely separate business for accounting purposes, even though the accountant may decide to add together figures for main shop and branch when preparing annual accounts for the inspector of taxes. Two major advantages gained are that a separate figure is produced for the branch for gross profit percentage on sales, helping to check the honesty and efficiency of the branch manager, and that a separate profitability table can be compiled, indicating among much else the best lines to stock for the branch's own location and surrounding area. Because every shop handles slightly different lines and at varying stockturn rates, the gross profit percentage of the branch will never be identical with that of the main shop, but it should never deviate significantly from that produced by the accountant after consideration of branch purchases, stock, and takings.

Discrepancies in branch takings or stock may be due to branch assistants: it is, therefore, best to allow a branch manager sole authority in selecting branch staff, so that he is responsible for shortages however they may occur. It is also necessary to define the branch manager's authority for buying, both in respect of extent and sources. It is common to charge purchases at selling prices, whether they come directly from suppliers or through the main premises. This aids control over efficiency and honesty of branch management: knowing opening stock, subsequent purchases and value of sales, all at selling prices, the notional value of closing stock at selling prices can be found quickly.

The accounts of the branch shop should be charged with a sum fairly representing the owner's time in supervision and administration. It may be a percentage of turnover if the work is closely in proportion to sales, such as doing all the buying and keeping most of the records. Where doubt exists, the charge should err on the higher side as this is easier to adjust subsequently without upsetting the branch manager.

A fair proportion of all running expenses, including such items as bank charges and wrapping materials, should also be allocated. It is important that the branch manager should know what costs are being allotted to his shop and that he should be allowed to see and comment on the accounts of his branch.

CREDIT TRADING

Whether or not a retailer should allow his customers to buy on credit is closely connected with his accounts. Credit trading requires extra book-work, and by permitting a considerable sum, probably made up of a large number of small amounts, to be owed to him the retailer may find that his own accounts show he is approaching insolvency or is granting credit which costs him a great deal in interest charges.

Custom sometimes determines whether a trader should grant credit. No one expects credit when they buy a bar of chocolate; everyone expects credit for at least one week for delivered newspapers, no matter how small their value. But usually it is for the retailer to lay down his own policy. The test is simple: will the profit on the extra trade so created be greater than the cost of financing the credit, bearing the loss of any non-payments, and recompense the extra work involved? The answer will depend largely on the type of merchandise sold (credit for expensive items naturally attracting proportionately more profitable custom than for goods costing little), on the class of customer catered for, and the policy adopted by competitors.

Credit trading does create extra trade and this is regular, if only because customers must enter the shop each week or month to pay off some of the outstanding balance. Other items are sometimes then bought, or at least noticed and bought subsequently. Credit customers tend to be loyal to a shop even when no longer in debt. The amount of trading on credit terms has grown greatly in recent years, and customers of many trades and in many localities have come to expect credit facilities as a matter of course. There are five main ways of selling on credit: weekly or monthly credit accounts; using one of the recognized credit card or check-trading systems; operating 'budget' accounts; and by offering hire purchase or credit sale agreements.

Credit accounts, settled weekly or monthly, are usually for relatively small amounts, often offered to established customers without

charge to retain their custom and build goodwill. No formalities
are normally involved beyond noting the prices, dates, and identi-
fying description of purchases on credit, together with amounts
and dates of payments, and outstanding balance.

Credit cards are issued by most banks and certain other large
organizations. Schemes vary slightly, but, in general, members
wishing to purchase on credit produce a special identity card and
sign the retailer's bill, which is sent to the organization for payment. Most organizations charge the retailer several per cent
commission for their service.

The shopkeeper must therefore decide before joining such a
scheme – there is sometimes a very small entrance fee or annual
charge in addition – whether the cut in net profit is worth the
extra business brought in. Shops agreeing to accept any of the
credit card schemes are listed in a directory issued to the organization's members and display insignia on the shopfront. This can
encourage trade that would not otherwise arrive, especially in
tourist centres because most operators of these schemes have
reciprocal arrangements in other countries. Credit cards are
normally issued to people of reasonable credit standing, who also
tend to be those, such as newly-weds, who need substantial
purchases over quite a lengthy period.

Credit card schemes have the advantage of reducing cash
handling, but the drawback of additional paperwork. Check-
trading systems are basically similar.

Budget accounts, sometimes called 'revolving credit', may be
offered to customers up to the limit thought safe by the retailer,
often eight times the monthly repayment, which is a constant
amount. The idea is to encourage customers to make purchases so
that this credit facility is used most of the time up to the agreed
limit, repayments being made ideally by monthly banker's
standing order. A small charge, such as a halfpenny per pound
owed each month, is common, or a suitable charge can be added to
the cash price at the time of purchase.

Larger shops issue holders of budget accounts with an identity
card which states the credit limit and includes space for noting

purchases, though this is only a rough check on the state of the account and does not replace the full accounting record, which needs to be consulted for sanction to purchase further items of substantial value. Purchases over the credit limit can be paid for in cash for the excess. It is good publicity to make known that any credit balance will always be paid out in cash on demand, a facility rarely requested.

Hire purchase facilities are frequently expected by customers for many relatively costly articles, such as furniture, large domestic electric appliances, and cars. A written agreement has to be signed by both the customer and retailer, naming the item concerned. There is normally a down-payment followed by payment of stated sums at weekly or monthly intervals for the duration of the agreement. The service charge for this credit facility, which includes interest on the sum involved, is fairly high.

The goods remain the property of the retailer until payment has been made in full, thus hire purchase is normally used for articles with reasonable repossession value. This gives the retailer greater security than any other form of credit selling, where the ultimate sanction involves the trouble and expense of suing for the debt.

Credit sale agreements are somewhat similar to hire purchase agreements, with which they are often confused. They are, however, another form of instalment selling: written contracts for outright sale at the time of entering into the agreement, with the purchase price being paid by stated instalments at stated times. They tend to be used for articles with relatively little repossession value, such as furnishings, bedding, and clothing, and because such items depreciate quickly, credit sale agreements are often for shorter periods than hire purchase agreements. However, in practice, where items such as bedding and furnishings are bought at the same time as furniture, for example, it is common to sell them all on the same hire purchase agreement.

CREDITWORTHINESS

Before allowing a substantial amount of credit to any customer it is common sense to check his character and ability to pay. The retailer can ask the customer to complete a credit application form, giving details of his occupation and employer, showing whether he is a householder, and whether he has hire purchase or other credit agreements in operation. Names of two or three referees, preferably other retailers and a bank, can also be requested.

A status inquiry by one of the recognized agencies can be initiated if the transaction is large, but often it will be sufficient for the retailer to make his own inquiries through banking channels, and perhaps the customer's landlord and other shops he uses, based on the credit application form information. If the retailer carries on much credit trading he may consider joining a local credit protection association, if one exists. Small amounts of credit are often given to respectable customers without any detailed checks being carried out, but at least some relevant information should be requested, if only to deter a potential defaulter.

If such precautions are carried out and the terms on which credit is granted are made perfectly clear when making the sale, there is comparatively little risk. To avoid attracting the wrong type of customer it may be better not to publicize that credit facilities are available, offering them only if requested.

Despite growth in use of cheque guarantee cards issued by banks, many creditworthy shoppers have never troubled to obtain one. To avoid creating two classes of customer – those with guarantee cards and those without, rather than those credit-worthy and those not – some retailers ignore such cards and ask all customers to write their name and address on the back of any cheque, as before introduction of guarantee cards.

OVERDUE ACCOUNTS

Occasionally, however, it is necessary to remind a customer that payment is overdue. As this may arise through forgetfulness, illness, or a disputed account, the first request for repayment should be polite. If this is ignored, the non-payment is almost certainly due to shortage of money or an attempt to avoid payment, so subsequent letters should be very firm. The first letter should point out the total amount outstanding as well as the instalment amount and date on which that sum was due, and should go on politely to ask for settlement of the instalment payment within, say, seven days or for notification of the reason. No honest customer is annoyed by such a request if it is politely written, pointing out that the retailer has had to pay in full for the goods to his own supplier.

If this produces no response a second letter should follow a week or two after the time limit set in the first letter has expired, pointing out that this is the second request and that, failing at least intimation why repayment has not been made, the matter will be put in solicitor's hands within a further, say, seven days. There is no point in dragging out matters: an honest person will respond at once even if it is only to ask by letter or in person for more time to pay. An exception may be made when it seems likely that the customer is away on holiday, but he should have remembered to mention this to the retailer in advance.

Requests for extra time to pay should be treated with caution and not agreed to unless there is a genuine excuse or unless it seems the best way to get the amount settled. Payments may then be reduced and spread over a longer period but they should continue to be regular. Extra time to pay should not be granted regularly as it is costly in the retailer's use of his capital and in his time in bookkeeping, while also being unfair to customers who keep their promise. Customers who take a very long time to pay off their commitments are usually doing business elsewhere; their custom, unless on normal trading terms, can be dispensed with.

Where a retailer has many credit accounts he may find it useful, as long as it is not an unnecessary complication, to spread the paperwork evenly over the week or month. Instead of making all payments due on, say, the first of each month, he can arrange for all credit customers whose surnames begin with letters A to D to pay during the first week of each month, those E to K in the second week, L to R in the third, and the remainder in the fourth week. This avoids a rush of payments on any single day of the month disrupting cash trading, and also gives the retailer more time to send out any necessary letters requesting repayment. A note of which customers have been sent which payment requests should be kept.

Checks should be made occasionally to see whether credit trading is worth the extra trouble and risk, and whether the proportion of bad debts incurred can be reduced. The latter may be achieved by taking more care when granting credit to little-known customers, by troubling to check up as thoroughly as possible on customers' creditworthiness and being extra cautious where this is not possible, by restricting credit to certain classes of goods or by lowering the limit of credit granted, or by adopting credit insurance for isolated transactions of above-average amounts. An accountant usually can suggest what proportion of bad debts to credit business turnover is reasonable, taking into consideration the circumstances of the individual shop.

FINANCING CREDIT TRADING

The amount of additional capital required to finance credit trading varies with the volume of credit business, proportion of the total price asked of customers as deposit, length of credit agreements, and the amount of service charge to cover the retailer's interest, extra overheads, and profit.

Many retailers do not finance their own hire purchase or credit sale agreement trading, though – provided they are prudent – it can be highly lucrative if they can spare the capital. It is usual to arrange that the extra capital investment necessary is provided by a hire purchase finance house through either the direct collection or block-discounting method. In the former, the retailer puts the customer in touch at once with the finance house, which buys the goods and so becomes the legal owner. The customer hires from the finance house, pays it directly and normally buys the merchandise in due course, the retailer dropping out of the transaction as soon as the customer and finance house are introduced.

When using the block-discounting method, the retailer enters into a contract with his customer but sells his contractual rights to a finance house, usually in a monthly or weekly batch or 'block' (hence the name), receiving immediate payment for most of the value of the goods together with deferred payments of the remainder due. In these circumstances the customer has no contact with the finance house, payments being made to the retailer, who passes them on. The retailer often has to guarantee his customers to the finance house, to which he is liable if his customers default, recouping his loss, if he can, from the customer who really owes the money.

Hire purchase and credit sale agreement trading tends to become self-financing once these sales have reached a steady turnover, repayments roughly covering outlay on merchandise. Any retailer interested in offering his customers hire purchase or credit sale agreement facilities may find that his trade association runs its own scheme. Alternatively, he may obtain the necessary information from the Hire Purchase Trade Association or Finance Houses Association, whose addresses are given in Appendix 8.

The legal position when selling on credit, especially through hire purchase or credit sale agreements, needs to be carefully understood by the retailer. There are several detailed books on the subject, as indicated in Appendix 11.

10. Staff Management

Most small shops employ at least one assistant; even those that do not at first, usually need to employ staff once trade has been built up sufficiently. Dealing with staff is the most difficult part of retailing for some shopkeepers: there is the continual problem of not only getting on happily with someone else, usually considerably younger and often with a different background and ideas, but also getting them to do willingly what the retailer wants. There is the need to arouse and sustain employees' enthusiasm for the job, as well as their friendship and respect for the retailer.

It is worth looking at the problem for a moment from the employee's viewpoint. Because assistants are more frequently female they are referred to here as 'she' but observations refer also to male assistants. She, or he, can obtain the normal retail assistant's wage anywhere and without much effort. If she is to be a hard-working and loyal employee there must be more to the job than simply the basic wage.

A 'pleasant' job is the usual first requirement. This has two aspects: interest in the work itself and, no less important, pleasantness in dealings with the retailer and any other employees. Other requirements are the chance to earn more money, an opportunity to improve status by taking more responsibility, and, sometimes, the chance to learn about retailing and the goods.

The retailer who can offer these requirements to an employee will never be without staff of above-average quality, helping his business to thrive and making his own work more enjoyable. By far the most usual shortcoming in what a retailer has to offer an employee is a pleasant human relationship. This is hardly surprising as the relationship between almost any two people is constantly in an uncertain state because reactions are unpredictable, while attitudes and even choice of words – including those of the retailer himself – frequently fall short of the ideal, especially during periods of temporary overwork.

It is all the more difficult for a retailer because in addition to being in constant close contact with an employee, giving greater opportunity for misunderstanding, he is also in the ambiguous position of being both master and friend. But there are techniques to help people get on smoothly with others and, to put it at its crudest, to get them to do willingly what one wants. Further help on this subject is given in Appendices 10 and 11.

From the purely business point of view, staff management is extremely important. Employees are a costly overhead, incurring more than merely the wage bill and thus representing a sizeable investment, while on them very largely depends increase in the goodwill the retailer is trying to build. Poor-quality staff also have the power to diminish goodwill actively: inefficiency loses customers, and lack of enthusiasm loses potential sales. Good staff selection, training, and relations are important to help the retailer earn more money and enhance the value of his business, not to mention moral considerations.

One of the secrets of getting the best results from staff is to choose the best material. This does not necessarily mean someone already highly trained and highly paid. So the first step is to choose from the most suitable people available, realizing that one is very lucky indeed to get exactly what one wants.

JOB ANALYSIS

But before the retailer can choose an appropriate assistant it is important to know exactly what he is looking for, otherwise there is no standard against which to compare. So it is necessary to consider carefully, precisely what will be required of the assistant and list the result in a 'job analysis'. This has the advantage of forcing the retailer to consider objectively all aspects of the assistant's work, of being able to provide applicants with a true picture of the job they are required to do, and of producing the necessary standard of comparison.

A retailer is not being fair to himself if he thinks of the assistant's job as 'serving and all the usual odd jobs'. He should consider what the odd jobs really are, what proportion of total time they take, and what training, aptitudes, and character are required. So a job analysis might look something like that shown in Table 12.

This reveals the qualities to look for when choosing staff and the degree of importance of each. Some retailers may be surprised to find that an attribute to which they attach great importance, for example early arrival, is of comparatively little real significance except in so far as it may indicate enthusiasm or reliability. Each ideal quality is required all the time, to produce consistency – even though the amount of time spent on tasks involving it may be small.

Table 12. A typical job analysis

Work	Approximate percentage of time	Ideal qualities
Selling to, and advising, customers	40	Knowledge of products and prices; selling ability; sympathetic, intelligent, truthful, patient, acceptable appearance, speech and manners
Wrapping goods	5	Simple manual dexterity
Handling cash	5	Honesty; reasonable arithmetic
Writing sales bills, special orders, etc.	5	Readable writing
Checking stock	5	Thoroughness, simple arithmetic
Arranging stock display	5	Neatness; elementary display sense
Writing price tickets, display posters, etc.	5	Ditto; able to do simple display writing or use display lettering kits
Unpacking; stocking shelves; cleaning shop	10	Willingness to do unskilled work; thoroughness
Answering phone; phoning orders	2½	Ability to understand, follow and convey simple instructions and requests; acceptable voice and phone manner
Etc.	Etc.	Etc.

Although the attributes of an ideal employee will vary with the retailer and type of shop, there are certain over-riding qualities required, such as a sense of responsibility; the desire to work in retailing for good reason; reliability; good health, including the ability to stand for long periods without discomfort (which reflects in sales proficiency); the temperament for working as one of a small group, and so on. Just as a retailer himself must be full of enthusiasm for his job and like the merchandise and type of customers of the trade in which he works, so must an employee. If she has not yet learnt about the trade or the techniques of face-to-face selling, she must be keen to learn. She must also be honest, be able to use the English language reasonably well, and be accurate with arithmetic, even if not quick with it. There will be some overlapping of ideal qualities listed in the job analysis for the various activities, as well as with the general attributes looked for, which are best noted before the first item in the analysis. Although contact with customers may occupy less than half an assistant's time, it is still by far the most important activity, and any candidate's suitability will be judged mainly on their capacity for making sales after the necessary training.

SELECTION GUIDE

From this list of ideal qualities it is easy to compile a suitable 'staff-selection checklist'. This will probably first list all the attributes the retailer considers essential for the particular job, and then continue with all those desirable. Particularly if he is to compare several applicants for the same vacancy, it may be worth scoring each applicant against the total possible marks he allocates in some reasonable proportion to each essential and desirable quality. This will help to overcome a common defect in staff selection, the 'halo effect', by which any applicant with one or two particularly strong attributes, beneficial or detrimental to the post, tends to be judged disproportionately in their light.

Once a staff-selection checklist for an assistant has been drawn up, it may remain of use with very little modification for many years, during which time a number of assistants may have to be interviewed. If the scoring method is adopted, it is also of use in making a detailed comparison between applicants for any particular vacancy, ensuring more accuracy than the part-remembered details of interviews, probably spread over several days and possibly each interrupted by the need to deal with urgent matters in the shop. It is not suggested that the retailer goes to greater lengths to devise his job analysis and scored checklist than is appropriate for his particular shop, but compiling them will clarify his mind about what he is really looking for, directing his attention to what is often one of the weakest areas of retail management.

The job analysis and staff-selection checklist will also make it easy to jot down a few questions to put to prospective employees likely to reveal the information required, such as 'Why do you want to work in a shop?' 'Why do you think work in this shop will suit you better than in some others?' and 'What position do you expect to be working in and how much do you think you will be earning in three years' time?'

It is important to realize that it is a first-class investment to pay a little more than may be usual and gain a good assistant than to pay the bare minimum and attract only the poorest quality. An extra, say, one pound a week represents a fairly small increase in the minimum investment necessary, yet it can increase the total value of that investment enormously if it is the means of attracting and keeping a good assistant. But a suitable applicant may not present herself when the retailer is choosing an assistant, so it is necessary to keep in mind what is the minimum standard one will accept as well as to establish what is the ideal, and to assess an appropriate wage for both levels of proficiency, and for inter-mediate grades.

There are minimum wages laid down by law for retailing in most trades. The shopkeeper can find out whether his trade is affected and, if so, what the minimum wages are, by writing to the senior wages inspector at any regional office of the Department of Employment, the address of which can be obtained from any employment exchange and some post offices.

FINDING ASSISTANTS

Some retailers prefer to train their own assistants, others like to take on staff already fully experienced. If a beginner is preferred, it may be convenient to approach the headmaster or headmistress of a local comprehensive or secondary modern school, or the local youth employment officer (the address of the youth employment service – which deals with people under the age of 18 – can be found from the telephone directory, employment exchange, or town hall), asking in a brief letter if they can recommend anyone suitable. The letter should mention the type of goods sold, the kind of customer served and when the assistant will be required to start work. As much advance notice as possible should be given. If an assistant is sought through an employment exchange, similar information should be given, if possible by a personal visit.

If a truly progressive career, perhaps leading to the position of manager, can be offered, it may be worth contacting a local grammar school. With the continuing trend towards employing more and more part-time, and especially part-time female, assistants, the role of the full-time, and especially full-time male, assistant grows more important – as the backbone of the staff, frequently the trainer of part-time assistants, and sometimes as the retailer's deputy. Many full-time male assistants at present working in this capacity entered retailing in the 1930s for lack of better career opportunities. As they are now approaching retirement age and it is difficult to attract young men of equivalent calibre, there is need for shops, including smaller establishments, to attract replacements as official or unofficial management trainees.

Occasionally it may be possible to obtain the assistant through recommendation by a friend or acquaintance of the retailer. Although this may be a good way to find the required person, it has the real drawback that it may not be easy to dismiss or fully control the assistant without risk of offending the friend or acquaintance.

Advertisement is often the best way to find an assistant. Sometimes a notice in the shop window is sufficient, especially if it is essential to employ someone living locally. Otherwise an advertisement in the local paper's 'situations vacant' column will be used. It may save the retailer's time if he states there just what he wants, particularly whether experienced or not, full-time or part-time, permanent or temporary, and the type of goods dealt in. The retailer can give the name and address of his shop if he does not mind dealing with applicants who may call when he is busy, nor it being known generally that he is the advertiser. Alternatively, he can use a newspaper's box number. It may be worth seeing all applicants because the most suitable assistant may not write a particularly good letter.

CONDUCTING AN INTERVIEW

An interview is held for three reasons: to outline the job and conditions of work to the applicant, to see how she measures up to the ideal standard, and to compare her with other candidates. It is desirable to hold the interview where the retailer will not be interrupted frequently, for example to serve customers.

It is usually best to start by finding out a very few facts, such as whether the applicant is experienced, wants full-time work, and so on. The retailer can then continue by stating the approximate wage, saying that the exact amount will be decided when he has had opportunity to consider the applicant's details. This can be followed by mentioning any special benefits, such as time off for study; the chance to meet a variety of people and help them; work being located conveniently near home; it being on the whole clean and 'light', with sufficient range of duties to stop it becoming boring. The retailer may also be able to offer a bonus or commission on sales, and a discount on staff purchases – which is often an important consideration for an assistant, perhaps more valuable than a bonus. He should then state what is expected in return from the employee, being precise about the hours to be worked, including whether the employee is expected to arrive a few minutes before opening time to prepare the shop and stay after closing to clear up, and about rest days.

The retailer can show the first two columns of the job analysis to the applicant if he wishes, but if he does not, he should carefully explain what non-selling duties, such as cleaning the shop and unpacking, are necessary and the approximate amount of time they take. It is pointless giving the assistant a false impression: the retailer wants to choose someone who will both stay and work willingly. But even so, the benefits of the job, such as variety of customers and better conditions than found in factory work, should be mentioned.

The retailer should then inquire whether the applicant is still interested and if so, after dealing with any queries, he can ask for more details. As well as those prompted by the job specification, he can ascertain the applicant's previous training and jobs, scholastic ability, and a little about her home life; for example, whether she has any relative in the trade or any disability in the family which might keep her away from work sometimes. Some shopkeepers also ask one or two mental arithmetic problems and sometimes put to a simple test the candidate's skill in parcel making, sales bill writing, and ability in salesmanship, with the retailer acting as a moderately difficult customer.

All the while the retailer has a chance to assess the applicant, making allowances for possible nervousness. Facial appearance, tidiness in dress, and pleasant manner are all important and, especially if the shop sells food, personal cleanliness is vital. Hands, especially finger-nails, and hair, are good indicators. An easy smile and cheerful disposition are great assets for an assistant, although these are not easy to observe during an interview.

The advantage of the retailer doing most of the talking first is that it helps to put the applicant at ease, making it easier to assess her correctly. By telling her the wages and conditions almost at once she is left free to concentrate on what for the retailer are more important matters: her duties. To choose the reverse order is to risk frightening the applicant with the recital of duties for which she may expect an unduly high wage, leading to disappointment.

It is important to discover why an applicant wants the job. If any shop assistant's post will do it is unlikely that the applicant will be the first-class employee hoped for. The same applies if she wants a job because she 'wants the money' or because she 'could never stand factory work'. There must be positive enthusiasm both for retailing itself and for the articles of the trade. This is even more important where a male assistant is engaged.

The interview is likely to be more helpful to the retailer if he can encourage the applicant to talk freely. Tactfully phrased questions that do not require a simple 'yes' or 'no' reply should invite the candidate to reveal important aspects of her motives, character, and attitudes.

Before taking on an assistant it is usual to follow up references from previous employers and, if the applicant is young, to see one or two school reports. A note to the candidate's doctor asking if he knows of any disability relevant to work as a shop assistant is also a good idea.

The shopkeeper may have to accept an employee who falls short of his requirements but he should continue to keep an eye open for the right person, specially if he can offer a progressive career for a really suitable assistant. Promotion will need to be on merit, not length of service, though regard must be had for employees who have given years of loyal service. In addition to offering them a continuing, relatively secure job with prospects of pay increasing at least in step with the rising cost of living, it may also be possible to arrange advancement in apparent status by widening slightly their range of minor responsibilities.

STAFF POLICY

The best way to keep good staff is to have a thought-out policy towards employees. They should be rewarded financially of course, their wages being reviewed automatically at least once a year, and it is worth telling them on engagement when the automatic review takes place. As the cost of living tends to rise every year a proportionate increase in wages is really giving away nothing, but a good employee has every right to expect more than just this increase. If the retailer aims to have good staff, his wages policy will be independent of official minimum wage regulations as he will be paying well above the legal minimum.

Encouragement can be an extremely valued reward. Every person wants very much indeed to be appreciated. If an employee works particularly hard one Saturday, thank her specially and say her efforts did not go unnoticed; if she makes a useful suggestion such as a new layout for certain goods, thank her enthusiastically, say it will be adopted, and if possible let her know a few weeks or months later that you remember it was her suggestion. Always give employees full credit for their suggestions, which should be welcomed at all times. A good suggestion is often worth payment: even twenty pence in these circumstances seems much more valuable simply because the retailer is not obliged to give it. If a suggestion is not practicable the assistant should be told the reason in a way which will not stifle further initiative.

As the retailer aims to have his staff doing what he wants, it is obvious that he must make his policy known. He should explain, for example, his attitude on the degree of substitute selling thought desirable.

Every week or so he should also quietly ask if everything is going well with the employee and whether there is anything she does not feel too happy about. This should be done in such a way that any grievance will be brought out into the open, instead of possibly festering into something more serious. Any complaint should be dealt with fairly and allowance made for the fact that something apparently trifling may seem very important indeed to the assistant.

A friendly relationship between employer and staff should always be the aim. It is the unbending employer with a constant 'keep in your place, you're my employee' attitude who invites mockery behind the employer's back, disrespect, and probably also dislike. A retailer who admits mistakes, apologizes to an assistant when an apology is due, and is tactful enough to let an employee save her face, wins respect and loyalty.

It should always be pointed out to staff that ability to pay wages depends on profits, and that high turnover does not necessarily mean high net profit. If an employee understands how a business operates and realizes how many overhead charges exist there is every possibility that she will work all the more harmoniously in the retailer's interest. Thus products carrying a good margin should be specially pointed out. Sometimes it is possible to chat with an employee about minor business problems, without disclosing confidential matters: they invariably feel flattered and it helps them see retailing in a wider perspective.

Such aspects of personal contact between proprietor and staff are all the more important these days: they are a major advantage which the smaller retailer has over his larger competitors and they ensure that employer and employee are not pulling in opposite directions. It goes without saying that a retailer should comply with his own declared policy. If, for example, it is one of 'customer always first' he should not call an assistant away from serving to ask her something which could wait.

Other aspects of staff policy which have to be considered include degree of restriction on smoking on the premises, whether suspicious-looking parcels may be taken home after work without question, and what type of clothes may not be worn. It is often a good idea to supply staff with overalls, which add brightness to the shop and give a continual impression of neatness and efficiency. But the overalls must always have a fresh appearance and look reasonably clean. Some shops expect assistants to pay a few coppers a week towards their laundering but this parsimonious attitude is not the best way to encourage unbounded enthusiasm and cooperation. Overalls provided by the retailer naturally remain his property should the assistant leave. As customers like to be able to tell at once who is a member of the staff it is advantageous for overalls to display the name of the shop, or for assistants and the retailer to wear an obvious badge.

It is necessary to teach the retailer's policy to an assistant. It may be necessary also to train her in the techniques of retailing and about the merchandise on offer; this is dealt with in the next chapter. But the job of the retailer is to inspire and lead as well as teach. Considerable tact is necessary at all times. If more than one assistant is employed it may be necessary at some time to patch up differences between them: inter-staff tiffs can be expensive for the retailer.

COMMISSION

Sometimes retailers pay their staff a commission or bonus on sales; whether this is an advantage or not depends on the shop's circumstances and its trading policy. It is a contradiction, for example, to instruct an assistant that substitute sales are not to be pressed and at the same time to offer an incentive markedly based on turnover or profit. Incentives based on individual effort are more appropriate where more than one assistant is employed, to encourage prompt service by each member of the staff. But drawbacks still exist: for example, it is necessary to be able to keep a check on the value of goods served by each assistant, the senior assistant may also demand first opportunity to serve if not herself already occupied, and there may be a tendency to 'oversell' customers.

If an incentive payment system is adopted by a small shop it is usually based on the increase in turnover or profit during a week or month compared with the corresponding period in the previous year, or alternatively, it takes the form of a fixed amount if a target figure for the week or month is exceeded. In either instance, the proportion of bonus or commission to total earnings should be small because the assistant must be able to rely on a regular substantial wage even if business is bad. Such payments should be made a week or month, as the case may be, in arrear to allow time for the amount to be calculated.

Many progressive small retailers consider that such payments are not worth the trouble and prefer to pay an above-average basic wage to keep up staff morale and initiative. If this is done and no reference is made at the time of engagement to any bonus payments, yet exceptional effort by an assistant during a particular day, week, or holiday period is rewarded by a small extra payment, it may bring even greater returns in increased incentive and gratitude, simply because such payments are unexpected and show that the assistant's efforts are noticed and appreciated.

SUPERVISION

One of the prime duties of a retailer employing staff is to supervise. This is not as easy to do properly as it sounds: badly performed supervision can very easily indeed cause bad feeling between shopkeeper and staff and can kill an assistant's initiative, to the retailer's own detriment.

Supervision on any particular task really consists of explaining clearly what is required and making sure the assistant understands; leaving her to do the job unwatched; subsequently checking that it has been done properly and complimenting the assistant on the way it has been done or explaining to her why it is not quite right. In the latter instance, the assistant should be shown again the right way, and where the task is suitable, at once given another chance to prove herself.

It is pointless for the retailer to lose his temper because a mistake has been made. The assistant has done her best, unless she is being deliberately obstructive, in which case the retailer has chosen his assistant badly – probably his own fault – or has not maintained good relations. The object is to get the assistant to do the particular job well, so patience and encouragement, not argument, are the qualities required. Praise for having done any part of the job properly goes a long way in getting the assistant's cooperation for subsequent attempts, and makes learning easier. Each new task then becomes a challenge to the assistant, though probably lying within her capabilities. Desiring self-respect and also to please, she will try to do it well for her own sake.

If a serious mistake is made, the retailer can say, if possible when no other staff can hear, that he is most annoyed and rather disappointed, but such chastisement should not be given bitterly and should be accompanied by helpful advice about how to do the job. Where the task is so important that the assistant cannot be left completely alone it is better to appear to leave her, and to busy oneself with some other duty while staying fairly near and keeping an eye on what she is doing, so that a really important mistake can be stopped in time. It is better not to interrupt if a minor error is being made.

General supervision as opposed to supervision of a particular task follows the same principles. It is important to find out why any work is done badly, to take corrective action – which may be a restatement of what should have been done but in the worst instances involves trying to find a better employee – and to check later that an improvement has occurred. Checking up, whether on a particular task or generally, is best done without being observed when this is possible, to lessen the chances of resentment by the employee and explosive comment by the retailer if he finds something wrong. But verification should never be done furtively: it is part of the retailer's job and there is nothing to be ashamed of if discovered by the assistant when checking up.

Instructions to assistants should always be clear, concise, unambiguous, and firm. They should never be given through third parties. The tone of voice, manner, and timing are also important.

It may sometimes be necessary to hear a grievance in private or to refuse a request for a wage increase. These situations call for tactful and sympathetic but firm handling. The retailer's attitude should be complete willingness to see the assistant in private and to hear all that she has to say. He should then let her know that her complaint is fully understood, give general encouragement and full credit for all the employee's good points. The decision should then be given firmly, along with the reasons.

Although some further discussion may take place and the retailer even alter his decision in the light of the new facts, he should never get into an argument. If the employee refuses to leave until she has had her way, the retailer can end with something like: 'You have told me clearly how you feel and it does you great credit that you have the courage and wisdom to come to see me about this; you have heard what I think and I have been at pains to explain why this is the best possible solution. Let us close the matter for the moment and we shall each think about it until this time tomorrow. If I have any new ideas on the subject I shall of course tell you, and if tomorrow you consider this solution is unacceptable perhaps you will tell me what you intend to do. Let us leave it like that until tomorrow.'

CHANGES IN STAFF

The reasons for an employee leaving are usually apparent but, if not, they should be discovered. It is useful to have a word with an assistant just before she goes, to find out also if the obvious reason is the only one. Such information can assist in future staff selection, training, or supervision and may even suggest a better method for performing some task in the shop.

Changes in staff are usually expensive. It takes time, often many weeks, before an assistant is working at full efficiency because at first she is unaccustomed to where goods are kept, which items are stocked, and the personal preferences of various regular customers. Her chances of making additional or substitute sales are also limited for similar reasons. Although she produces less benefit to the retailer she has to be paid at the full rate. In addition, there is the cost, in time and trouble, of teaching and supervising her.

But costs of staff changes do not end there. The assistant who is leaving rarely works properly up to the last minute, and sometimes a week's money may be given for which no value is received, rather than have her in the shop because of damage she may do to goodwill or in other ways. There are also the costs of advertising, the time spent interviewing, and the inconvenience until the vacancy is filled. The total cost of staff turnover can be high if assistants come and go frequently, and this is yet another good reason why it is not at all expensive to pay existing good staff an above-average wage to ensure that they continue to work well and want to remain with the retailer.

From time to time a retailer will be asked to give a reference concerning an assistant who used to work for him. He is not legally forced to, except in the rare instance when he has entered into a legal agreement to do so. Nevertheless, it is usual to give a reference when requested and it should be truthful. Even if it is unfavourable the retailer cannot be sued for libel or slander, unless it is both untrue and malicious, because such occasions are legally privileged: even so the retailer will take care that what he says is undoubtedly true. He is also theoretically liable for damages if a good reference is given falsely and the new employer suffers by acting on it.

Because of the legal implications few employers give a detailed reference in writing, but if any written reference is given, it is wise to include the statement that it is given to the best of one's knowledge and belief, and a copy should be kept. When asked to give a reference it is better to speak to the prospective employer on the telephone, where information can be given more freely, telling how long the assistant was with the retailer, why she left, mentioning good qualities and only the most major faults. These principles apply in reverse also: when engaging staff, little attention can be paid to written testimonials, it being far better to telephone the previous employer.

ENGAGING A MANAGER

Engaging a manager is basically similar to taking on any other staff but it is necessary for both parties to be more detailed and particularly important for the retailer to investigate references. Because the retailer will not want to disclose trading and accounting details unnecessarily, it is better to hold preliminary interviews with all applicants first, explaining to each that should he appear to be a likely candidate after all have been seen he will be asked to come for a more detailed discussion later. Probably the best two candidates will be invited for a second interview, but if none is really suitable it will be necessary to advertise again.

The advertisement should give such important details as size, class of trade, and locality of the branch, whether living accommodation is available, and method of remuneration. An informative advertisement placed where it is likely to be seen by the most suitable type of man is essential when seeking such a responsible employee.

The candidates have the right to expect more detail at their second interview about trading conditions and competition at the branch, the degree of supervision, what costs will be charged to branch accounts, manager's authority over staff, buying and other matters, the extent to which he will be allowed or expected to contribute ideas on improving the main shop as well as the branch, and whether he will be permitted to examine and comment on the accounts of his branch. The second interview, although even more important than the first, should be less formal. The working relationship between retailer and manager must be friendly: it is best to start off with the correct attitude.

It is usual for a manager to be paid a substantial basic salary, as a guarantee of reasonable security, together with a relatively small commission based on the new profit of his branch. This is better than basing payments on turnover as increased turnover does not necessarily indicate increased profit. The commission should be paid monthly rather than as an annual bonus to avoid being minimized when the manager considers his income, and it is important for the manager to be able to verify the amount of commission to which he is entitled.

If the retailer decides to take the manager into partnership or to allow him to buy shares in the company he will consult his accountant and solicitor about the best method, which may include allowing the manager to make his financial contribution by regular deductions from his salary. Tenancy of any living accommodation that is provided should be made a condition of employment to ensure that the premises will be vacated if the manager eventually leaves or is dismissed, irrespective of general tenancy legislation. It is reasonable to deduct the rental value of the tenancy and associated expenses such as rates and repairs from the manager's salary, though it is rare that the full economic value of the premises can be charged because the resulting salary appears unattractive.

The chosen manager should spend, where possible, two or three days at the main shop with the retailer before starting at his branch, enabling the retailer to better judge his capabilities and the manager to accustom himself to the merchandise and any special ways the retailer may have. Subsequently, there should be regular consultation between retailer and manager on problems which arise and on ways to improve efficiency and net profit, including possible new lines. It is wise to encourage comments on the main shop from the manager just as from assistants: all that this chapter says about employing staff applies to managers just as much as to assistants.

A notebook should be kept for recording details of all staff, including name, address and any phone number, date of joining, wage, date of leaving, and reason. There are also various legal requirements concerning staff outlined in Chapter 16.

Many small retailers lag behind industry in their staff relations, all the more surprising because it is in shops that assistants are in direct contact with customers. No shop is too small for a thought-out staff policy: the smaller the number of assistants the more closely do customers identify each with the retailer himself. Advantages of a progressive staff policy include providing employees with satisfaction in their work so that, apart from moral considerations, they work well and stay, with the consequent increase in sales and goodwill redounding to the retailer's own benefit. Personal contact between proprietor and assistant, and lack of staff regimentation, are big advantages small retailers have over chain store competitors.

11. Selling

Really good face-to-face selling is difficult: it is not possible to go back one step in the sequence of events, nor to stop for a while to consider carefully the next move. To make matters more difficult the buyer is just as flexible in possible 'moves' as is the seller, so the outcome frequently cannot be foreseen. Thus, good selling requires real skill in addition to knowledge.

Every retailer must ensure that his staff are properly skilled in sales techniques, and, if not, arrange that they learn; otherwise they can never fully earn their wages. Worse still, their presence excludes that of someone who might be much better at increasing profits and building goodwill. To deal fully with this vital aspect of retailing the author of this book has written another concerned solely with personal salesmanship,* suitable as a training manual for all who serve and as a detailed refresher course for the retailer himself.

TRAINING

Three types of training are required: knowledge of what is stocked, where it can be found, cash handling procedure, how to make parcels, and similar matters; knowledge of products, their uses, benefits to buyers, prices, advantages over competitors; and knowledge of sales technique.

Training in the first category is largely a matter of practice. The assistant may never have used a cash register before and no matter how experienced, will certainly need time to find her way around the shelves. If goods are arranged logically this task will be simplified. Patience is necessary in explaining all the many intricacies involved in selling from the particular shop, but an assistant can

* *Better Retail Selling* by Alan Fiber, published by Management Books.

hardly be blamed for not knowing them if she has not been clearly instructed in the first place.

It is best to explain the more important points first, leaving final details until the assistant has settled in. Positive instruction by either the retailer or a competent assistant is necessary: it takes much longer to learn by simply picking things up and meanwhile bad mistakes may occur.

Product knowledge may be gained from school, friends in the trade, books, catalogues, trade magazines, even indirectly from customers themselves, but the retailer must see that it is sound and up to date, and if necessary help with the instruction. Even experienced assistants will not know about new lines, so when these first arrive in the shop the retailer should explain in detail the products and the benefits that they bring the purchaser, and also indicate specifically the main sales points.

Training in sales technique must also be given by the retailer. Even experienced assistants may have gaps in their knowledge or they may have faults requiring correction. The best way to do this is for the retailer to act the part of a customer while the assistant sells to him. This can be done conveniently during a quiet trading period. Some retailers give a regular session lasting ten minutes or so almost every day.

During the period of instruction the retailer can imitate different kinds of customers – the talkative, silent, fussy, undecided, and so on – to give the assistant practice in dealing with them. By appropriate questioning he can also make the assistant tell him about particular products and their advantages and disadvantages compared with others. From this he can discover how much the assistant knows and can train her to make the correct response to questions by customers. If the assistant handles the encounter well, he should agree to 'purchase', and compliment her.

PREPARING TO SELL

As most customers are women the feminine gender is used here, but selling to women is sometimes slightly different from selling to men, a point worth mentioning to assistants. However, whether serving women or men, the assistant should be taught to create a favourable impression, which begins even before the customer enters the shop. The assistant should have a reasonably well-groomed appearance and an alert attitude. As the assistant stands for most of the day, shoes should be comfortable; it is difficult to be pleasant with aching feet.

The assistant should be trained to make every customer feel welcome, to greet them, and to smile. It is easy for even experienced assistants to forget this, but it helps customers feel important and the assistant gains their confidence. Most of all it depends on the assistant's attitude: the wish to be helpful. An excellent way of creating a happy sales relationship and building up goodwill is to greet a customer by name when it is known, but it is safer not to do so if there is any doubt; many people are far more annoyed by having their names mispronounced than by an assistant not remembering the name at all.

A junior assistant is sometimes extremely shy and the retailer will have to help her overcome this. One way is to encourage her to attend clubs and other group activities outside business hours where she can meet people and develop confidence in herself. But although the retailer can point out occasionally and tactfully that belonging to clubs can help the assistant in her work, he must avoid the impression of nagging her to accept this advice in case it is construed as unwarranted interference in her affairs. With practice in selling, a shy assistant will gradually grow confident, but perhaps the greatest confidence is engendered by the assistant realizing that she knows how to handle sales and knows the merchandise. Thus, to counteract shyness, teach the assistant her job as quickly and clearly as possible and give encouragement.

ASCERTAINING REQUIREMENTS

Every retailer realizes that few customers when they enter a shop know exactly what they want and make their requirements completely clear. So staff must be taught to find out the full requirements of each customer, and trained to listen to and observe customers, asking pertinent questions. Only then can the assistant offer the right merchandise.

It is usually a great psychological help to an assistant to realize that she is not so much selling as guiding a customer's choice. The customer shows she wants something and is in a buying mood by entering the shop.

SELLING BENEFITS

An assistant cannot be told too often that she is not selling merchandise but the benefits the goods can bring. A dress is not merely a means of keeping warm, but expresses the customer's desire to show she can choose something suitable, knows current fashion, and can treat herself to an article to match moods, clothes, or occasions. Soap is not only a combination of unpleasant fats and oils but an article to make her more attractive. The same principle applies to all products and just as much to men and children as to women.

The successful assistant is one who learns at an early stage to talk in terms of benefits to the customer. A sale becomes far more likely, desire is strengthened, and price becomes less important. Value for money always seems greater if the benefits are fully realized before the price. For this reason an assistant must be taught that it is usually better not to ask what price the customer has in mind when obtaining fuller details after initial welcoming.

But as price will clearly affect the eventual purchase, the assistant should be trained to produce a medium-priced article in the first place, unless the customer has stressed that she wants 'a good one' or 'something not too dear'. The article should be handled carefully by the assistant to emphasize its value: the more expensive the merchandise the more care should be taken, holding the goods up to eye level, letting the customer see it in a good light and displaying its best points to maximum effect. The assistant should be taught to allow the customer to handle the article herself: this adds greatly to her desire to possess it and thus aids the sale.

Every article bestows many benefits so an assistant should never be at a loss to find suitable sales talk if the retailer has ensured she is properly versed in product knowledge. This includes not only the advantages of having the article, how it should be used and how it stands up to use, but also understanding its materials and manufacturing processes so that the customer can be shown how to judge its quality. In addition to more specific benefits, the quality and long life of more expensive merchandise should be stressed, and any good after-sales service for mechanical products should be made known. Although a good assistant will know the many advantages of each product she should not reel them off, but choose one or two and concentrate on these. A customer's own questioning, if not the original statement of what she is looking for, usually reveals the point she wishes most to be reassured about.

By emphasizing the benefits obtainable from the product the idea of value for money is instilled in the customer's mind. There can even be a hint that a product is slightly more expensive than it really is so that the customer has a pleasant surprise when she eventually learns the price.

SALES TALK

Type and amount of sales talk should be suited to the customer. As this calls for experience, the retailer can suggest that his assistant pays particular attention to how the retailer himself handles sales. She should also be told never to disparage merchandise, even a low-priced article: she may have to serve it a few minutes later. And in any case, a customer's confidence in more expensive articles can be reduced by the thought that poor-quality goods are also sold in the shop.

The assistant must also be taught not to display too many articles at once, to narrow down the customer's choice to only one or two possibilities, and to bring the transaction to a successful close before interest flags, by summarizing the benefits of each or concentrating on a single article when the customer hesitates. During a transaction it is common for a customer to raise objections: it should be pointed out to the assistant that these, far from opposing her will, are helpful in that they indicate clearly what the customer has in mind. Even when a customer says that the demonstrated goods are not what she really wants it is an opportunity to find out exactly how the merchandise differs and so helps to narrow the choice further. Sometimes the displayed articles are precisely what is wanted and the customer only needs reassuring about certain points.

OVERCOMING OBJECTIONS

Specific objections should always be met truthfully: it helps to agree with a customer over an objection before going on with a 'but . . .'. The assistant should always wait until the full objection has been stated, avoid lecturing the customer, and never argue. Having overcome the objection she should continue with the conversation and demonstration so that the customer does not lose face nor have time to argue or think up further objections.

If the objection is that the same article can be bought more cheaply elsewhere the assistant should first of all establish that the article is identical and, if it is, thank the customer for the information, saying that the retailer will take up the matter with his suppliers to check that he is getting the best terms.

CLOSING THE SALE

There are several ways of closing a sale and the assistant should be taught in which circumstances each has the greatest effect. Probably the most common is the 'alternative close', that of summarizing the benefits of two articles followed by a direct question about which one the customer will take. Occasionally, it is possible to say that a particular article is extremely popular and to give specific reasons: this often acts as a spur because many customers like to follow the majority. Less frequently the assistant may be able to offer a temporary price reduction as an incentive, or possibly emphasize the difficulties the customer may find herself in if she does not buy at once.

Voice and actions should reveal the assistant's confidence that a sale is about to be made and with the type of customer who constantly wavers it is necessary to be quite firm. Whichever method of closing a sale is adopted it is necessary to make the customer feel that she has made the decision to buy and that the final choice has been hers.

From time to time a customer cannot be suited; staff must be instructed firmly never to show resentment nor feel they have worked in vain. It should be stressed that goodwill has been built up and that losing the sale is trivial compared with losing a customer, which may well result if the customer notices that the assistant is cross.

SUBSTITUTE SALES

The retailer should explain to his staff his policy concerning substitute sales. It is usual to suggest similar products to those requested but not in stock, but the customer should not be pressed, to avoid any appearance of high-pressure salesmanship. There must also be a policy concerning the exchange of unsuitable goods. If the article is undamaged it should be exchanged – it is an excellent means of winning a permanent customer.

It is important for the retailer to impress upon his staff that they must never misrepresent goods. It is illegal and an extremely short-sighted trading policy. Similarly, no assistant should promise more than it is possible for the shop to do: the customer must be made to feel she can rely completely on the shop, all who serve in it, and the merchandise it sells.

Other points about which a retailer should caution his staff include the danger of overflattering customers, most of whom see through the device and despise the assistant for thinking they could be influenced by flattery; not to oversell, in either price or quantity, as the memory usually lingers a long time and goodwill is lost; and not to use clichés and technical jargon, nor to talk so much that the customer may be confused or feel she is being over-persuaded. The importance of politeness at all times as well as of good English should be stressed. If circumstances warrant, the retailer may suggest that his assistant should attend evening classes to improve her grammar, diction, or general powers of expression.

Training assistants in sales techniques requires imagination. They are more likely to maintain interest if, for example, the retailer compares skill in guiding a customer's choice with that of mind-reading experts and magicians seen on television who successfully lead members of their audience to choose the desired playing cards or other objects. Once the assistant has learnt the steps leading up to the successful closing of a sale, how to handle different types of customer, and how to demonstrate the goods, the tuition can be extended.

ADDITIONAL SALES

One successful sale is the foundation upon which to build another, but the retailer should discourage the assistant from adding 'Anything else, madam?' Every suggestion for a second sale must be specific, although never a reeled-off list. Greatest chance of success lies in offering an article related to the completed purchase, introduced by mentioning its benefits in this relationship: thus a shoe shop assistant might offer another pair of shoes for an occasion different from the one for which shoes have just been bought, while a men's outfitters might offer a tie with a new shirt.

In the same way, additional sales are likely if they prolong the life of the original purchase, as with shoe-trees or polishing materials for a pair of shoes, or a clothes-brush for a suit. Sometimes the assistant can point out that a saving occurs if the original article is bought in a larger size; at other times it may be possible to draw attention to some special offer being made by the shop. These additional sales can usually be made conversationally before the first sale is fully completed, for example, while the first purchase is being packed up. Associated sales should never be pressed too hard, and the retailer should make an assistant realize that these additional sales should not be attempted always – if, for example, it is clear that the customer is in a hurry.

Every assistant will have to deal sooner or later with more than one customer at the same time; she should be taught how to welcome the second customer by breaking into her sales talk and asking if she would be good enough to wait just a moment or two – or possibly a friendly glance will suffice. The assistant can be taught during training sessions how to act if the first sale is still some way from its conclusion, for example, by leaving the first customer to handle and examine possible choices while finding choices for the second customer to consider as the assistant completes the first sale.

Checklist 11. Steps to a sale

1. Be prepared: know the merchandise and techniques of selling.
2. A pleasant approach, including appearance, smile, manner, and speech.
3. Discover customer's exact requirements.
4. Select one, perhaps two, suitable articles.
5. Handle and display the merchandise carefully to enhance its apparent value.
6. Talk about its major selling points, in terms of benefits to its eventual owner.
7. Allow the customer to handle the product.
8. Answer questions truthfully, noting which particular requirements or anxieties they indicate.
9. Build the customer's confidence by indicating that the merchandise and customer's problems are both thoroughly understood.
10. Explain, in relation to all requirements now known, differences between articles under discussion, or if necessary, between them and other broadly similar products, still stressing benefits in every instance.
11. Mentally assess customer to decide the most suitable method to guide choice and successfully make a sale.
12. Hint that one of the products is the correct choice in the circumstances, focusing attention on its benefits and then mentioning its price.
13. Without rushing the customer or forcing the sale, give reasons why the customer will not regret the purchase, e.g. long life, after-sales service, etc.
14. If the customer is still hesitant, find the reason and dispel uncertainty. Often it is doubt about which of two articles displayed is better value for money: the benefits and price of the other article can be enumerated, compared with the first article, and the customer asked directly which is preferred.
15. Sequence of selling and method of closing may vary a little, but the attitude and tone on asking for the decision should always indicate that a sale is confidently expected for good reason.
16. If a sale is made, consider attempting an additional sale; if no sale is possible, remain courteous and helpful.

The retailer knows the importance of good face-to-face selling. So much of his business activity is directed towards getting the customer into the shop that it is clearly foolish to miss possible sales at such a late stage. This stresses the importance of good staff and good sales training, and emphasizes what sound investment it is to offer wages and surroundings better than average for staff who are better than average. Some retailers complain that margins are too small to allow them to pay above-average wages but this is to ignore that good staff can create an extra profit greater than the extra expense involved.

A first-rate assistant can be made by selecting someone only slightly above average, training them well, giving them happy surroundings, a fair wage and eventual opportunities for promotion.

Ability to offer each of these rests with the retailer himself. Training, for beginners as well as allegedly experienced assistants, is frequently skimped and unimaginative even by retailers who do realize its importance. Periodic re-training to keep up knowledge and skill and to maintain enthusiasm is even more uncommon in smaller shops, but nevertheless important.

Each sale ought to promote positive goodwill. A customer is either satisfied with the service and product received or she is not. First-class salesmanship is essential if the retailer is to reap the benefits of increased sales per person and progressively improving trade. Thus employment of competent sales staff and provision of good training is the only sensible policy for today's competitive trading conditions.

SERVICING

Many articles need periodic inspection and adjustment, and sometimes repair. Such occasions are usually expensive to the retailer after allowing for the high labour cost involved. Charges need to reflect this, except when it is judged that by paring profit a new customer can be won. The manner in which products for servicing are accepted and returned to the customer is a major opportunity to build further business. Work done should be fully explained, verbally or on the bill, and often it can be worth discussing the intricacies of the article with the owner, perhaps mentioning how later models have been improved.

Arrangements about servicing and charges should always be clearly stated when accepting the work to avoid customers being dissatisfied without cause. Prompt repair to products clearly needed urgently can be an excellent way to gain loyal customers, who then often recommend the shop to others. Where after-sales service is really part of the original sale, it should be given cheerfully.

CONSUMER PROTECTION

The consumer protection movement has grown rapidly in recent years and its activities clearly affect retailers. Although the basic precept in law is still 'Let the buyer beware', this principle is increasingly being modified in practice. It is now customary for progressive retailers to deal with customers having a genuine complaint generously and with good grace, instead of relying on any strict legal rights. Suggestions for handling complaints are given on page 238. The three chief effects of the consumer protection movement are that shoppers tend to be more aware of their legal and generally-accepted rights, are more knowledgeable concerning articles for sale, and are more discriminating in their choice of alternative products.

The Consumers' Association, particularly through its magazine *Which?*, has an important influence on the consumer protection movement, and many retailers may find it well worth reading this publication to keep in touch with consumer affairs and attitudes. It will also indirectly help by providing much information on products, including many selling points on goods stocked. Other bodies closely associated with the Consumers' Association are the Research Institute for Consumer Affairs, which issues various specialized publications, and the National Federation of Local Consumer Groups, a constituent of which may be active in the retailer's area.

Other organizations connected with the national consumer protection movement include the government-aided British Standards Institution; the Retail Trading-Standards Association, financed largely by textile manufacturers and department stores and perhaps best known for its investigations, often followed by prosecution, of complaints about false trade descriptions applied to textiles and other products; the citizens' advice bureaux; and various regular columnists in newspapers.

One result of increased consumer awareness has been growth in the number of firms and organizations issuing a seal of approval or guarantee for appropriate products. These make strong selling points. The honest retailer should welcome the consumer protection movement: its effects can only be to drive out of business his less scrupulous competitor and to encourage shoppers to recognize good service and value-for-money products.

12. Shop Layout

Rent, or its equivalent in freehold purchase, is a major overhead, especially if the shop is in a main street; it is common sense to utilize the space it buys to pass the greatest possible volume of profitable goods through the shop. Ability to do this depends to a considerable extent on the layout and use made of display, the latter being dealt with in the next chapter.

Layout is of course governed by the existing shape of the building, although this is not necessarily the shape of the shop. Partition walls may separate stockroom or office from shop, and while it is not suggested that major building work is resorted to lightly, it is worth remembering that alterations may sometimes pay off. Occasionally, selling area can be increased and given a better shape by converting stockroom into shop and keeping stock in a convenient and adequate basement, garage or outside building.

A wide frontage to the pavement is a great advantage but most small shops are fairly narrow and sometimes rather deep – an awkward shape. The problem then is to attract customers in and to make the shop appear to be bigger than it is. A good shopfront undoubtedly helps to create an impact on potential customers when they pass the shop, but much can be achieved by having a light, cheerful, clean-looking, and orderly interior that is visible from the street. Good lighting is cheap to run and not dear to install, while any shop which hopes to survive competition should in any case be clean and orderly.

The judicious use of mirrors can increase the effect of displays of goods and lighting, in part by reflecting the natural light of the shop window, and also help to make the shop look bigger.

Another inducement sometimes adopted to tempt passers-by is to have the front door and main window at an angle to the pavement, especially where pedestrians tend to move in one direction more than the other when shopping. This has the advantages that passers-by receive the full impact of the window display and that it seems more natural to enter the shop, while, once inside, customers are directed naturally to a counter some distance from the entrance without the position seeming too far away. The benefits from this are that customers can be subjected to more displays, the shop interior can be arranged in a more dynamic manner, and the doorway remains unobstructed even when there are several customers in the shop. A secondary window that faces passers-

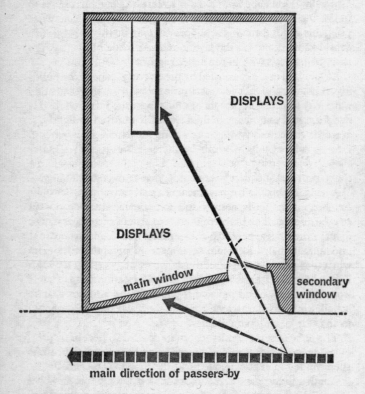

Diagram 2. Better display and easier access may result if the shopfront is set at an angle to the pavement

by coming from the opposite direction usually can be included in the layout. Windows at an angle to the pavement also provide more window display space than is available otherwise.

Placing of counters and displays controls directions in which customers move about the premises. Most shops have at least two groups of customers: those wanting very quick service and those wanting to select or discuss the articles. The selling area should be laid out to separate these 'streams' to ensure that the slower customers are not troubled by the others and that those wanting quick service can get it by not having to walk very far into the shop. Subject to this, it is normally desirable to place lines in regular demand towards the rear of the shop, to encourage customers for them to notice and perhaps purchase other items also, and in addition to leave room towards the front of the shop for displays, changed from time to time, of articles whose rate of sale is noticeably affected by sales promotion. Within this framework, it is best to arrange associated product groups adjoining each other to encourage customers to make additional purchases.

SELF SERVICE AND SELF SELECTION

Before the retailer can evolve his best layout he must decide to what extent, if at all, he intends to adopt self service or self selection. Self service is more suitable to some trades than others and it has made greatest headway in shops selling heavily advertised, branded, and pre-packed goods, such as food and household articles. Self selection avoids use of a checkout, and assistance is available to help customers seeking advice, although they are able to examine and select goods without being approached. Other shops sometimes display products to help customers make their choice before taking up the time of assistants, though they are demonstration articles that cannot be removed: this is sometimes called pre-selection.

Almost every shop can use to advantage self selection in some degree. Whether self service is beneficial depends on such factors as the type of goods sold and the shape of the selling area. The greatest advantage of self service and self selection is that they reduce staff costs in relation to turnover. Because there must be at least one person even in a self service shop to deal with money and generally supervise, self service for small shops rarely leads to a reduction in staff. It does however enable the same staff to handle a larger volume of trade, so long as this can be induced into the shop, and it also exposes customers to scientific sales techniques based on impulse buying.

In addition, it forces the retailer to display his merchandise well. Less time is spent wrapping goods because they are pre-packed, while space is better utilized – counters are eliminated – and there is less double handling of goods because stock is often kept in the shop itself, on display. Stockrooms sometimes can be turned into selling areas by knocking down a wall or by simply opening the room to the public – taking care not to display items that are small enough to make pilferage much more possible. Also shoppers may be served more quickly, an advantage to the retailer as well as the customer, and the time of the retailer himself or his knowledgeable assistant is not wasted serving goods which customers can easily select for themselves.

Self service and self selection also are greater inducements to passers-by than counter service. Bookshops discovered long ago the advantage of getting customers to come in and browse. Further information about the advantages of self service for any specific shop can be obtained from some trade associations, or voluntary groups and chains where applicable to the trade. Some associated advantages of conversion to self service or self selection, such as new display fittings and modern shop lighting, can of course be gained simply by investing in such new equipment when necessary, without in fact converting.

Conversion may cost a fair amount of money, especially if it involves building work. A change to self service also detracts from the idea of personal service, one of the few remaining weapons the small retailer has against his larger rivals. It is unsuitable for some trades – jewellery, for example – and even ironmongers have not always found it successful because many items are either too large for easy removal or too small to stop pilfering, while other lines still require considerable personal salesmanship in matching the required product to the need of the customer who is unable to recognize it. In addition, there are still some people who are a

Checklist 12. Advantages to customers of self service

1. Products can be seen and handled.
2. Less obligation to buy.
3. All articles priced.
4. Display usually better.
5. Service often quicker.
6. Suggests a progressive retailer, therefore customer more likely to obtain what she wants and value for money.

little frightened or bewildered by self service and its attendant clamour of competing products.

Losses through pilferage vary considerably with the type of goods, staff, and customer, but chain stores sometimes accept a loss of a half per cent of turnover as normal. This includes losses caused by short deliveries that are not noticed at the time. Self service, and to a lesser extent, self selection, provide more opportunities for theft: losses tend to increase when either is first adopted. Some stores have reported pilferage as high as five per cent of turnover, though much can be done to reduce losses, by proper administrative procedures, good staff selection and training, anti-thief mirrors and, where justified, detectives – often women – circulating among displays as if shopping. Supermarket procedures sometimes include 'frisking' of suspects for pocketed articles, pointing out suspects to staff by using coded words or dialogue known to all staff, and various other devices. Customers are of course unaware of what is happening. Such activities may seem justified from the retailer's viewpoint, but they raise important ethical, and possibly legal, questions, especially as innocent customers may suffer defamation of character through a staff member or detective being mistaken, or even wilfully accusing falsely.

COUNTER SERVICE

Although a great deal of time is wasted by using counter service – the retailer waiting for the customer to make up her mind or the customer waiting to be served in the first place or while requested items are brought – related and substitute sales are more easily made and a closer relationship between customer and shop is established.

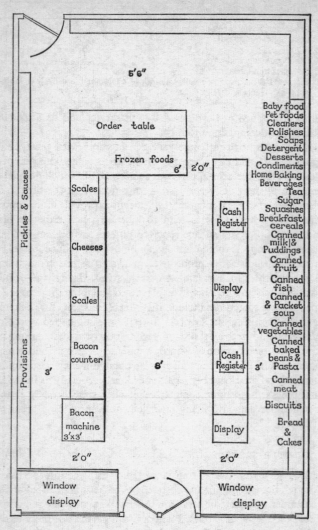

Diagram 3. Full counter service: typical layout of a 700 sq. ft total area grocery shop for full counter service

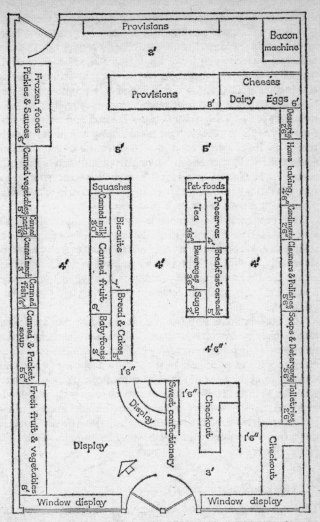

Diagram 4. The same shop planned for self service but with personal service retained for certain merchandise. This layout shows the much larger area for customer circulation (approx 370 sq. ft instead of 170 sq. ft) and vastly increased opportunities for persuasive displays

Once it has been decided whether to employ self service, self selection, or counter service, attention can be given to detailed layout within the shop. Even where counter service is fully maintained, the trend is to make the counter as small as possible, consistent with providing enough space for transactions, demonstrating the goods, and a few point-of-sale promotions. Space behind counters is used relatively uneconomically, it often being necessary to make the width between counter and wall sufficient for two people to pass without disarranging any display on the rear wall. It is often a good idea to place the counter directly against the wall, the retailer serving from the same side as the customer. Having no impersonal barrier between customer and retailer adds to the feeling of friendship and can help to overcome psychological resistance to salesmanship.

Most customers like to move freely among merchandise, but aisles must be sufficiently wide. Displays in the centre of the selling area, whether shelving or goods themselves surmounted by showcards, should be kept below eye level to avoid customers having the impression of being shut in or of shopping from a warehouse. This also helps the retailer to keep everything under surveillance.

The quicker a line sells the more it should be displayed: customers clearly want the product. It is now usual to apportion display space in relation to turnover. Fast-moving lines are best given prominent positions: near the entrance, close to the cash register, or at the back of the shop with special lighting to draw attention to them. If self service or self selection is adopted it will be found that goods move more quickly from the ends of island shelving than from the sides, so shorter units may be preferable as they provide more ends, though this may be counteracted by loss of shelf space.

CUSTOMER CIRCULATION

The pattern of circulation by customers depends on how the retailer arranges his layout. Positioning of counters, displays, cash register, and lighting are his means of making customers move as he would like. Patterns on the floor covering occasionally may help also to guide customers subconsciously. Except perhaps when providing instant service, as for papers or cigarettes, the aim should be to draw the customer well inside the shop. In self-service shops it has been found that centre aisles are used much less than along the outer walls. Studies have been carried out in many countries but it has not been determined whether customers prefer to saunter in a clockwise or anti-clockwise direction. Women tend to browse more than men.

Grouping of merchandise is the most effective method of controlling customer circulation. Except where a special display is being arranged of one manufacturer's products, merchandise should be grouped by its use or type of product, not its maker. Thus, a chemist might have separate sections for pharmaceuticals, dispensing, toiletries, baby goods, and general merchandise; an ironmonger might arrange departments for tools, decorating materials, heating or gardening equipment according to season, household goods, and screws and similar items.

These departments should be well signposted, by written or illuminated signs or by prominent displays of products, packs, and showcards. Customers can then go straight to the section which interests them and, once there, are subjected to displays of related items, saving retailer or customer having to walk unnecessarily about the shop for service, while also helping to build up extra sales. Ideas for lines which sell well through impulse in association with others can be gleaned from chain competitors, especially self-service stores.

If self service or self selection is used, displays should be of differing height to avoid monotony and to create interest, thereby slowing down the customer as she passes. Quick-moving lines can be stacked to considerable height against walls, saving valuable horizontal space. Island shelving is sometimes placed at an angle to shop walls, providing variety and interest; space at the wider end is then used for dump bins and similar displays. All articles of course must be clearly priced, either by the retailer himself or manufacturer, and it is worth remembering that many women with poor eyesight do not wear glasses while shopping.

FIXTURES FOR MERCHANDISE

Display fixtures themselves, whatever method of service is adopted, should be as unobtrusive as possible, leaving the merchandise and packaging to do the selling. It pays to have better quality fittings: they must withstand constant use, while cheap fittings disparage merchandise and are a danger to customers through faulty brackets, broken glass, splintered wood, and unprotected corners. Thus good-quality second-hand display fittings and furniture are better than new but cheap material. Glass-fronted counters help to display goods and also to create an atmosphere of lightness and dynamism.

It has become more acceptable to display multi-packs once they are opened; manufacturers aid this trend by producing well-designed outer packaging. Even where full counter service is the policy, self-service dispensers can be placed on counters to advantage.

There should be no dead space at all in a shop. The retailer should so arrange his displays and customer circulation that every inch is well used, for example, by exhibiting items on pegboard attached to the wall or on frames which swing out from the wall. Customers like to be out of the way when browsing, so a dead corner can be brought to life by adopting the 'catalogue corner' technique mentioned previously.

Where a stockroom cannot be converted easily into a normal selling area it is good sales psychology to invite customers wanting to look at goods stored there to come behind the scenes. The customer feels privileged to be taken to the stockroom, which in any case should be clean and tidy, and it also saves the retailer carrying items about the building unnecessarily.

PRACTICAL CONSIDERATIONS

Practical points concerning layout include floor-covering material and shop heating. Floors take much wear and the ideal material depends on the class of shop and goods, and of course on the available money. First-quality lino is often best, while rubber and plastic tiles are also common. Extra matching material should be bought when the floor is first covered as certain areas, especially just in front of the door and the cash register, wear out more quickly than others: patches that are not too obvious can then be made.

Mats help to keep the floor clean and reduce wear but they must be well secured and recessed if customers are never to trip over them. All floor surfaces should be non-slip. Steps inside a shop or at the entrance are dangerous and a subconscious barrier for customers; where possible, they should be replaced by a ramp.

Except for food shops, the best shop temperature is about 18° C (64° F). Premises much warmer in cold weather appear overheated to customers coming in from the cold and returning there fairly quickly. A heater above the door and directed downwards has the advantage of warming air as it enters. If necessary, other heaters can be placed strategically inside the shop but they should always be out of the way of customers' clothing, and of children's reach, and should not interfere with customer circulation.

METHOD STUDY

Layout should be considered also from the viewpoint of saving the retailer time and effort. The technique of method study,* widely adopted in industry, is at last becoming accepted by retailers. It is the systematic recording and critical examination of existing or proposed ways of doing work to make tasks easier, reduce costs, simplify staff training, and give customers better service. It can be of great assistance at any time, but especially when planning a new layout. Any retailer can easily carry out method study at no cost except a little of his time and often saves himself considerable sums of money and a great deal of unnecessary effort.

The technique consists of choosing a particular problem for examination, noting the relevant facts, seeing if a better method

* Method study is not the same as work study although confusion has arisen in the past through diversity of definition. Terms used in this book are in accordance with definitions laid down by the British Institute of Management and the British Standards Institution (BS. 3138); distinction between method study and work study is made on page 197.

can be devised and, if so, installing it, and checking later that all is working well. It sounds so easy and obviously sensible that it can be overlooked, yet the profitability of a business and the ease with which it is run often can be improved greatly, not necessarily by any single spectacular change but by introducing many small improvements.

Any task that takes a long time, is messy, inconvenient, or tiring suggests scope for improvement, but priority should be given to problems whose solution is likely to give greatest benefit. No problem can be judged objectively until the unbiased facts are known: it is often best to jot down details in case the retailer is interrupted or if inspiration does not come at once. It also helps the retailer to think logically.

Facts can be recorded by making lists of actions or diagrams indicating what is necessary to carry out any particular task, or by taking a fair sample of activity to see how time is being used. A revealing method is the 'flow-process' table in which each activity is noted on a separate line of notepaper, to the left of which is written the letter D if the action causes delay, or the distance, in feet or yards, if movement is involved. Activity incurred in selling a length of electric cable, for example, might be as shown in Table 13.

This example shows just how much movement is necessary for an apparently simple operation. If electric cable, to continue this illustration, is sold frequently, probably it would be better to modify the shop layout by bringing the cable-storing location closer to the main serving point, by siting the yard measure at the serving point and, possibly, by moving the cash register and wrapping-paper hook so that less walking and effort are involved, taking all the shop's trade into account.

There is a minimum of wasted time, other than in moving about, in this example. Only one D is listed and that for a reason over which the retailer may have no control, although, possibly, he could have displayed his reels of cable so that the customer could have chosen while another customer was being served. If analysis of a selling operation produces several D's – because it is difficult to pass behind another assistant at a certain point behind the counter, or because it is necessary to wait while the customer

Table 13. Extract from a flow-process table

24 ft	Walk to corner of shop where reels of cable are stored
	Select two qualities
24 ft	Return to customer
	Show to customer
D	Await customer's choice
15 ft	To yard measure
	Measure five yards
15 ft	Return to customer
	Cut off five yards
	Coil five yards and tie up
	Collect payment from customer
8 ft	To cash register
	Ring up sale and collect change
8 ft	Return to customer
	Give change to customer
4 ft	To wrapping-paper hook
	Select paper
4 ft	Return to customer
	Wrap sale
	Give to customer
24 ft	Return reels of cable to corner
Total 126 ft	

stands aside to allow the assistant to pass to the customer's side of the counter – the table will pinpoint where procedure falls short of the ideal and also indicate where effort and time are required to cover distances. It is often possible that certain selling activities can be improved without recording the series of movements – merely by observation.

Another method study technique which may be useful for a retailer is that of 'activity sampling'. This is performed by choosing periods at random and seeing how time is employed by assistants. The periods must be true samples, not all slack periods. They can be of any length (the longer the total, the more accurate the result), need not be continuous, and can be timed with an ordinary watch. An example in a stationer's might be as shown in Table 14.

Like the 'flow-process' table, an activity table indicates distances travelled – in yards or feet. The column 'number of customers in shop', which should not include those browsing and, therefore, not desiring immediate attention, reveals bottlenecks in serving.

Checklist 13. Why people buy

Some factors influencing purchases, whether needs or on impulse:

1. To save, or make, money.
2. To gain comfort or convenience.
3. To save time or effort.
4. To be in fashion.
5. To show that they are not inferior to others: pride.
6. For seasonal or topical reasons.
7. To boost their morale, e.g. by being extravagant.
8. Through fear of later being without the article.
9. To please others.
10. As an outward symbol of what they approve.

An analysis of the 'activity' column may enable an assistant's work to be arranged more economically.

The most important step in method study is the critical consideration of the tables or of the unrecorded observations. The retailer should ask himself whether each operation is necessary and, if so, whether it could be made easier. Method study is essentially a critical examination of existing operating methods so that they can be improved and so that time and effort can be saved. The saving in money follows automatically.

Table 14. Extract from an activity-sampling notebook

Time	Activity	Distance in yards	No. of customers in shop
10.34	Arranging stock on shelves	16	
10.38	Serves customer from shelf-stock	3	1
10.41	Takes payment to cash register and returns change	7	1
10.44	Makes up order from shelf-stock	24	
10.52	Welcomes customer; goes to stock-room for typewriter cover; returns	72	1
10.55	Writes bill		1
10.56	Takes payment to cash register and returns change	7	1

Method study and its aims should be explained to assistants at the outset. It should be emphasized that the purpose is to make their work easier: they cannot lose, but stand to gain a great deal.

Their cooperation can thus be won and their advice sought on the most pressing tasks for study. There is no suggestion of slave-driving because it is no part of the scheme to make staff work harder: only to make more effective what they already do. This is where method study differs from work study: the latter employs method study and uses the findings to establish a standard time for a qualified worker to do a specific job at a defined level of performance; a matter for conveyor-belt factory work and in no way related to work in a shop.

Where an improved method of working has been devised – it may be nothing more than storing certain items closer to the main serving point or at a more accessible level – it should be installed and checked up on later. Snags may occur until the new routine becomes habit, while sometimes even the new system itself can be improved.

POSSIBLE IMPROVEMENTS

Improvements commonly adopted in a wide range of shops as a result of method study include placing floor-level displays on a slightly raised platform so that floor sweepings are kept clear of merchandise and so that brooms do not knock or chip goods; keeping blank bill forms, spare pencil, scissors and other items for shop use in a regular place so that they can always be found quickly; mounting reels of flex, string, and similar articles for sale on a simple wooden spool under the counter close to the yard measure, to save uncoiling and recoiling, to avoid knotting and damage, and the need to take it to the measure and to return it subsequently; storing cylindrical goods on shelves which slope backwards to stop them rolling off; using similar price tickets for groups of lines to make it easy for customers to recognize the series, compare, and pre-select; displaying staple lines by sample near eye level, if possible with reserve stock underneath; and planning general layout to minimize movement, both horizontally and by climbing and bending, and to avoid leaving the selling area unattended.

Periods of peak activity are particularly inefficient, as well as trying. They also make it difficult to give the personal service which is the mainstay of the small independent trader. Although shopkeeping can never be a steady flow of work, there are steps a retailer can take to smooth the work load; method study will help to uncover and solve problems of specific premises but one solution which applies to very many shops is pre-packaging. Whether selling sweets or screws, china or cheese, most shops are asked during busy periods for certain standard items which can be weighed or counted out as necessary and packed in preparation for the rush. It may even be advantageous to do more work than the theoretical minimum, such as part-emptying a bulk-supply case to fill shop shelves to their limit, if this saves time or effort during the peak period.

It can be seen that method study is largely common sense. Often it can produce worthwhile results without being applied rigidly. Perhaps the most important of its contributions to the efficiency of small shops is its demonstration of the considerable benefits possible, if only the retailer adopts the correct approach.

13. Display

Good display in shop windows and interiors calls for knowledge of the merchandise, ideas to provide suitable themes, an understanding of major principles of display, and some finger dexterity. Every retailer should know his merchandise, this chapter should help with the next two requirements, and while those without manual skill are at a disadvantage, they can still create first-class displays. Help is available from various sources, occasionally free, if the retailer feels totally unable to tackle his own displays; but whether he does so himself or employs others, really good displays should be made, and replaced when necessary.

A shop's windows are its cheapest and most effective form of advertising. Not to use them to full advantage is to discard a considerable asset. A look at the windows of most independent small shops reveals how very few retailers use this invaluable sales aid successfully. A glance at the windows of any chain store shows that none of these powerful competitors would dream of throwing away such major sales opportunities. The lesson for the small retailer is inescapable.

The purpose of window display is not to make the shopfront look attractive: it is to promote sales forcefully. Window displays well planned and executed do just this. They attract attention; stimulate interest; create a desire for goods which leads to purchase, even if not always instantly, and they promote confidence in a shop and its merchandise. These are precisely the same functions of salesmanship as in selling face-to-face or through any other form of advertising.

Bad display is worse than no display, just as bad salesmanship is worse than none at all. The absolutely minimum achievement of window display must be to impress the shop's trade and class of goods on the memory of passers-by. But a great deal more than this is possible without much trouble or expense. It is not unreasonable for most types of business to spend one to two per cent of turnover on this important advertising medium.

KINDS OF WINDOW

Some trades, especially those selling large articles such as furniture, have eliminated the need for window dressing by arranging that the shop interior is seen easily from outside. They use interior displays and lighting to sell through the window to passersby as well as to customers already inside the shop. The method is clearly unsatisfactory for articles at the other extreme of size such as jewellery, but merchandise of many trades falls into an intermediate category. Here, the advantages of a backless window often can be obtained, without sacrificing sales impact, by using a window layout related to the interior display. Items in the window should be spaced apart rather widely to aid the impression of perspective, colours in the window should be strong, and objects should be arranged to lead the eye to focus on the display inside the shop.

All shop windows, but especially those without backs, should have panes of glass as large as possible. The glazing bars required by smaller panes can ruin otherwise effective displays while they also suggest an unprogressive retailer who has not troubled to bring his window up-to-date.

SHOPFRONT APPEARANCE

To a lesser extent the same is true of the whole shopfront, which frames the pictures created by display windows and has an important influence on the total effect. In addition, the shopfront is usually noticed before the details of window display because of its size, while it impresses itself on the memory of shoppers because it is unchanging. It is taken by most passers-by – potential customers – to be an accurate reflection of the shop's character. The retailer should ask himself candidly what his shopfront represents: does it indicate the kind of goods that are sold, attract the class of customer catered for, and show that the retailer is progressive and prosperous? Flexibility is possible through choice of materials, colour, and design.

The fascia can be put to good advertising use: only if a shop is extremely well known and long established should it contain merely the retailer's name or trading name. By saying what is sold, in only one word or two, new business can be won from a glance by a passing stranger. The lettering material and style should also reflect the character of the business.

Shop-window surfaces should be completely free from lettering or advertising signs or stickers, unless put up for a short period to draw attention to some very special offer. Even then, care should be taken not to spoil the overall effect of the window display. The billposted appearance of some supermarket windows is not normally suitable for a small shop, where less reliance is placed on price reductions and considerable advertising impact available through good window display. It is however usually a good advertisement to have the name of the shop low down on the inside of the glass where it does not detract from window displays, preferably near the shop entrance.

Sunblinds may be necessary to protect window displays: similar information to that on the fascia can be written on them if thought worth while. It is better to fit the blind box below the fascia where possible, so that the fascia can be read across the street even when the blind is down.

LIGHTING FOR EFFECT

Lighting plays an important part in window display. It should give good general illumination without dazzling the shopper or casting shadows on the goods, and should be supplemented by flexible spotlights to focus attention on specific points in displays and to emphasize the three-dimensional nature of the merchandise. Fluorescent lights are usually best for general lighting because they are much cheaper to run, emit less heat, and give fewer shadows. But fluorescent lights may discolour merchandise. Where possible, various lighting tints should be tried out on samples; it may be best to match differently-coloured fluorescent tubes.

Naked lamps usually cheapen the shop's appearance. Recessed lamps, baffle boards, louvres, or special fittings can be used to suit the circumstances, such as shallow, corner, or backless windows. The same principles apply to display inside the shop. Considering how they can help sales and how long they last, lighting fittings are not expensive and it is false economy not to take full advantage of them. Advice on shop lighting can be obtained from local electricians and in addition is provided free by local electricity board showrooms, from the marketing department of the Electricity Council (the address is given in Appendix 8), and from some of the major lamp and fittings manufacturers who, on request, will send their representatives to inspect, advise, and submit quotations either without obligation or for a small charge.

Table 15. Shop window and interior lighting

Typical good lighting for a closed-back window 12 ft long in the main shopping street of an average town is 600 W (watts) of appropriate high-lighting, plus general lighting of eight 80 W fluorescents in suitable fittings, or equivalents, such as twelve 100 W incandescent lamps in mirrored reflectors. Less is required in suburbs; much more for city shopping centres.

Good general lighting for a shop interior is between fifteen and thirty lumens per square foot (or foot candles), supplemented in display areas. A shop of 1,000 sq. ft requires 2,000 watts, possibly divided between six double-lamp fluorescent fittings (960 W) and seven 150 W spotlamps.

The following data on typical incandescent reflector lamps may be useful:

Wattage	Throw (in feet)	Maximum illumination (lumens per square foot)	Diameter (in feet) of lighted circle where illumination is not less than one fifth of maximum
150 W spotlight	3	360	2½
	6	90	4½
	10	35	7½
150 W spotlight (24 V)	3	1,100	1
	6	275	2
	10	100	3
150 W floodlight	3	240	3
	6	60	6¼
	10	20	11
100 W	3	150	2¾
	6	40	5½
75 W	3	110	2¼
	6	30	5½

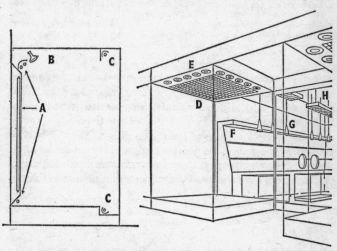

When outside light is stronger than the lighting inside, the windows will reflect the street. To prevent this, it helps to have a well-lighted white background. For backless windows, the shop interior should be well lighted. Display lighting should be left on as long as people are passing the shop: if necessary, a time switch can be used to turn it off.

It is very poor salesmanship to exhibit dirty windows. Condensation is sometimes a problem when the glass is cold and the atmosphere moist. If the window display space is totally enclosed it may be possible to control the condensation by ventilating the window interior; if this is insufficient or impractical an inconspicuous tubular heater can be fitted to warm the inside of the pane.

Diagram 5. Shop-lighting fittings. *Left,* a cross-section of a typical single-aspect window, showing: A, fluorescent tubes behind 'picture frame' – either reflector type tubes, or normal tubes in external reflectors. B, adjustable reflector spotlamps. C, white or coloured fluorescent tubes lighting the background. *Right,* multi-aspect windows of the backless type, showing: D, fluorescent tubes above 'egg-box' louvre in false ceiling E, recessed filament lamp fittings or adjustable spotlamps. F, a pelmet screening fluorescent tubes which light the stock shelves and walls above to produce the bright interior essential with backless windows. G, deep pendant fittings screening spotlamps lighting showcases. H, fluorescent fittings end-on to windows – least obtrusive view when seen from the street.

Checklist 14. Tips on shop lighting

1. Lighting is of three types: incandescent (as used in the house) which brings out sparkle in merchandise, gives warm appearance and is good for spotlighting as its high intensity can be beamed; fluorescent, which is good for general illumination; and cold cathode, sometimes used for showcases as it emits less glare than fluorescent lighting.
2. Colour lighting must not alter true colours of merchandise but is useful for backgrounds to displays, setting moods.
3. Window-lighting fittings should be very flexible to suit changing displays.
4. Display lighting should be as close to merchandise as possible.
5. Brightness depends on the reflective powers of merchandise as well as intensity of lighting.
6. Dark objects are seen more easily if against a light background, and vice versa.
7. Attention is usually attracted to the brightest items in a display.
8. Light emphasizes shape and detail: the smaller and more delicate the merchandise, the more intense the light required.
9. Glass-enclosed showcases, like shop windows, need extra brightness to counteract reflections of external objects which obscure the display.

Totally enclosed window areas keep dust down to a minimum and are, therefore, good for displays of unwrapped articles. Good displays are all the more essential for enclosed window areas because attention is then focused on articles in the window, unless the window back consists of clear glass panels. There should be more than one door to the window enclosure otherwise the whole display must be changed at once, as arrangement of the portion furthest from the door usually involves upsetting that in front of the door.

DISPLAY THEMES

The theme of a window display is the equivalent of the sales story: there should be only one theme for each display. Scope for originality exists, but all themes should stem from the merchandise itself, emphasizing its benefits or topicality or showing a group of related lines, latest fashions, a special offer, or perhaps demonstrating the breadth or depth of the range in stock.

Successful window display calls for planning. Although many themes cannot be prepared months in advance because they depend on unexpected events or new products, the retailer can be certain of the number of displays he will need each year and their approximate date. He knows he will have a special display for Easter, Christmas, summer holiday periods, and at the onset of autumn. Periods in between can be allocated in advance, but flexibility is required as weather and other factors cannot be foreseen. Similarity between successive displays should be avoided.

The frequency with which a window display should be changed depends on the trade and the retailer himself. Fishmongers, bakers, and others need to change their display daily; grocers perhaps weekly; many retailers in other trades change monthly. But most displays lose their impact after two weeks, so ideally this is the maximum period.

Possible themes can be jotted down in a notebook so that the retailer is never at a loss for ideas. Any subject likely to attract potential customers and easily linked with the merchandise is suitable. For example, a tailor's shop specializing in fashionable suits for young men might build its display around a sporting rifle and large target board with a prominent showcard urging potential customers to 'Be on target with our personal tailoring'. The rifle is likely to attract the attention of the right audience, the idea of leisure shooting has overtones of luxury and 'quality' which spill over to the merchandise itself, the potential customer is likely to be very conscious about whether his clothes are up to the minute or in tip-top condition, and the theme is tied in very easily with the merchandise.

Topicality makes the greatest impact so themes associated with the weather, seasons, and current world or local events have punch though the display must exhibit the merchandise without the connection appearing contrived, and it is important that a topically based display should not linger for long after the event has occurred.

Many topical themes can be prepared in advance. The list below is merely an indication of what can be compiled from a good diary, *Whitaker's Almanack* (available in every good library), and similar sources. The items are basically regular calendar events, supplemented by major national sporting events, exhibitions, festivals, royal occasions, famous anniversaries, and activities common at the time of year.

January:
  New year resolutions
  Pantomime and circus season
  Summer holiday planning
    begins

February:
  St Valentine's day
  Waterloo cup
  Spring fashion shows

March:
  St David's day
  St Patrick's day
  Boat race
  Grand National
  Preparations for pleasure
    motoring
  Spring begins
  Ideal Home exhibition
  Mother's day

April:
  All fools' day
  St George's day
  Shakespeare's birthday
  Spring cleaning
  Easter
  Gardening activities

May:
  May day
  Queen's official birthday
    ('Honours' list)
  Trooping the Colour
  Chelsea flower show
  Cricket begins
  Football Association cup final

June:
  Summer begins
  Father's day

June (*contd.*)
  Wimbledon
  Derby
  Ascot
  Royal tournament
  Midsummer day

July:
  St Swithin's day
  Independence day, U.S.A.
  Eisteddfod
  A.A.A. championships
  Henley regatta
  Open golf championships
  Holiday season

August:
  Bank holiday
  Cowes week
  Edinburgh festival
  Soccer starts

September:
  Back to school
  Preparations for a warm winter
  St Leger
  Michaelmas day

October:
  Trafalgar day
  United Nations day
  All Hallows eve
  Motor show
  Horse of the Year show

November:
  Guy Fawkes' night
  London's Lord Mayor's show
  St Andrew's day

December:
  Christmas

To these regular events can be added the shop's own anniversary, clearance sales, and introductions of new lines or merchandise. Popular television series and well-publicized plays and films, items in newspapers and trade magazines, and similar sources provide many other ideas for suitable window-display themes which remain topical long enough for them to be prepared and fitted into the display schedule.

Benefits of merchandise can be shown in a number of ways, ranging from a step-by-step photographic display lent by the manufacturers showing how a product is made and quality built in at every stage, to a dummy representing a housewife relaxing in an armchair in the kitchen conveying the idea of extra leisure gained by buying ready-prepared foods.

Subjects for window-display themes are basically the main selling points of the product, so the retailer who knows his merchandise will never be at a loss for ideas. But it is essential not to try to cover too much ground in a window display: customer attention must be concentrated on a few major points. 'How it works' displays of products are usually popular, while a live craftsman, for example, a chair upholsterer working in the window of a furniture shop, will certainly arouse interest. Impact often can be created by displaying articles related to the items being promoted. Thus gardening implements, weed killer, and flower catalogues may be used to promote a display of books on gardening, overcoming the bookseller's problem of promoting the sale of books that look very much alike.

As the purpose of window display is to increase profit, most goods shown should be best sellers. A line carrying a particularly good profit can be displayed sometimes as the extra publicity boosts its sale, but this should not be done so often that a misleading picture of the character of the business is built up for passers-by.

UNDERLYING PATTERNS

The secret of attractive window display lies in the underlying design. Good arrangement and spacing of shapes, colours, textures, and so on, grips attention and leads the eye in the required directions. This is the visual equivalent of the retailer's verbal salesmanship and is essential if the window shopper is to be left with a logical sequence of reasons for buying that culminates in an

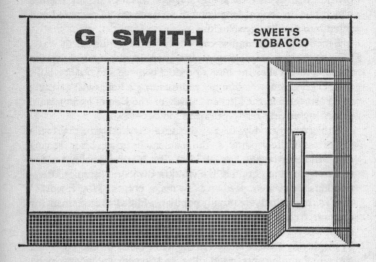

Diagram 6. Finding key points for a window display

impulse to enter the shop. Few retailers are sufficiently artistic to know instinctively whether certain arrangements of goods make a well-designed window: their talents usually lie in other directions. But there are a few guiding principles.

Every window has four key points to which the eye is naturally drawn. By locating major products or sales slogans in these positions, or slightly below them, and building up the rest of the display to emphasize these points, impact is assured. These positions can be established visually, or on paper by sketching a layout, by dividing the width of the window into three equal parts and the height similarly; the four intersections of the dividing lines are the four key points.

But good display can lead the eye to any point. One powerful method is to place the product in the desired position and arrange for a number of lines of sight, possibly formed by smaller versions of the same product, to converge on it. In this way, no matter where the eye first picks up the display, it is led inevitably to the required spot. Such focal points should never be in the exact centre of the window unless a completely symmetrical display is being attempted, though the last is not recommended for most displays because of monotony.

Displaying articles in groups has the advantage of showing more products while still allowing space between masses to play its proper part, and of creating more impact than would one article by itself. Another technique sometimes used is that of repetition, in which identical objects are spaced out regularly, the repeating pattern acting as a magnet to passing eyes. A variation of this is alternation, using two products alternately.

Merchandise arranged to form the rough outline of a pyramid is an effective display technique: not the laborious building-block method of stacking tinned foods so often seen in grocers, but a mere impression of a pyramid formed of different items that do not necessarily touch each other.

It is important to remember when designing a display that it has to catch the potential customer's attention before she reaches and passes the window if the display is to be an effective advertisement. This means that the effect of a dressed window can never be judged by the retailer standing directly in front of it.

The relationship of one colour mass to another is also important. Contrasts in colour attract attention and give the impression of movement, while colour can give optical balance to objects very different in size, a small object in a strong colour offsetting exactly a large but pale mass. Some colours are complementary, others contrast: the retailer can use his own experience and judgement to arrive at satisfactory solutions.

SHOWCARDS

These in a display are an integral part of the composition and need to be considered at the planning stage; added as an afterthought they upset the prearranged balance. Messages should be as brief

Checklist 15. Advantages of frequent changes in window display

1. Attention of potential customers constantly attracted because display does not become stale.
2. Customers more easily realize the width and depth of stock carried.
3. Greater opportunity to emphasize the shop's class of trade and specialities.
4. Less chance of damage to displayed stock from sunlight, etc., while article remains fresh in appearance.
5. Name and merchandise of shop more likely to be recalled by passers-by.
6. Indication of a lively and progressive retailer.
7. More sales and increased profit.

as possible, making each word – especially adjectives – full of punch. Vague phrases such as 'Good value' should never be used: the specific benefits should be mentioned, for example, 'Will last a lifetime'. When the price is on the showcard instead of on a separate ticket it should be the last item to be read.

Various kinds of lettering outfits are on the market, ranging from stencils to interchangeable letters sliding into grooves in the showcard. Continuity can be obtained by using only two styles of lettering: one for headlines, the other for details. Lettering should be of a suitable size as well as easily legible. Except when dealing with really exclusive lines, every item in a window should be priced, preferably shown beside each article instead of on it.

Merchandise normally should be displayed as it appears in use: thus a raincoat might be shown on a model and pinned upwards at the hem on one side, suggesting that the garment is being blown about on a blustery day. A certain number of fittings are necessary to create good displays: glass shelving of various lengths on attractively simple metal stands, pegboard fittings, models, and a wide variety of special equipment for individual trades.

A few stage properties also may be incorporated, but these should be changed when the merchandise display is changed, otherwise the window may not look very different. Stage properties can enliven a display and create an atmosphere, but the merchandise itself must always be paramount. It is sometimes possible to borrow props from goods sold by fellow retailers in exchange for a mention on a showcard that they have been lent by that trader, giving the address of the shop. This joint advertising should be used in reverse also as it can be a means of tapping

Checklist 16. Displaying impulse merchandise

1. Present the products well, including position, surrounding space, and possibly, lighting.
2. Draw attention to them with showcards, etc.
3. Make benefits of products immediately apparent.
4. Gain extra impact by linking displays with other current advertising, by manufacturer or retailer.
5. Choose, on the whole, inexpensive fast-moving lines to exhibit.
6. Use topical showcards with the merchandise, e.g. 'Warm up winter with soup'.

another sector of the market: those who regularly pass the other trader's shop but never one's own.

Backgrounds to displays should also be changed from time to time. A wide variety of display papers is available, imitating everything from quilted silk to stone sculpture; scenes such as countryside or a beach are also available in paper rolls. Greatly enlarged photographs can be very effective but may be rather costly. Crêpe paper looks tawdry unless used sparingly and kept new-looking.

Because most women are greatly attracted by their own reflection it is a good idea to incorporate a large mirror into some window displays, when some of the merchandise will also be noticed. Any shop selling products which affect the appearance of women – clothes, accessories, cosmetics, and so on – should also have a large mirror conveniently located inside the shop where women can glance at themselves while being served: dissatisfaction with some element in their appearance (and most set themselves a high standard) can be the spur for them to ask for additional articles.

CHANGING DISPLAYS

Having decided on a theme, thought about the atmosphere to be created, sketched a layout, and improved upon it as necessary, before tackling the job of changing the old display the retailer should ensure that the window enclosure is completely clean and that everything he will require is to hand, including tools. The check from outside on completion should not be entirely for self-congratulation. It is very easy to place an article upside down when dressing a window from the rear; obviously it is important to correct such slips and to modify the arrangement if it can be improved upon.

Merchandise in short supply should not be displayed, and articles should always be sold from the display if the product requested has run out of stock. It is preferable that further supplies of display lines should be available quickly and it is worth remembering that the impact of special promotion often continues after the display has been changed. Additional benefit therefore can be obtained from window displays if on occasion the principal lines appear in a subordinate position in the next window arrangement or are incorporated into an interior display. It is important for all staff to know what merchandise is included in each window display so that they are prepared when a customer asks for 'one like that in the window'.

It is hard to judge accurately the effectiveness of a display but it may be possible to take spot checks from time to time to notice the proportion of passers-by who disregard any display, glance at the window, or stop to look carefully. These samples are subject to factors other than the effectiveness of the display; people going home at night, for example, tend to be in a greater hurry than housewives shopping during the day. But if it is clear that a display is not effective it should be changed before its allocated time. The retailer should ask his wife and others he can trust for their opinion and honest criticism of displays both in the window and inside the shop.

INTERIOR DISPLAY

The principles of window display apply equally to display within the shop. The background colour scheme should suit the type of trade carried on and should not attract attention away from merchandise. The shop interior and its equipment should look clean, as well as be clean.

Display inside the shop is important because customers glance around while being served and thus can be encouraged to make further purchases. They are also influenced for other buying occasions. Eye level and a little below is the most effective height for interior display and placing products between waist height and eye level will encourage customers to pick up a pack or product for closer examination, especially if a notice urges them to do this. Shelving behind the retailer, facing the customer as she is being served, is an excellent position: other good positions are close to the door, where products can be seen both on entering and before leaving, and close to the cash register.

In spite of distances within a shop being bigger than in a window, the idea of grouping instead of dotting about displays, or references to a particular product, remains important. The larger any display, the more likely it is to attract attention. Remember to include useful information about the product as part of the display – whether this is simply the price of a well-known line or occasions for, and methods of, use if it is something less commonplace. Where children are served regularly, as in a sweet shop, it is worth making a 'children's corner' where cheaper lines can be shown in a display low enough for them to see.

Some retailers find display work difficult or uninteresting. Freelance window dressers operate in some districts and other traders may be able to put the retailer in touch with them.

Many manufacturers offer to take the work off the retailer's hands by arranging special displays of their own products. This is useful from time to time, especially where the products are those of an agency the retailer has, but if they are already fast sellers it should not be permitted too often. Display space, both window and interior, is for the retailer to demonstrate his whole range and to emphasize the character of his shop; the fact that so many manufacturers fight for the privilege of putting up displays without charge should be a warning to the retailer of how important is this aspect of salesmanship.

14. Promoting Sales

Increased sales, which may bring increased profit, can be had by every retailer for very little trouble and at no expense. A host of methods exist by which the shop and its products can be brought to the notice of potential customers. The word 'advertising' may be inappropriate, partly because some of the methods go beyond what is usually thought of as advertising, and also because that word may summon up an idea of paying a large sum of money for advertising in a newspaper without any increase in business resulting. Effective advertising for the retailer is something quite different.

Advertising which costs money is no good. A shopkeeper may set aside small sums for short periods to cover promotional costs, but unless profit, clear of all expenses, resulting from additional sales amply covers these outlays the advertising has been a waste of money and time. It is always difficult to assess exactly what extra sales are due to advertising, but, as will be seen, an estimate can usually be obtained sufficient to decide whether it is worth continuing to advertise, and if so, to what extent and in which ways.

ADVERTISING METHODS

The more usual methods of advertising include:

Notices to bring to the attention of customers and potential customers the fact that certain lines are now in stock, that the shop specializes in certain types of goods, that a new line is now available, that particular products are being offered at reduced price, and similar facts. These notices can be displayed in the shop window or inside the shop. If the latter, they will probably be seen by only those customers already inside.

Any notice in a shop window, whether by window sticker or other means, should be brief and clearly seen at a distance. The aim is to impart information to people hurrying by, perhaps on a bus, and to induce them to enter the shop on that occasion or subsequently. Notices inside a shop can be placed on the counter, on top of relevant goods, or hung from walls, display fitment or ceiling.

Most manufacturers supply such point-of-sale advertising for their own goods, and some of this may be very useful; but there are occasions when a shopkeeper has to write his own. Probably the easiest method is to write with felt-nibbed pens on stiff white or light-coloured cardboard; charcoal or crayon can also be used if there is no risk of the notice being brushed against by customers' clothes. No retailer need worry that such notices may look amateurish: in an increasingly mass-produced world, they can be much more effective than machine-printed advertisements because they convey the personal touch and have much more immediacy. 'Special offer: buy today while stocks last' in the retailer's own handwriting will always be more effective than precisely the same wording on a manufacturer's mass-produced, carefully prepared, lavishly coloured announcement. For those occasions when the retailer prefers to use words with a more printed appearance there are on the market several types of stencils and transfers.

Handbills can be a cheap form of advertising if used sensibly. A local duplicating agency will produce a hundred for around £3, including cost of paper and typing the 'master', but extra copies can be made at the same time for a matter of pennies a hundred more. Exact cost depends on method of duplication: photo-offset usually looks far superior to wax stencil. Handbills are most effective if they are brief, and colour-tinted paper, costing only a few further pennies a thousand, is more effective than plain white.

They can be distributed door-to-door, to pedestrians in the street, or at places where crowds gather such as football matches or cinema queues. Although door-to-door distribution takes longer, it is more effective; not only do householders give more attention to a leaflet received through the letterbox, but they are more likely to be receptive to its information. In addition, they can more conveniently keep the leaflet for future reference. One low-cost method of distribution is to use reliable schoolchildren. Some manufacturers help with this form of publicity by providing free leaflets about their products overprinted with the retailer's name and address to indicate the nearest stockist.

Direct mail is an extension of the door-to-door leaflet idea but, for the extra cost of postage and envelopes, can be even more effective. Letters for direct mail should be to the point, whether it is to announce an old business under new management; the recent delivery of a bargain line; a reminder that the shop holds the local agency for certain branded products, sells a certain range of goods and believes in giving above-average service, or anything else. Letters should have an opening sentence which will particularly interest the reader and thus gain full attention. The letter should end, possibly in a postscript, by urging action – a visit to the shop, phoning through an order, and so on. Occasionally a follow-up letter can be sent, but the retailer should avoid the impression of badgering his potential customers.

Most people glance quickly at direct mail letters in a neutral frame of mind. Any slight annoyance at finding that what appears to be a letter is a piece of advertising is usually offset by the thought that if a businessman considers it worth while to send a sealed letter addressed to the householder personally, there is a good chance that the announcement will be of benefit to him. There is, therefore, scope for more words than are appropriate for a window sticker or handbill, but the letter should not be long nor cramped in appearance. Suitable handbills already in existence can be enclosed also.

The key to success in the use of direct mail is to have up-to-date lists of appropriate potential customers. For example, it is a waste of money notifying flat dwellers about a sale of lawnmowers. Lists of addresses suitable for direct mail for different purposes can be built up by the retailer himself. If he carries on any credit business he already has a list of existing credit customers. A knowledge of the neighbourhood from which his customers are drawn will show which householders, or their wives or children, are the most likely target for letters selling specific goods; roads can be classified according to approximate income of inhabitants and this together with the type of house can indicate much about the wants and desires of people living there.

Some shops write receipts for each sale, asking all customers for their name and address: building direct mailing lists is then straightforward. Other shops can offer to note details of the customer's tastes. Booksellers, for example, can arrange to notify them each time a new book appears on appropriate subjects or by favourite authors.

Another useful source for direct mail lists is the local electoral register. This can be seen at the town hall and copies obtained there for a small charge. The register lists, house by house and street by street, almost everyone in the district over eighteen. Streets where some existing customers live are worth particular attention because people with similar income and, to some extent, general tastes, tend to congregate. Other sources of names and addresses include local street directories and the local telephone directory, most subscribers being of some financial standing.

Exchanging lists with retailers aiming at similar customers but who do not directly compete can also add to the number. Further methods for certain merchandise include, for example, 'birth' announcements in local papers for the many shops selling baby requisites (linen, chemists, toyshops, and so on). Yet another means is to ask friendly existing customers if they care to give the names and addresses of one or two of their friends in the neighbourhood who may like to receive personal notification of special attractions likely to interest them when next offered by the shop.

If direct mail is used often – for several trades it is one of the most effective forms of sales promotion, other than window display, in relation to its cost – it is worth preparing a card for each existing and prospective customer whose details are known. No elaborate equipment is necessary: cards can be ordinary postcards and they can be filed in a shoe box. Each card should be marked with a C, if a customer, or P, if a prospect, and, in addition to name and address, details such as special interests in relation to the shop's merchandise, and whether a parent, can be added.

The date of each direct mail letter sent can be stamped or

written on the back of each appropriate card and a tick later inserted if a purchase is known to have resulted, although this may be possible only in a small proportion of instances. Some idea of the response to direct mail efforts is then available, giving guidance in preparing subsequent mailing lists. A copy of each direct mail letter sent out can be kept for reference, comparison of which with response may help in wording future letters.

Cards, which should be classified by major interest in relation to the shop's merchandise, must be kept up-to-date, otherwise customers may still receive letters aimed at prospects suggesting that they visit the shop for the first time. The great advantage of direct mail is that if all recipients are selected high-potential customers it can be a very effective method of advertising for very small outlay. Hand delivery may sometimes be convenient and cheaper than postage.

Letters may be duplicated by local advertising agencies or secretarial bureaux, by some printers, or by direct mail agencies. Most will also quote a separate price for addressing envelopes, inserting the letter and posting, while advertising and direct mail agencies will also draft appropriate letters for a further fee. Readability of all copies, overall appearance and layout, quality of paper and suitability of letterheading are all important.

Catalogues are a further possible source of publicity. It is rarely economic for a small shopkeeper to have his own catalogue prepared, showing or listing most of the lines he handles, because this is expensive and tends to become out of date. But some manufacturers or suppliers may offer catalogues or brochures of their own products for which the retailer is sole local agent: these, with the name and address of the shop overstamped, cost little or nothing and can be hung in the shop where customers can browse at their leisure, placed on the counter where interested customers can help themselves, enclosed with large orders, given to inquirers about one of the major products listed, or used in direct mailings or door-to-door distribution. In this way cheap publicity is obtained for at least some of the lines a shop handles.

Press advertising is of two kinds: classified and display. Classified advertisements have the advantage of being placed under certain headings, just where potential customers may be looking for the retailer's products or services. Well-worded classified advertisements can convey a fair amount of information at very little initial expense.

Display advertisements are considerably more expensive and strive to catch the eye of readers. Thus while a quarter-page display advertisement perhaps 10 in. by 7 in. in a local paper with a circulation of 25,000, which might cost about £18, may be a good way to publicize a special event at the shop, it is not economic for routine announcements unless the retailer has decided that his advertisements in that particular paper bring in sufficient extra business to cover this outlay. Except for special occasions such as a sale or an opening under new management, display advertising is a longer-term project, an attempt to insert the name of the shop and its type of merchandise into the semi-consciousness of potential customers. This cannot be achieved with intermittent display advertising; there must be a regular campaign, each advertisement consistent, though not identical in message, and concentrating on a simple theme. It is usually best to leave such promotion until a shop is fairly well established before incurring the relatively high expenditure.

Most of the cost of display advertising is in buying the space in which the retailer's message is to be printed. Typical advertisements include illustrations, and are reproduced by a printer's 'block', the making of which costs a few pounds. This block, once made, becomes the property of the retailer and can be used over and over again, although its message cannot be altered.

Some manufacturers offer free ready-made blocks of their products to which retailers can add details of their shop. Occasionally, manufacturers also pay half the cost of the display space. Additional advantages of such support by manufacturers are that familiar brand names catch the reader's eye more easily than the less familiar name of a small shop, while the suggestion of quality or value for money associated with specific brands tends to be linked with the shop selling and advertising these goods. Some advertising agencies also offer, for about a pound each, the exclusive use, within a defined area, of blocks showing unbranded products to which the retailer's own details can be added by means of either typesetting or a second block.

Choosing a newspaper in which to advertise needs care. The number of potential customers likely to see and act on an advertisement is what matters, not a newspaper's total circulation. For example, an evening paper circulating over a wider area than a shop normally serves may possibly provide better value for advertising expenditure than a local weekly paper with a smaller circulation: in spite of considerable wastage of readers of the more popular paper because they are not near the shop, and in spite of possibly higher advertising rates to match the greater circulation, a greater number of readers of the evening paper who are near the shop may be induced to buy for one reason or another.

So circulation figures, even when independently audited to guarantee their truth, are an inaccurate guide to what is best for a particular retailer. Advertisement managers also offer free advice, some of which may be very sound, but every advertisement manager is biased in favour of his own paper. The best course of action is for a retailer to consider independently which papers might be best, obtain details of costs of advertisements, number of readers, district in which the paper circulates, and the type of person who reads the paper. The last is important because it is pointless advertising, for example, ladies' hairdressing in an evening paper bought mainly by working men for sports results. Close scrutiny of the papers under consideration, and of their rivals, should indicate likely readership.

Advertising rates and other details for most newspapers can be found in *British Rates and Data*, *The Newspaper Press Directory*, or *Advertiser's Annual*, which, as explained on page 278, may be available at the public library. The advice of a local advertising agency is useful when display advertising is being considered; as explained on page 229, this costs nothing if the advertising is inserted eventually because agency commission is included in newspaper rates.

Cinemas can help shopkeepers advertise in many ways. On the screen, slides have generally given way to two types of advertising films: fifteen-second live-action commercials and sixty-second productions. Fifteen-second live action commercials of a general nature can be hired, to which the retailer can have added, for about £10, his own shop's details on sound and screen. The shop-keeper has to commit himself to hiring the filmlet for 26 alternate or 52 consecutive weeks but the exhibition charges, including hiring, are usually little more than £2 a week.

One-minute dealer films are of two types: those of a general nature devoted to a trade, such as hairdressing or dry-cleaning, and those sponsored by a manufacturer devoted to one of his products. Details of the retailer's shop can be added at the end on sound and screen. It is usual to show such films during one week in six, for which exhibition charges, including hiring the film and producing the dealer's individual ending, are around £15 for the week. But dozens of manufacturers who have a film about their own products usually pay half the cost that the dealer would otherwise incur. Cinema managers can be approached for full details of screen advertising.

Off the screen, cinemas help retailers advertise through com-petitions and joint promotions. In the former the shopkeeper supplies a prize, not necessarily expensive, which becomes the subject of the competition. An example might be for a household shop to supply four sets of cups and saucers with different patterns, contestants being asked to match the most suitable patterns to the character of the four stars in the current film.

For the retailer this means free advertising of the products together with name and address of his shop in the cinema foyer and again on any leaflet handed out by the cinema. The shop gains further publicity if, for example, the editor of the woman's page of a local paper agrees to serve on the panel of judges. The com-petition details, including the shop's name, would probably be mentioned in an article on the subject and possibly a second time in the caption to a photograph of the winner receiving the prize. Such competitions can have many variants.

Joint promotions similarly offer opportunities of useful cheap publicity where a genuine link exists between goods on sale and the current film. A simple example might be to devote a window to a special display of household lines with appropriate 'stills' from a current film called, say, 'Wedding Bells' well arranged at the back of the display. Cinemas pay all or most of the display cost but the shopkeeper's aim is to make passers-by look in his window and to promote his own goods, not merely advertise a film. Occasionally, similar joint displays are allowed in the cinema foyer: this is even better for the retailer as he gets a useful extra showroom for a week for nothing.

Cinema managers have considerable freedom in arranging joint promotions and competitions, and retailers interested in such publicity methods should let the manager know that they are open to suggestions. Arrangements for joint promotions and competitions take time, especially if they involve the printing of leaflets, so it may be too late if a retailer waits until he knows what films will be shown the following week: cinema managers know their own scheduled films many weeks in advance.

Collaboration with other shopkeepers can also bring cheap or even free publicity through joint promotions. A grocer might, for example, prominently announce that every fiftieth pack of a certain line he wishes to clear quickly has had inserted in it a voucher worth, say, fifty pence that can be used at a near-by jeweller. Appealing to the same instinct in passers-by which makes football pools and lotteries so popular, the goods would be sold more quickly and probably new customers enticed into the shop for the first time also. The jeweller may be happy to contribute half the value of the voucher in return for bringing extra customers into his shop, all of whom would probably not have visited him for many months because of the nature of his trade. Also, because relatively few articles in a jeweller's can be bought for fifty pence there is every prospect of the winner spending a good deal of his own money in addition to the voucher.

Estate agents, if they will cooperate, can often be of use to shopkeepers by passing on the name and address of new residents as they join the community. Most newcomers have immediate requirements such as household hardware and ironmongery, probably curtaining and floor covering material, possibly domestic equipment and furniture. In addition, they may want the services of a decorator, window cleaner, or electrician. Retailers in suitable trades can send in their trade card or circular letter, if they have one, about their services or even call at the door and greet the newcomer by name.

TV advertising is still too costly and unselective for independent shopkeepers. Even national chain retailers use TV only on special occasions. Local commercial radio may be more practical.

Posters are not likely to be sufficient advertising in themselves but if well-sited can be a reinforcement to other advertising. Their message must be brief. Useful sites may include bus shelters, railway stations, walls, the shop's delivery van if there is one, and, if carrying a special announcement, perhaps also the shop window. Local advertising agencies and printers can provide details of costs and further advice.

Advertising by cards placed above bus seats is another possibility within the probable budget of small shopkeepers, details being available from the local offices of the bus company. Some local authorities permit street litter bins to carry metal advertising plates and council offices know the address of the contractor responsible. A typical charge is around twenty pence per bin per week, which includes the initial cost of the plate to the retailer's own design, but as it is usually necessary for the shopkeeper to commit himself to a three-year contract, he should first be convinced of the merits of this advertising method.

Miscellaneous. Parish magazines, programmes issued for football matches and other local events, and restaurant menus are further ways of advertising at small outlay, but these will only be remunerative if advertisements of the shop's products or services are placed there for good reason. An advertisement for a shop selling the latest popular records would interest few readers of a church magazine, yet the same publication may be an excellent medium for attracting highly potential customers to a shop selling serious books, dictionaries, and devotional works. In the same way, advertisements placed on the menus of local restaurants should be appropriate to the clientèle of the restaurant: one frequented largely by comfortably-off women during morning or afternoon shopping may be an excellent means of publicizing handbags or fashion shoes; the menu of a restaurant that does most of its trade in the evening, after the shop placing the advertising has closed, may be a waste of time.

Other cheap yet effective means of publicity include making full use of the entry in the telephone book and the fascia above the shop; having informative letterheadings which mention the shop's specialities, agencies held and telephone number; and displaying eye-catching signs outside the shop. The cost of the latter may be defrayed by one of the shopkeeper's normal suppliers in return for it carrying his own advertising as well as the retailer's name. A delivery van can also be a good advertisement by being in reasonable condition and having the name of the shop, trade carried on, address and telephone number prominently displayed.

ADOPTING A HOUSE STYLE

Retailers using some of the above means of publicity can have a further method at no cost beyond a little forethought. This is by introduction of a 'house style': a consistent appearance in all publicity material, intended to convey the character of the business even to potential customers who have never seen the shop. A house style is obtained by using regularly the same style of lettering and colours wherever they can impress themselves on the public: shop interior, shopfront and fascia, delivery van, all kinds of advertising and stationery, wrapping paper or bags, labels, and staff overalls.

Chosen lettering and colours should be consistent with the type of merchandise sold and the 'personality' which the retailer wishes his business to have. It is not a question of the retailer's own favourites: old-fashioned Gothic script would not suit a modern electrical shop. Lettering and colours should be chosen also bearing in mind where they will appear, and as only one style of lettering can be selected for all purposes it must be equally suitable for small letterheadings and large shop signs.

Some lettering gives an appearance of solidity, other styles have a feminine appeal, or can give an impression of dynamism. Examples of the different styles of lettering can be seen at any printers, or perhaps in a typographical book, such as the *Ency-*

clopaedia of Type Faces, from the local public library. Colours can also be suited to the trade carried on: pastel shades for baby linen and strong primary colours for shops catering for handymen, for example. If the shop's legal trading name is long it can be shortened for almost all occasions.

House styles sometimes also feature a house mark: the retailer's equivalent of a manufacturer's trade mark. It may be a symbol indicating the trade or some other fact associated with the shop, or it may be, for example, an adaptation of the capital letter of the retailer's surname. The symbol is to help customers automatically link the shop with its products or services, so it should be neat, simple, and easy to reproduce. The value of a house mark can be appreciated from the use larger retailers make of it.

The great advantage of a house style is that it costs nothing. The shopfront must be painted some colour; letterheadings have to be printed in any case; if bags are being printed with the shop's name they might just as well be helping to create a consistent appearance of the shop and its products, and so on. Once chosen, the house style should remain basically the same for at least several years to achieve long-term impact of the chosen 'public character'. Any branch shop should adopt the same trading name and house style as the main premises; publicity for each establishment helps the other.

SPECIAL EVENTS

There are additional ways of promoting sales on special occasions. Opportunities for a special event can occur quite often, as when the retailer obtains a bargain line, either a product at a reduced price or the normal article accompanied by a free gift. The advertising potential is being wasted if these bargains are offered merely to existing customers, where they would create only a little extra goodwill. Instead they should be publicized and used to attract new customers into the shop. And new customers or old, once they are inside, the retailer has the opportunity to make sales which otherwise would not have occurred.

On a few occasions free gifts for patrons may be an economic form of sales promotion, for example, giving away pocket calen-

(i)

ABCDEFGHIJKLMNOPQRSTUV
abcdefghijklmnopqrstuvwxyz

Specimens showing

(ii)

ABCDEFGHIJKLMNOPQRSTUVW
abcdefghijklmnopqrstuvwxyz

five of the many

(iii)

ABCDEFGHIJKLMNOPQRSTU
abcdefghijklmnopqrstuvwxyz

type faces available

(iv)

ABCDEFGHIJKLMNOPQRSTUVWXYZ
abcdefghijklmnopqrstuvwxyz

to the modern printer

(v)

ABCDEFGHIJKLMNOPQRSTUVWXYZ
abcdefghijklmnopqrstuvwxyz

in a wide range of sizes

Diagram 7. A small sample of different type faces: (i) Baskerville, (ii) Perpetua bold, (iii) Bodoni bold italic, (iv) Gill sans italic, (v) Rockwell bold condensed dars each Christmas. A local printer may quote a low price for producing the following year's calendar on a piece of white or coloured card which also bears the name and address of the shop. These can be placed on the counter for customers to pick up. Most would be kept for a whole year and the shop's name brought to the attention each time they were consulted.

One way to get the shop talked about, attract publicity and draw crowds is to use celebrities to open a new shop or extension, mark the shop's anniversary, or to inaugurate a 'season' or special display. Celebrities need not be nationally known: a local councillor or beauty queen may well be sufficient. More notable people can be asked to appear if thought desirable: if they live locally a telephone call will determine whether they are willing and what they would charge.

Alternatively, the approach can be made through a local advertising agency, but they will charge a commission, often fifteen per cent on any booking. Charges for use of a celebrity vary greatly with their fame and what they have to do. All local papers should be informed whenever an important person cooperates in this way. They may publish a photograph of the celebrity against the background of the specially arranged shop window or interior display. The name and trade of the shop would certainly be mentioned editorially and in captions.

The crowd which gathers at such events is not transformed into customers: it is the associated publicity, in the local papers and as a topic of conversation for days afterwards, which makes this method of sales promotion occasionally worth while. It is of greatest use where the type of person likely to take a particular interest in the celebrity is a potential customer; thus, it is more satisfactory for a shop selling, for example, lingerie to teenagers and young housewives than for a gentleman's outfitter directing his appeal to the more conservative and elderly in the district. Suppliers sometimes help; publishers, for example, sometimes arrange for authors of new books to be present in certain bookshops to autograph any copies of their books sold at the time.

Opening day for a shop or branch merits a substantial investment in publicity. The sooner potential customers buying elsewhere realize that a new shop has been opened, or that a shop is under new management, and discover the types of goods and services available, the quicker the retailer builds up his trade to a profitable level and obtains a good return on his investment in capital and effort. The amount to spend on the opening promotion depends on such factors as the degree of competition and whether a going concern has been taken over. Including a direct mail or poster campaign for two or three weeks before the opening day and further special publicity for another fortnight, even a small shop may find it worthwhile to spend £100, perhaps £250, if there is strong competition or if the shop serves a wide area. Suppliers, particularly manufacturers, sometimes offer advice and practical help such as providing free catalogues and a financial contribution towards their mailing, or assistance with methods of joint advertising.

GAINING EDITORIAL REFERENCES

Editorial columns of a newspaper are better places for promoting sales than advertising spaces in the same paper. They have a better chance of being read, believed, and acted upon and, above all, editorial references cost nothing. Such 'mentions' cannot be bought in any reputable newspaper; the editorial publicity is obtained only because the item referring to the shop is likely to interest readers. But enterprising retailers can turn otherwise unremarkable events into interesting material for newspapers: news of a joint promotion scheme or competition; the first of the new season's lines; the sale of the hundredth washing machine, and so on.

Just as the interest of customers must be borne in mind when framing advertisements, so should the interests of newspapers and their readers be remembered on such occasions. A bald statement to the press about the hundredth washing machine may not evoke any response: add a sentence pointing out that this is one of several recent indications of the increasing prosperity of the district and this not only rates as news for the newspaper but is likely to interest every reader also. Similarly a new season's lines may not be outstanding but they probably differ from those of the previous year and perhaps this indicates a newsworthy trend.

Such editorial references benefit the retailer by getting published the name and address of his shop together with details of some of its products, often just at the time when publicity does most good, as at the start of a season.

When opportunities arise for getting an editorial reference, a shopkeeper should write a short note of the fact to the editor of all non-national newspapers circulating in the district. When a specific event is the reason for the approach, as it usually is, the newspapers should be informed well in advance: a fortnight if possible in the case of a weekly paper. If the paper intends to publish something on the subject they will usually contact the retailer for additional information and perhaps arrange for a photographer to be present. Even in instances such as 'the hundredth washing machine', advance notice can be given when the, say, ninety-eighth has been sold.

It can be seen that there are many possible ways to advertise on a small budget. Window display, discussed in the preceding chapter, is probably the most effective method of advertising in relation to its cost and should have its own budget.

FIXING BUDGETS

One common way to set the advertising budget is to allocate a small proportion of annual turnover, usually between one and five per cent. Back-street shops and those selling luxury goods need a larger advertising budget than others. If this is too small to permit a regular weekly campaign, the most effective periods of the year should be chosen. These may be determined by the weather or the seasonal nature of the trade. Some retailers use their limited advertising to boost sales when trade is beginning to slacken off, others prefer to employ it at the beginning of a busy period when people are in a buying mood.

It always pays to advertise quick-selling lines rather than slow-movers, except when the latter are being sold off cheaply. It is usually uneconomic to advertise lines already heavily promoted by the manufacturer, unless there is a price reduction.

Local advertising agencies usually do not charge for giving advice about or placing advertisements because their commission is included in the newspaper's rates: but for advice and work on catalogues, leaflets, and other promotional matters they are likely to expect about fifteen per cent on printing and similar costs. Because commission varies considerably with the amount and cost of work involved, a fee always should be arranged before any work is placed. Charges often are disproportionately high unless the agency can expect a minimum volume of business regularly, such as £500 a year.

Some idea of the effect of advertising may be obtained if results for a week for which advertising has been used are compared with the same week for a previous year when it was not. But this must be done sensibly: there may be many other, perhaps more important, factors influencing sales figures. But any retailer can judge response to his contact with newcomers to the district, the effect of a joint promotion, or of any bargain line he offers. Many customers brought into the shop through a direct mail letter may say that they understand from a circular letter that a certain new line is now in stock, indicating the effectiveness of the mailing.

Results of advertising should always be remembered or noted so that comparisons can be made in the future. After an experimental period, each retailer will find his best advertising methods. Although he will normally concentrate on these, he should not be afraid to experiment on a small scale with other methods at a later date: he may find that conditions have changed.

FRAMING AND PLACING ADVERTISEMENTS

Although all aim to sell more goods, there are three distinct types of advertisement: those announcing special offers or other non-recurring facts, those telling potential customers of the business and location of the shop, and those reminding existing customers of these facts. The wording, placing, and timing of advertisements, as well as the kind of goods it is desired to promote, depend on which aim is being attempted. Often an advertisement will try to combine two or all three types. But to make advertising effective, the retailer must be clear about who he is trying to reach.

A usual line of thought is to consider existing and potential customers in the district, decide what they may be induced to buy, and consider how best to get them into the shop. Another is to begin with goods the retailer would best like to sell, then think about how these products affect people, narrow down the potential to specific groups or types of people, then decide how they can be influenced.

No one knows better than the retailer how his products affect people and he also knows the needs and desires of those served by his shop. His success in promoting sales depends largely on his skill in selecting the best method and time to put his message over and to phrase advertisements so that they compel. Brevity is always an advantage while clarity of expression is vital.

It always pays to think in terms of customers' interests. Most domestic electrical appliances for example are to potential purchasers primarily a means of doing necessary and repetitive tasks with comparatively little effort; they may also be a source of pride, putting the purchaser ahead of her neighbours. It is these benefits to the customer which must be sold, not merely the machine itself. This principle of 'benefits, not the article itself' applies to every product in every trade.

Many products also confer advantages which are unique: these are also well worth publicizing. Exaggerated claims and old-fashioned or pompous language should always be avoided, while reference to how long the shop has been established is a waste of space.

Gaining attention for advertisements can be achieved by clever wording and effective layout, as well as good positioning. This is a further reason for phrasing advertisements with benefits to the customer to the fore: the opening words catch the eye and immediately win interest.

Persistence in advertising pays off in the long run so long as the advertisement is well sited, well phrased, and well timed. But persistence does not mean that all advertisements must be the same. Even in classified advertising it may be better if wording is slightly altered for each insertion; in such instances it is wise to see whether the reduced rate applies for a series with varied texts. For all methods of advertising and especially where space is limited, specific information must be given: vague terms such as 'reasonable prices' waste space and kill effectiveness.

The cost of advertising is no guide to results. A cautious two pounds a week on a classified advertisement may eventually waste as much money as a large display advertisement in the local paper badly thought out and ill-timed. Once initial experimenting to find the best methods of advertising is over, outlay on promoting sales should be of little importance. All that does matter is that there should be every chance of the promotion bringing in far more profit than the advertising costs. Charges incurred in promoting sales are of course allowable expenses for tax purposes.

Any retailer with a lively mind will find any number of possibilities to promote extra sales. It is always worth watching the advertising of competitors, both to get ideas and to foresee any effect on one's own trading. One final point: if any specific products are advertised, be certain that an adequate stock is held.

15. Increase Your Profit

Many ways exist to make an established business more profitable. This chapter lists a few; others particularly suited to the district and trade may be suggested by the retailer's accountant or through informal conversation with fellow shopkeepers, possibly at meetings of the local branch of the trade association or chamber of trade.

EXTRA SALES

Rackjobbing is a practice started by supermarkets but can be applied to most kinds of shop. It consists of agreeing with a supplier, often a local wholesaler or other retailer, that he will be allocated a unit of shelving, display stand, etc., in a given position within the shop on which he will maintain a stock and display of agreed lines – normally those of a different trade to the shop yet likely to appeal to existing customers, such as kitchen gadgets, small electrical goods, toys, or cosmetics in a grocer's. The rackjobber, using his knowledge of his trade to display fast-moving lines – changed from time to time – bought at competitive prices, calls as necessary to maintain stock levels, change displays, etc., undertaking responsibility for shopsoiled items and price marking if required.

The retailer sells the goods in the normal way, paying the rackjobber an agreed percentage. This might yield the shopkeeper a 25 per cent margin on goods normally offering retailers 33⅓ per cent, though arrangements vary considerably. The reduced margin reflects the shopkeeper's payment for the rackjobber's knowledge and, in effect, the sale or return supply facility, perhaps for quantities too small for direct supply by wholesalers in the normal way.

As long as the retailer cannot use the space for better-paying lines of his own, this is clearly a useful source of extra income. However, retailers attracted by a margin substantially larger than common in their own trade must remember that the stock-turn rate is likely to be slower than for their own goods. The amount of space rackjobbed – there may even be more than one rackjobber – can vary to suit the retailer's requirements.

On a much larger scale this becomes the renting out of a counter, perhaps staffed by the 'rackjobber', or the creation of a 'shop within a shop'. Rackjobbing can be a source of increased profit also through the retailer himself being the rackjobber in appropriate neighbouring shops.

Home workers – men and women, working part time or full time, making an enormous variety* of products, ranging from handicrafts and soft toys in the living room to articles produced from a plastics moulding press in the garage – abound in many districts. Arranging to display in the shop such items likely to interest existing customers can be an additional source of profit. Goods are supplied on a sale or return basis, involving the retailer in no risk, and the commission received on making a sale usually provides the equivalent of a margin well above average. A small advertisement in the local newspaper, or perhaps in the shop window, stating willingness to discuss sale of home-made items is often the best way of making contact. Products need to be of a fair standard to avoid spoiling the shop's reputation for normal lines.

An exceptionally wide range* of services are also provided by home workers. The retailer can gain commission by acting as a sales agent. Some services may be directly connected with the shop's trade – a stationer's shop recommending a home-typing agency, a bookshop knowing qualified tutors to coach students privately, a draper's being able to pass on details of a home-visiting corsetière, for example – and in some instances it is likely that the home agency will buy supplies from the retailer as well as pay a

---

* Details are given in *Be Your Own Boss* by Alan Fiber, published by Management Books.

commission on business introduced. Other services the retailer might make known for commission may be of a more general nature, such as those of a good gardener, alteration needlewoman, or dog trainer. Where suitable, a well-designed notice can be displayed in the shop or window inviting inquiries from customers and passers-by for the home-based service, providers of which may be found as suggested above.

A hiring service for equipment associated with the trade can be a useful way to provide customers with a valued facility at the same time as helping to make a well-paying additional sale on many occasions. Customers of many trades have need of expensive equipment for short periods only, for which they are prepared to pay a substantial rental. Examples include an ironmonger hiring garden barrows or electric hedge clippers; a chemist handling photographic lines offering hire of a film projector; a builder's merchant renting out ladders, scaffolds and such equipment as floor sanding machines, both to do-it-yourself enthusiasts and to the trade; an electrical goods shop making available an additional TV set by the day or week, and so on.

It is always necessary to show customers carefully how the equipment is to be used, to take a deposit, and to inspect for damage on return. It may be possible to hire out the shop's appropriately trained delivery boy or other suitable person as the sole operator of the equipment. Care should be taken that the hiring facility does not harm the normal sale of similar equipment: the relationship of the hiring fee to the purchase price normally overcomes this.

Mail order is a logical development of direct mail advertising. It is simple to enclose an order form with any direct mail letter, drawing attention to this additional service. Although not suitable for every trade, it often can bring in additional business at no extra cost except that of postage or delivery, while having the further advantages of helping to fill slack trading hours profitably and providing customers with a supplementary facility.

A follow-up letter after a large purchase by a customer can create goodwill by the thoughtfulness of the retailer and also be an effective advertisement for future sales. A short note saying in effect 'Hope you are pleased with your purchase; thank you, and we are always at your service', sent, say, one month after the purchase, is all that is required. In such instances, and with other forms of direct mail, it may be worth having the letter signed by the assistant who served the order if the retailer did not do so himself, and so strengthen the personal touch.

Correspondence should always look dignified, which implies a reasonable quality paper and well thought out text. A typewriter can be useful; second-hand machines can give years of good service, but it is important that however bad the machine looks, the type itself should not be damaged nor the lines of typing appear irregular. Letters should always be replied to promptly and queries fully answered, but never write a letter in anger. All business papers should be kept tidily so that relevant facts can be found easily: this is a matter calling for self-discipline rather than expensive filing systems.

Customers should never be told that trade is bad. If they ask, never understate the volume of business and always look on the bright side. Not only do people like to shop where it seems that many others are gaining satisfaction, but many customers only ask to make conversation and want to hear a cheerful response.

Trading up by constantly aiming to sell higher-priced merchandise pays off by widening the range of potential customers, enlarging turnover and increasing chances of gaining repeat-business because more expensive articles are more likely to give customers fuller satisfaction. This policy should not be confused with over-selling customers with dearer articles than they really want. Trading up eventually offers customers greater variations between the cheaper and dearer articles a shop sells. Because the normal principle of handling only the most profitable lines remains, taking into account both margin and stockturn, trading up helps the retailer find the most beneficial price levels to stock for each range of his merchandise.

Multi-packs. Extra sales can be made more easily and without the appearance of doing so by offering multi-unit and extra-large packs once the desired product has been ascertained. Customers are not talked into buying something they do not want, they do not spend more per article or quantity than they originally intended (there may even be a slight reduction) yet profits are raised.

Music softly playing in the background is said to make customers less hesitant to enter a shop, less tense during a sale and more likely to stay for a second purchase. The music, planned to suit all tastes, helps to advertise the shop as customers tend to talk about it. Staff morale is also improved. Several firms supply suitable tapes of music, changed regularly, along with the hire of a tape-playing machine and amplifying equipment as necessary. Systems vary slightly and cost from about £2 a week.

New lines create interest so it is a good idea to have a permanent prominent position for the latest merchandise. Customers and, if conveniently placed, passers-by, then get the habit of looking for it.

Special promotion of some article or other should constantly be taking place, giving an always-something-on air to the shop.

Win back lost customers by mentioning in any suitable advertising that 'customers old and new' are welcome to see, try, and so on, whatever is being promoted. Such a phrase is sufficiently ambiguous to make it seem as if one is not admitting publicly that customers have been lost. Another approach might be 'When did you last visit us? Come and see what we have done: you'll be surprised.'

Previews. Regular customers can be favoured, and thus retained, by being invited personally through direct mail to visit the shop on a certain day or days between given hours to a special preview of new lines just arrived, asking the customer to bring the invitation as the admittance ticket. Previews can be held in a room at the back of the shop, increasing the 'special treatment' appeal. Those at the preview should be allowed to handle and, where appropriate, try the goods, but although all sales points should be brought out, no direct sales talk should be made. Orders given on the spot can be accepted, but there should be no hard selling: it is sufficient to have the chance to demonstrate to good customers and to make them feel privileged by being treated specially.

Occasional complaints are inevitable: well handled they can build goodwill. Be apologetic and generous: a complaint is better than a lost customer. If merchandise is genuinely faulty, apologize and explain what action will be taken to correct the fault and to see that grounds for complaint will not recur. It usually pays to replace the article at once and trust that the manufacturer will be equally generous with the retailer. If the customer is to blame, it is necessary to explain this tactfully. If only a small amount is involved, an awkward customer judged to be worth keeping can be given a new article. Where a complaint has been settled, a letter to the customer a month later trusting that all is now well can be an indirect way of advertising the good service of the shop.

Not all complaints come to light. If it is noticed that a good customer appears to have transferred her custom, a personally-addressed letter can be sent along the lines of

Dear Mrs Brown,

You have been kind enough to patronize my shop and it has been a pleasure to serve you. As I have not seen you lately I am rather worried in case any items you have obtained or service you have received have not been up to the expected standard. If we have been at fault the matter will receive immediate attention. I look forward very much to being able to serve you again.

Yours sincerely,

This brings the fault to light and may win a customer back even more firmly than previously.

Disputes in retailing rarely warrant legal action but there is a trend towards independent conciliation and arbitration, offering for the more serious disagreements an impartial hearing and justice to both sides without the anxiety, delay, cost and publicity of a court hearing. It is probable that more trade associations, and perhaps chambers of trade and commerce, will offer this service where members are involved in serious disputes, paying for a hearing by a completely independent arbitrator nominated by The Institute of Arbitrators (see page 283) if conciliation by an official of the trade association or chamber fails. Conciliation is also offered by the weights and measures inspectorate in certain areas.

Telephone calls can boost sales. Regular good customers can be telephoned during slack periods and asked if the shop can supply them with anything, mentioning any current special offers. This reminds customers of their wants, ensures that a competitor does not supply them, is an extra service often appreciated and may help to ease trade during peak periods. Best results come when telephone-selling can be relied on by customers as a regular service at approximately the same time each week or month, and when combined with a delivery service.

Even if no sale is made, the call acts as an advertisement, while the customer is encouraged to use her phone also to place orders, enabling the retailer to win business even though the client is nearer a competitor's shop. Telephone calls, counting for tax purposes as a business expense, are not costly. Any assistant entrusted with telephone-selling, or even merely answering the phone, should be trained in its correct use. The G.P.O.'s free booklet *The Telephone in Business* may be helpful.

Telephone-answering machines may also be worth consideration. They are basically a tape recorder attached to the retailer's telephone; the machine answers the phone with a pre-recorded announcement and records any message. This saves the retailer being called away from work to answer the telephone, while immediate answering encourages customers to phone in orders. The equipment, of which several models are available, shows when a message has been recorded: at a convenient time the retailer can play back the tape to deal with the messages.

It is usual to leave the machine plugged in all the time so the shop is virtually open twenty-four hours a day, including Sunday and early closing day. Incoming messages, both business and private, can be recorded also while the retailer is out. The machine does not stop the telephone from being used normally and the tape operates only when it takes a message. Hire of a machine, including full maintenance, costs from under £2 a week.

Delivery service can be expensive but it is a facility often much appreciated by customers. It is worth estimating the cost of this service from entries in the analysed cash book, unless obviously trivial. If the service is expensive to run the retailer should charge extra for delivery, stating the additional cost when asking the customer if she prefers delivery. Because the service builds goodwill it is not necessary to make a profit on deliveries. Some retailers may prefer to fix a low charge, being content to offset merely part of the costs involved. Full charge may reduce the demand for delivery so much that those deliveries still remaining may cost far more than originally calculated so that a loss is still incurred: when this seems likely it is clearly better to charge less and please more customers without losing any more money.

If delivery is offered it may be useful to map out the area covered by the shop to make sure that the most economic route is taken. It may be possible also to use return journeys to pick up items for stock, for example from a cash-and-carry warehouse. Sometimes it is practicable to arrange with one or more neighbouring shops to pool a delivery service, sharing the costs. Any delivery service offered by the retailer must be completely reliable. The assistant making the delivery needs training, just like any other staff: points requiring particular attention include procedure when a customer for a cash-on-delivery parcel says that payment will be made next time the shop is visited, and the additional points of courtesy such as wiping shoes on the mat before entering a house.

A mobile shop may be worth consideration if the retailer already has a delivery van. By travelling to an outlying estate it can widen the shopkeeper's clientèle. Once there, whether calling door-to-door or staying at one or more fixed points, it is important for the service to be regular, and preferable to circularize houses in the district announcing the start of the service. Before taking any action a visit to the local authority of the district to be served is important, to check that no regulations will be infringed. Objections from other retailers, however, must be expected.

Flexible sales outlet. Sometimes the same end can be achieved without the expense of a mobile shop. An enterprising bookseller, for example, can arrange to exhibit selections of suitable books at local schools, factories, and hobby clubs, reaching his potential market where it is relatively densely packed, without any significant overheads. In many trades there are opportunities to gain worthwhile extra business by going out to get it instead of waiting for it to arrive at the shop – selling to large office blocks and institutions as well as factories, and so on.

Using assets to the full usually provides further sources of profit. This may vary from hiring out the retailer's own van for light removals to accepting postcard advertisements for display on a board in the shop window. The principle is the same: the retailer should consider carefully what his assets are, and whether they are fully used. He should not forget such intangibles as the attention of certain categories of people – his customers – while they are in, or perhaps only near, his shop, and also the retailer's own knowledge.

BETTER MANAGEMENT

Delegation of duties should be practised as soon as the shop is large enough to employ staff, otherwise too much work accumulates for the retailer, who is then too busy to be able to stop and consider his business methods and future. Delegation also helps the retailer in his staff policy as an assistant sees the extra duties as training for promotion, which indeed they are. The speed and amount of delegation depends on the quality of the assistant and her, or his, particular duties, but it should work up eventually to include most of the retailer's own functions, perhaps even including the buying of some lines. However, control should never be delegated completely: the retailer should check at irregular periods that all is well. Before delegating, thought should be given to which aspects of the task are likely to give difficulty to the assistant; what the consequences of errors are likely to be, and the acceptable limit of errors; how often, to what degree, and in which ways the work should be checked; how long mistakes might remain undetected; and which aspects of the task are likely to give the greatest satisfaction to the assistant.

The shopkeeper should explain to the assistant that he is being given more responsible work and that the level of income and status he will achieve in life depend on his willingness and ability to deal adequately with progressively difficult duties. Some assistants will not accept responsibility, even if refusal means forgoing advancement; such staff cannot be forced, but if the retailer has plans for expansion he may well have to consider whether his assistant is the most suitable employee available or what would be the reaction to a more go-ahead assistant joining the business and eventually overtaking his colleague.

The purpose of delegation is to have tasks done properly by an assistant, which does not mean that the retailer's own methods and ideas have to be followed implicitly if the assistant can improve on them. Originality should be encouraged.

Leadership can be exercised in many 'styles', the most suitable depending to some extent on the retailer himself. Most assistants respect a boss who is tactful, patient, consistently fair, never moody, and who clearly knows his job.

Good health is important. The retailer cannot afford to be away from the shop because of illness, but poor health can be detrimental to business even without this by impairing selling ability. He should take regular exercise – walks around his district may also help him to discover new lines to sell, and potential customers – and avoid unnecessary exertion in the shop in lifting boxes and climbing ladders, etc. Method study may help here. Above all, he should have the right approach: trifles are not worth anxiety, and major problems are not solved by worry but by deciding what exactly the problem is, its causes, possible solutions, and the best course of action.

Progress reviews. Ideas for improving the business in any way are

Checklist 17. Curing causes of complaint

Among the more common:
1. Faulty merchandise – take up matter with supplier.
2. Merchandise wrong size, shade, etc. – better selling technique: ascertain customers' complete requirements.
3. Legal liability towards customer – consult proper source of guidance, e.g. trade association, chamber of trade, solicitor; if retailer at fault, greater care and knowledge are required.
4. Damaged, soiled, or stale merchandise – take more care in storing and display: sell older stocks before new; do not over-order.
5. Poor service, late delivery, delay in obtaining special order – ensure that no promises are made that are unlikely to be fulfilled: improve business organization.
6. Mislaid order, article delivered to wrong address, etc. – attend to administrative system, including staff supervision.

valuable: they should be jotted down as they occur in an 'ideas' notebook and reviewed regularly each week. Some will then seem foolish and should be crossed out: others can remain for subsequent reconsideration if not acted upon at once.

Improvements to the business are always possible and there is never a limit to sales and profits. Complacency can ruin a shop's trade: it is necessary to think continually of improvements, merely to match competition, and to keep up-to-date. Regular periods should be set aside for reviewing business progress, perhaps monthly, at a time when there will be no interruptions.

Consider where the shop is heading, how best to attain targets and what is going on in the world outside which may affect the shop. Study the latest trading results and financial position and let the mind wander idly on business matters for a few moments every now and again during these review periods: the subconscious sometimes comes up with the answers. This is the nearest anyone ever gets to inspiration: the surrounding conditions must be suitable and the thought focused on the subject, yet relaxed. Do not worry if inspiration does not come: it will do so on some occasions. Progress of the business can of course be considered at any time: these regular periods merely ensure that a minimum of review is given.

Diversification is the next step once the retailer is certain that no more scope exists for expansion of trade in his present lines – but this rarely occurs. Diversification usually takes the form of selling associated lines likely to appeal to existing customers, for example, toys as well as sweets, or office machines as well as business stationery, but an opening may exist for a completely different trade for which customers in the district are not well supplied. Perhaps the insufficient custom does not warrant a shop in that trade, but what business is available may make it profitable to open a separate section of an existing shop that is already well known in the district.

Selling rackjobbed goods or acting as agent for services and products supplied by home workers, as referred to on page 234, are an elementary form of diversification. This might be taken a stage further without involving much shop space or capital by offering, where appropriate to existing customers' needs and if not provided by other local traders, any of the wide range of possibilities mentioned in one of the author's other books, *Be Your Own Boss*, such as a ticket agency or one of the many types of 'bureau' business. On a larger scale still, it may be possible and profitable to open a sub-post-office in part of the shop. This involves extra space and perhaps extra staff, though in addition to receiving payments on the standard post-office scale for official business transacted, there is the advantage of attracting into the shop many extra people – especially beneficial to trades such as stationer's and tobacconist's.

Additional capital will be required where diversification involves buying stock in the subsidiary trade.

The retailer must always remember that it is necessary to know something of the new trade: without this knowledge he may easily make costly mistakes in buying, although the risk is slightly less than when first setting up a shop because the diversified lines are additional to the established business.

Expansion of any business, by diversification or otherwise, brings further problems but they are mainly a scaling-up of those besetting any smaller retailer. Probably the greatest is shortage of finance, especially ready cash, followed by lack of retailer's time because he has not delegated sufficiently. Answers to these problems are to be found earlier in this book.

There are dangers in too-rapid major expansion. Increased business must be built on a firm foundation. The retailer's accountant and bank manager should be asked for advice early in any expansion plans.

Competitors need constant watching, but not slavish imitation, and elementary market research as detailed in Chapter 4 should be carried out from time to time to ensure that the shop keeps up-to-date with its potential.

The retailer's attitude to competing traders should be reasonably friendly: there is always a living available for any progressive retailer who knows his business. It is helpful to take part in local affairs, clubs, trade associations, and the chamber of trade. It broadens the retailer's views; gives him greater self-confidence; keeps him up-to-date with local trading matters; assists in making his business aims felt, as one of a group of traders, by the local council and others; and helps in making more friends and customers.

Success comes from hard work, ever-improving efficiency, and the realization that there is always much to learn. The retailer may find the appendices to this book a helpful guide to further study and information.

16. Legal Matters

The legal obligations of retailers are considerable, but because they are varied and particular circumstances sometimes alter normal liability it is impossible to give a comprehensive summary that will be an always-accurate guide. This chapter merely sets out the more important legal obligations so that the retailer can appreciate the need to at least skim through a good book, for example one of those recommended in Appendix 11, devoted entirely to retailing law. It is not necessary for the retailer to know thoroughly the intricacies of law, but he should have a good idea of the general principles, know what are his retailing obligations and where he can find help if necessary.

A number of legal points have been referred to throughout this book where appropriate, while those concerning licences or registrations to trade, and planning permission, are grouped towards the end of this chapter for ease of reference.

DEALINGS WITH STAFF

In practice, the majority of retailers are brought into contact most frequently with the law when dealing with staff. Firstly, under the Contracts of Employment Act any employee working twenty-one hours a week or more must be given a written note containing the chief points about the terms of employment, such as rate and frequency of payment, hours of work, holidays with pay, and period of notice on either side. Full details of this Act's requirements are available from the Department of Employment.

National insurance cards normally need to be stamped for each employee. The cards themselves contain the main instructions and further information is supplied by the Department of Health and Social Security. One legal point worth remembering is that an employer is not entitled to deduct money from an assistant's wage for being away ill, not even if sick pay is received from the National Health Service or any other source, unless the assistant has signed a document permitting this to be done. A simple agreement allowing this therefore should be entered into before taking on staff: otherwise they may receive more money for being away than from working. It is usual to allow three days' absence on full pay, after which a note from the doctor is requested and sick pay deducted.

Income tax usually has to be deducted from wages under the pay-as-you-earn system. Any assistant who has previously paid income tax will normally present on their first day the P.45 form completed by the previous employer. This gives instructions for the new employer. Full information on all tax matters can be had from the office of the local inspector of taxes.

The retailer is likely to be governed by regulations about minimum wages decreed by wages councils set up for various trades under the Wages Councils Act. Even though he is probably paying well above the minimum it is worth discovering his legal responsibilities in this direction. Details can be obtained from the senior wages inspector at any regional office of the Department of Employment, whose address can be found through any employment exchange and some post offices.

If nothing is otherwise agreed in writing, it is usual to make holiday pay proportional to the period worked.

Information about restrictions on the employment of school-children, for example for deliveries, can be had from the local youth employment officer or education officer. Their address can be found from the town hall, where they may have their office, if they are not listed separately in the telephone directory.

Legal liability for working conditions of staff is governed chiefly by the Offices, Shops and Railway Premises Act and the Shops Act. The former covers such matters as cleanliness, a reasonable minimum temperature of 16°C (61°F), adequate ventilation and lighting of the premises; provision of sufficient and reasonable sanitary conveniences, washing facilities, and a supply of drinking water; accommodation for clothing not worn in working hours; provision of appropriate eating facilities if staff have to take meals on the premises, and an easily accessible first aid box or cupboard used solely for first aid requisites; and regulations about keeping passages, stairways, etc., as free from obstruction as practicable.

This Act also deals with fire precautions and lays down rules for administering the Act, which include the need for the retailer to inform his staff about the Act's provisions, either by posting up the prescribed printed notice in a prominent place or by giving each employee a copy of the official explanatory booklet. It is not always realized that there must be at least one convenient seat in the shop for every three employees, of either sex (and similarly a seat for one or two employees in total, or in excess of a multiple of three), and staff must be allowed to sit down whenever it does not interfere with work. The Shops Act deals with regulations concerning early closing day, Sunday trading, closing times in the evening, and various other matters affecting conditions of work for employees.

The local authority has power to inspect to see that all shops conform to this and several other Acts. They can provide further information and, where appropriate, issue certificates of exemption where particular requirements are impractical. There are usually substantial penalties for failing to comply with such legal obligations, sometimes involving fines for each day the retailer remains in breach of the law after he has been warned. In practice, however, local authority inspectors give shopkeepers a reasonable time in which to put matters right before they severely apply the letter of the law.

In most legal matters concerning staff conditions, a manager counts as an assistant, but close members of the family working in the shop, in general, do not.

The retailer's accountant can often advise on such general legal matters involving staff, as can some local chambers of trade and trade associations, who may also provide members with staff agreement forms and other help. More information about their services is given in Appendix 7.

Other laws of direct relevance to employing staff include the Payment of Wages Act, allowing the retailer to pay by cheque or credit transfer if the employee agrees to it in writing, and the Theft Act, which applies to staff pilfering. Staff can involve the retailer in legal obligations in other ways also. For example, certain actions by employees in relation to customers, suppliers, and others, may be legally binding on the retailer even though he was not previously consulted. Negligence by an assistant in serving a customer, contracts of service such as may be given to a manager, and accidents at work, are further common matters where the retailer may find himself threatened with legal action through his staff.

LIABILITY TOWARDS CUSTOMERS

Buying and selling goods can involve the retailer legally in many ways. A contract is made when an article is sold and the law has a good deal to say on contractual liability. In particular the Sale of Goods Act stipulates that, unless otherwise specifically agreed between buyer and seller, the goods must correspond with their description, be of merchantable quality if sold by a dealer normally trading in the type of goods concerned, be up to sample, fit for a particular purpose if the buyer makes the purpose known or if it is obvious so that the seller is called on to exercise his judgement on goods he is accustomed to selling, and be free from defects. This Act deserves particular attention.

The Trade Descriptions Act is also very important, particularly in relation to the accuracy of the principal kinds of information, written or verbal, given to prospective customers about goods or services offered. These include references, either incorrect or misleading, to the quantity, method of manufacture, composition, fitness for purpose, strength, performance, and behaviour of goods; where they have been made and by whom; how they have been processed or reconditioned; and to the approval or testing of what is offered. There is also the requirement that price-reduced articles must have been sold at the indicated former higher price for a continuous period of at least twenty-eight days during the preceding six months, unless the contrary is indicated.

This Act applies to all methods of supply, not only straightforward shop sale, and to claims in advertisements. The local weights and measures authority has the duty of enforcing this Act, which, being part of criminal law, does not debar a civil action by an aggrieved customer against a defaulting retailer in addition.

A retailer can render himself liable for an action for negligence or for not warning customers of known defects in products, even if these are due to the manufacturers' inherent design. He is also under a duty, through the Occupiers' Liability Act, to make his premises safe for all who enter legally. In this he must allow for children being less careful than adults. For example, he needs to see that children do not stand where they may be hit by the shop door: he will normally be liable if the child is hurt, even if it was really the child's fault for playing with the door.

The Weights and Measures Act naturally applies to all shop-keepers. It provides for inspection of all measuring, including weighing, devices, and indicates penalties for short measure. It also stipulates that measurement details of contents of packs, weight, number, etc., must be available for customers to see, either on the packaging or by measurement in front of the cus-tomer: particularly important where the retailer makes up his own pre-packs.

The Hire Purchase Acts and the Advertisements (Hire Pur-chase) Act have widespread application. Any trader selling by hire purchase or credit sale agreement should understand thoroughly the legal positions of shopkeeper, customer, and, if used, finance house. The Disposal of Uncollected Goods Act affects many trades, and guarantees are becoming increasingly usual, bringing their own legal complications. The Consumer Protection Act, Resale Prices Act, Race Relations Act, and Shops (Early Closing) Act are further measures of interest to many retailers. There are also a number of Acts applying to specific trades, such as the Seeds Act, the Assay Act, and for food shops, the Food and Drugs Act, and the Food Hygiene Regulations.

A problem affecting all trades is pilfering. To sustain a legal action against a customer for shoplifting it is usually necessary to prove that the goods were taken away, that no payment was offered, and that there was intent to avoid payment. It is therefore always advisable to wait until the suspect has left the shop before making the accusation, otherwise they may claim they intended to pay before leaving.

A retailer or member of his staff is entitled to arrest personally on the spot, someone reasonably suspected of theft of goods or cash, though they should be sure they can prove their allegation. Damages will not be incurred for unlawful arrest if the decision to prosecute, or not, is taken without delay – that is, if necessary, after consultation with a solicitor or shop's director. The suspect's agreement is required before searching their clothing, bag, etc.; the police can be called if they refuse. It can be made one of the terms of employment that staff will agree to this where there appears to be cause.

The retailer is free to decide for himself whether to prosecute or to let a thief go, and can legally threaten prosecution to obtain return of the goods or cash. The police sometimes prosecute if called in and at other times leave any action to the retailer. Equally, even if the police intend to prosecute, the retailer is not obliged to cooperate – if, for example, legal proceedings are not worth his time and anxiety, or if he feels his evidence may be insufficient to ensure conviction so that he might come out of the case badly.

Other legal points involving customers include the extent to which married women can pledge the credit of their husbands, and the fact that a retailer cannot refuse to hand over goods, such as articles brought in for repair, as a lever to obtain payment for an unpaid bill.

GENERAL RESPONSIBILITIES

A contract is made when the shopkeeper or an assistant makes a sale, when the retailer buys supplies, when staff are engaged, and on many other everyday occasions. Contracts do not have to be written: they can be inferred from people's actions. Thus the general law of contract is particularly relevant to retailing. It has been established, however, that the price ticket on an article is merely 'an offer to treat'; the 'offer' part of the contract created when making a sale comes from the customer and the 'acceptance' from the trader, so a retailer can refuse to sell an item wrongly price-marked.

The shopkeeper needs to appreciate the difference between civil and criminal law as this affects legal rights and procedures. Some incidents in retailing may involve both kinds of action at the same time. When criminal law is involved, legal proceedings are brought by the police, or other official body, as the prosecutor. In a civil action, the retailer is the prosecutor. In civil disputes, it may be possible to avoid going to law, using conciliation or arbitration instead, as referred to on pages 238, 264 and 283.

As mentioned on page 51 it is often advantageous to trade as a limited liability company or in partnership: both methods of operating a business have their own legal implications. Even if a shopkeeper carries on business as a sole trader he may have to register under the Registration of Business Names Act. Details of when registration is necessary and what is involved – it is quite simple – can be obtained from the Registrar of Business Names, whose address is listed in Appendix 8. Registration, where applicable, must be within fourteen days of the start of the business, and a heavy penalty can be imposed if a trader does not register when he should do so.

There are many other legal matters that may affect a retailer, in both his business and private life – in relation to landlords, cheques, neighbours, and wills, for example. The need to read a good book on retailing law is obvious.

LICENCES AND REGISTRATIONS

Before a retailer can sell certain merchandise or offer certain services he is often required to notify the proper authority and, in some instances, obtain a licence: local conditions must be ascertained, from the various bodies mentioned below or through the retailer's trade association, because the legal requirements are not always consistent throughout the country due to local Acts and legislation which local authorities can adopt or ignore at their own discretion. In London, powers are distributed between the G.L.C. and metropolitan boroughs on a special basis.

The addresses of appropriate bodies can be found from the

local telephone directory, town hall, or public library. Newcomers to retailing are advised always to inquire, whatever their trade, at the town clerk's department in the town hall, where they can be informed of any local legislation and guided in these complicated matters. The most usual items requiring registration or a licence in England are:

Goods or services:	*Make application to:*
Beer	Customs & Excise and Licensing Justices
Chemists in the National Health Service	N.H.S. County Executive Council
Cider and perry	Customs & Excise and Licensing Justices
Confectionery	Council of county, county borough, borough, or urban district with over 40,000 population
Dry cleaners (with machine on premises)	Factory inspectorate
Firearms dealers	Police
Fireworks (maximum quantity normally 100 lb.)	County (including London), county borough, urban or rural district council
Food (all types)	Council of county, county borough, borough, or urban district with over 40,000 population
Game birds	County (including London) or county borough council.
Methylated spirits	Customs & Excise
Pawnbrokers	County (including London) or county borough council
Poisons noted in Part 2 of the Poisons List (including certain insecticides, preparations for horticulture, rodent killers, concentrated ammonia and caustic soda, etc.)	County, county borough, or metropolitan borough council
Petrol filling stations	Council of county borough, borough, urban or rural district, or G.L.C.
Pets	County borough, borough (including metropolitan borough), urban or rural district council

Goods or services:	Make application to:
Pharmaceutical chemists*	Pharmaceutical Society of Great Britain
Restaurant with liquor licence	Customs & Excise and Licensing Justices
Spirits	Customs & Excise and Licensing Justices
Wine (including tonic wines, cooking sherry, etc.)	Customs & Excise and Licensing Justices

PLANNING PERMISSION

Permission from the local planning authority is necessary when a retailer wishes to begin to trade as any of the following:

Car showrooms
Catsmeat shop
Fried-fish shop
Petrol filling station
Pet shop
Public house
Repairing garage
Tripe shop

Permission is not required for the above if the retailer merely takes over an established business so that no change in type of use of the premises is involved. The local planning officer, whose office is often in the town hall, will answer all inquiries in these matters.

INSURANCE

It is common sense to minimize the risk of loss due to legal liability by insuring against normal business risks. Similarly, it is

---

* By law only qualified and authorized pharmacists may call themselves retail chemists, druggists, pharmacists, or certain other titles. Shops selling broadly similar merchandise but operated by retailers who are not qualified in pharmacy are sometimes called drug stores. They are not permitted to dispense prescriptions nor to sell certain pharmaceutical products, but, unless dealing in items listed above such as tonic wines, they do not need to register or obtain a licence.

foolish not to be insured fully against other hazards of trading, such as fire, burglary, the loss of cash in transit, or of profit following a fire.

Insurance requirements vary and need to be discussed in relation to the retailer's own circumstances. This can be done directly with an insurance company or through an insurance broker. The advantage of using a broker is that he can advise on a wider range of policies because he is in contact with several insurance companies. His services are free to the retailer as he is paid a commission by the insurance companies on the business he places with them. He therefore has a financial interest in selling insurance, and may be biased in favour of a particular company. As with choosing other professional advisers, where it is not possible to have a broker recommended by a reliable friend, business acquaintance, etc., it tends to be safer to select a member of one of the principal bodies – in this instance, the Corporation of Insurance Brokers or Association of Insurance Brokers.

Appendices

The following information is presented here, rather than in the appropriate chapters, to make it easier for the reader to use this book as a work of reference. Small variations in some details may be found, but the sources of information about local conditions or the means of verifying addresses are usually apparent. Public reference libraries, trade associations, and the trade press are a fund of information whenever in doubt.

The detailed index and contents list will also prove helpful for quick reference.

Appendix 1. Professional advisers

It is essential for the purchaser of a business to employ an accountant, solicitor, and, normally, a surveyor. None should act for the seller also. An arbitrator may also be required by a retailer on occasion.

All solicitors and arbitrators, many accountants, and the majority of surveyors belong to an appropriate professional body: if the retailer is choosing unknown professional advisers it is safer to engage properly qualified men. Some members of recognized professional bodies are better than others, and not every member will give faultless advice and service on all occasions, but professional qualifications are an indication of a minimum standard of knowledge – often very high – and of a reasonable standard of business conduct. Unqualified advisers may be equally suitable but it is more likely that they will not be. To employ an unknown unqualified adviser is to increase risk of error, nullifying the very reason for employing a specialist, without compensating advantages: fees charged are often the same and may be even higher for an unqualified man. Good advisers save a retailer the cost of their fees many times over.

Choice of professional advisers is an extremely important matter. The retailer should choose, wherever possible, advisers who have been recommended for good reasons by those whose judgement he trusts.

Membership of a professional body means that the adviser cannot advertise at all (except in very restricted circumstances for a surveyor), carries on his business without the safeguard of it being a limited liability company – a constant reminder to him that his personal effects are at stake if he makes a serious error – and can be called to account by his professional body for his actions, advice, and fees charged. Full details of how clients are safeguarded are available from the secretary of each professional body. When a professional body is formed it usually admits as members, without written examination, anyone who is currently practising and who meets the body's standards (which can vary) of minimum experience and integrity, and it is often only after many decades that a body can claim that all its members have both passed all its written examinations and attained the minimum practical experience currently demanded for full membership. Other things being equal, the qualifications demanded by an older body are likely to be higher than others in its field because all bodies aim constantly to raise their standards.

A free estimate of likely fees can always be obtained, and where a fee depends on time taken which cannot be calculated accurately in advance, the basis of the charges should be stated in addition. The scale of fees can often be varied by agreement between retailer and his adviser but this should be done at the time instructions are given and not left until the account has been rendered. A broad indication of the usual costs are included in Appendix 3. The seller pays all fees for the sale of the shop; the buyer pays only those fees incurred by his own advisers in checking the seller's statements.

How to find suitable advisers and what lies behind the various designations is set out below. Small variations may occur outside England but local conditions can always be verified by consulting the secretary of the corresponding local professional body, where this differs from that given. Advice on how to make contact may also be available from a local public library.

It is always possible to send a letter to the secretary of the appropriate professional body requesting the name and address of qualified members in the retailer's district. However, these organizations will always reply with a short list of local members: they can never advise on the merits of one member compared with another, or recommend only one member.

ACCOUNTANTS

The importance has been stressed throughout this book, and especially in Chapters 2, 3, 8, and 9, of using a trained independent mind, skilled in particular in relation to financial matters, to ensure that the retailer gains the maximum from his investment and efforts. Accountants understand business matters and what lies behind figures appearing as a result of day-to-day trading and in annual accounts.

Shopkeepers can benefit greatly from professional guidance about business methods in general and especially about records required, for assistance in daily operations as well as for preparation of annual accounts. Adequate financial information of the kind accountants can readily provide enables retailers to make the most of their opportunities; without it, a business can all too easily get into difficulties.

Annual accounts prepared by competent accountants assist the shopkeeper in raising further capital or overdraft facilities if these become necessary. The accounts are also important for tax purposes. A wise businessman will have his tax assessments negotiated by his accountant. The need for skilled and independent advice from a professional accountant when buying a business is vital and has been stressed in Chapter 3.

Accountants provide these and many other services for the whole range of business enterprises from the smallest one-man business to the largest industrial groups. Accountants usually provide their services for any type of retail business; the principles underlying their work are not greatly affected by the precise nature of the trade carried on. There is, therefore, normally no need to look for an accountant who specializes in any particular retail trade.

All members of the recognized accountancy bodies are required to treat as strictly confidential the knowledge they obtain as a result of having access to their clients' records.

Accountants' fees are based on the skill and knowledge required for the type of work involved, the calibre of the persons engaged on the work, the time occupied, and the responsibility which the work entails. Fees may, therefore, vary considerably according to the nature of the work. Before undertaking work for a new client an accountant will normally be prepared to indicate the approximate amount of his fees, but to do this he must first ascertain what the client requires and be given sufficient information about the nature and the size of the business, the records available, and so on.

The best method of finding an accountant is through a recommendation from a friend or business acquaintance. If such an introduction is not possible, reference can be made to the 'yearbooks' of the recognized accountancy bodies, available in most local public libraries, or inquiries can also be made of the local district societies of the recognized bodies. Help can also be obtained, if necessary, by writing to the secretaries of the professional bodies.

Although anyone may practise in the United Kingdom as an accountant, he may not use a description indicating membership of a recognized accountancy body unless he is a member of that organization. The recognized bodies in England are the Institute of Chartered Accountants in England and Wales, whose members use the description 'chartered accountant' and the letters A.C.A. (for Associates) or F.C.A. (for Fellows), and the Association of Certified and Corporate Accountants, whose members use the description 'certified accountant' and the letters A.A.C.C.A. or F.A.C.C.A.

Chartered accountants. Membership can be obtained only by training for a long period, usually four years, as an articled clerk with a practising chartered accountant in the United Kingdom and passing the Institute's professional examinations. Before the training can commence the candidate must have reached a high standard of general education. The Institute's examinations cover not only such subjects as accounting, auditing, and taxation, but also cost and management accounting, commercial knowledge, and English law. An Associate can become a Fellow only after ten years as an A.C.A. or after five years' continuous practice as a principal of his firm.

The Institute of Chartered Accountants in England and Wales was incorporated by Royal Charter in 1880. Its headquarters are at Moorgate Place, London, EC2.

The Institute of Chartered Accountants of Scotland (27 Queen Street, Edinburgh 2) and The Institute of Chartered Accountants in Ireland (7 Fitzwilliam Place, Dublin) are broadly similar to the

English institute. In 1957 the Society of Incorporated Accountants, then a recognized body, arranged with the three chartered institutes to go into liquidation. Certain of the members admitted to the English institute under this scheme continue to use the description 'incorporated accountant' and the letters A.S.A.A. or F.S.A.A.

Certified accountants. Membership can be obtained only by training for a long period, usually five years, and passing the Institute's professional examinations after attaining a high standard of general education. The Association of Certified and Corporate Accountants differs from the chartered institutes in that its candidates may obtain their practical experience in industry or commerce or outside the U.K., instead of as an articled clerk in the U.K. under a practising chartered accountant. An Associate can become a Fellow only after five years as an A.A.C.C.A.

The Association of Certified and Corporate Accountants was founded in 1904. Its headquarters are at 22 Bedford Square, London, WC 1.

SOLICITORS

Chapter 3 shows how a solicitor can help a retailer when buying a shop and there are also many other occasions when a solicitor's advice is invaluable. Only those whose names appear on the Roll of Solicitors maintained by the Law Society can call themselves solicitors: a guarantee of considerable ability, as the Law Society sets high standards of entry to, and continued membership of, the profession. A solicitor can be found by consulting *The Law List*, published annually, and available at most public libraries and citizens' advice bureaux. This book contains details of all solicitors, grouped by towns.

Fees for certain work by solicitors are laid down by statute, but charges for many of the services likely to be required by retailers depend on the time taken and the complexity of the work. Advance estimates always can be obtained. The Law Society, whose address is The Law Society's Hall, 113 Chancery Lane, London, WC2, was founded in 1825.

ARBITRATORS

Retailers involved in serious, though not criminal, disputes with customers, suppliers, staff or others can, with the agreement of the other party, arrange to refer the dispute to an independent arbitrator, as outlined on page 252. Arbitrators are often doubly qualified, having passed examinations in law as well as being qualified in the sphere of professional or commercial activity involved in the dispute. Both parties having agreed to abide by his ruling and the Arbitration Act, the arbitrator decides the points at issue as would a court judge, backed by all the authority of the High Court, though usually with much less formality in proceedings – in an office instead of a courtroom, without legal jargon, and often without need for lawyers or others being present. The parties can make conditions in appointing the arbitrator, gaining far more flexibility than with a court hearing: for example, that the arbitrator holds the hearing locally, quickly after appointment, at convenient hours, and views for himself the shop involved if this is relevant.

The arbitrator having knowledge of the trade, best practice in retailing, etc., as well as legal knowledge, proceedings are also likely to be shorter than a court hearing, where the judge has to be told about the customs of the trade and other technical matters by one of the parties, witnesses or counsel. Costs may also be far less than those of a court hearing, and, being held in private, neither the dispute nor the result is publicized. Especially as most retailers cannot afford to be away from their business to attend long-drawn-out court proceedings, arbitration offers many advantages. The process is welcomed by the courts, who themselves sometimes submit to arbitration legal actions requiring specialist knowledge. An arbitrator holds a judicial inquiry to settle a dispute and his award can be enforced directly by the court, as distinct from, for example, a valuer whom the parties may appoint to give his own opinion on some matter, where a legal action may have to be brought to enforce the decision.

The only body of arbitrators in Britain, all of whose members are qualified, is The Institute of Arbitrators, whose address is 16 Park Crescent, London, w1. The Institute was founded in 1915, arbitration being a twentieth-century development to combine the increasing technicality, complexity and pace of life with the continued authority and justice of the law.

SURVEYORS AND ESTATE AGENTS

The services of a surveyor may be required by a retailer to report on the structural condition of premises, to help the retailer fight an excessive claim by a landlord for dilapidations at the end of a lease, or to draw up a plan for alterations to business premises, including obtaining the necessary permissions from the local authority and others, and supervising the building work. An estate agent may be required when the retailer is about to sell a shop.

Many estate agents are also surveyors, but by no means all surveyors are also estate agents. The difficulty is that anyone can call himself an estate agent or surveyor – or both, just as anyone can also call himself a business transfer agent. It is, therefore, all the more important, when engaging a man for these services, to look at his qualifications: they will certainly be displayed prominently if he has any.

Various sets of letters after a man's name reveal which body he belongs to and thus which aspects of the wide field of surveying or estate agency he tends to specialize in, but there is considerable overlapping both in day-to-day work and in qualifying examinations. Membership of more than one of the professional bodies is common.

A suitable surveyor or estate agent can be found by observing the shop used as his office (or name plate on the door if a house or office building is used), noting the name and address from a board outside a property for disposal, through advertisements or entries in local papers, directories or guide books, or by reference to a list of members of the professional body concerned, published as a book and sometimes available at public libraries or town clerk's department of a town hall. Many of these lists include an index of members grouped by districts.

Royal Institution of Chartered Surveyors. Practising members are either Professional Associates (having the letters A.R.I.C.S. after their name) or Fellows (F.R.I.C.S.). Only a member of one of these categories is entitled to call himself a 'chartered surveyor' and no firm may call themselves 'chartered surveyors' unless all the partners are so qualified. Members belong to one of many separate sections of the Institution according to their principal work: estate agency, auctioneering, valuation, building surveying, and quantity surveying sections are those most relevant to retailers' needs.

Minimum qualifications to attain A.R.I.C.S. include passing three examinations of the Institution, covering about twenty subjects, and several years practical experience. No Professional Associate can become a Fellow until he is over thirty years old and has completed at least five years as a practising surveyor in a senior position in his firm.

The Royal Institution of Chartered Surveyors was founded in 1868. Its headquarters are at 12 Great George Street, London, SW1.

The Incorporated Society of Valuers and Auctioneers. Practising members are either Associates (having the letters A.S.V.A. after their names) or Fellows (F.S.V.A.). The Society was formed in 1968 through a merger of the Incorporated Society of Auctioneers and Landed Property Agents, founded in 1924, with the Valuers' Institution, founded in 1929, entry to either body not necessarily involving written examination, until recent years, for estate agents or valuers with acceptable practical experience. Written examinations are now held for new entrants, and the education and practical training required of these younger members to attain Associateship and Fellowship is not very different from that approved for members of the R.I.C.S. The Society's headquarters are at 3 Cadogan Gate, London, SW1.

The retailer will probably find a suitable surveyor to carry out his work concerning structural survey, dilapidations, or alterations among the surveyors or estate agents in the district with one of the above qualifications, but surveyors with one of the following designations may also be accustomed to performing such work:

F.I.A.S.: Fellow of the Incorporated Association of Architects and Surveyors, being a surveyor.

A.I.A.S.: Associate of the Incorporated Association of Architects and Surveyors, being a surveyor.

F.I.Q.S.: Fellow of the Institute of Quantity Surveyors.

A.I.Q.S.: Associate of the Institute of Quantity Surveyors.

F.F.S.: Fellow of the Faculty of Architects and Surveyors, being a surveyor.

A.F.S.: Associate of the Faculty of Architects and Surveyors, being a surveyor.

The headquarters of the I.A.A.S. are at 29 Belgrave Square, London, sw1, of the I.Q.S., 98 Gloucester Place, London, w1, and of the F.A.S., 68 Gloucester Place, London, w1. All now demand substantial standards of educational and practical ability although entry by written examination only did not commence for the I.A.A.S. until 1954 and for the I.Q.S. until 1941.

Appendix 2. A typical prospectus

BUSINESS: Chemist's shop at 93 Carlton Road, Camberwell, London, SE5 trading under name of 'Jones the Chemist'. Situated in centre of a busy local parade of seven shops, located in a working-class/lower middle-class residential area.

TRADE: All types of chemist's sundries including a high proportion of branded pharmaceuticals and cosmetics, a fair trade in certain fancy goods, and some sale for baby foods, health drinks, and photographic materials.

There is a substantial dispensing connection accounting for about thirty per cent of turnover and there are six doctors in the vicinity.

Several leading agencies are held for cosmetic, photographic and other goods.

COMPETITION: Another pharmacy exists in the area and a national chain of dispensing chemists has an important branch approximately one mile away, in the heart of a main shopping centre.

HOURS: 9 a.m. to 6 p.m. Early closing day Thursday.

ESTABLISHMENT: Business established about twenty-five years. Present owner took possession four years ago and now wishes to open a business in another area.

STAFF: Two full-time and one part-time assistant are at present employed in addition to the owner, who works full time in the business.

FINANCE: Turnover during the last trading year, ending 30th June, was £24,971; gross profit £6,430. This was the third successive year to show an increase in both turnover and gross profit. Audited accounts for the last four years are available.

FIXTURES: Traditional mahogany fixtures and fittings and cash register. Estimated value £950.

STOCK: Last valued in June. Estimated to be worth £4,800.

PREMISES: Double-fronted shop 18 ft frontage by 32 ft, dispensary at rear. Large dry basement used as stockroom. Living accommodation comprises four rooms, kitchenette, bathroom, separate W.C. Small yard at rear.

TENURE: Approximately 8 years to run of 14 year lease at rental of £880 p.a., including rates at present level.

REMARKS: This business should offer scope for improvement to a man younger than the present owner. In addition, several new blocks of council flats are being erected in the locality, increasing the potential trade.

VENDOR: John Smith at 93 Carlton Road, SE5.

PRICE: £4,450 for lease, goodwill, and fixtures. Stock at valuation.

The above details have been supplied by the vendor. They are not guaranteed correct nor do they form part of any contract.

This example shows what details a prospectus should give, but it is not perfect. From the prospective purchaser's point of view it would be far better if it gave, for example, the audited turnover and gross profit figures for each of the last five years (even though the present owner has been trading less than this period) and stated whether either of the competing shops has opened only recently. Many trades have their particular quirks: dispensing chemists for example often have to stay open late some evenings on a rota system for the district and in this instance the prospectus should have stated whether rota duties were involved. The reason for sale of 'wanting to open a business in another area' is ambiguous and calls for more detailed explanation.

Nevertheless, this is a prospectus which gives a fairly good idea of what is for sale. But as mentioned on page 60 every statement in a prospectus should be checked before a purchase is agreed.

Appendix 3. Typical costs in starting a shop or branch

This example assumes that the business outlined in Appendix 2 is being bought as a going concern and that the purchaser's professional advisers have enabled certain reductions in the original price to be agreed with the seller. As mentioned in the commentary on pages 40–44, costs vary widely according to circumstances.

	£
Goodwill, including remainder of 14-year lease for shop and living accommodation, but excluding rent, rates, etc.	3,325
Redecoration of shopfront, and part of shop interior and living accommodation, including necessary minor repairs	300
Solicitor, for all legal work involved in short leasehold premises as outlined in Chapter 3	35
Accountant, for all investigation work involved as outlined in Chapter 3, assuming audited accounts by firm known to buyer's accountant are available and buyer instructs acceptance of figures at face value. (Preparation of accounts and complete investigation of business finances might double this figure – yet still be excellent value for money, saving buyer hundreds of pounds.)	50
Valuation of stock (assuming fee shared equally by buyer and seller)	30
Valuation of equipment	10
Surveyor, for structural survey report as outlined on pages 72–4	35
Formation of a limited liability company	50
Equipment:	
Bought from outgoing retailer	610
New equipment required	200

carried forward £4,645

£
brought forward £4,645

Stock:

Taken over from outgoing retailer, including purchase tax	4,085
Additional necessary, including purchase tax	400

Running costs (allowing for a 13-week period):

Wages, including national insurance, for two full-time and one part-time assistant, and drawings of owner and wife	1,300	
Interest on borrowed capital and all bank charges	80	
Rent and rates	220	
Electricity and gas	25	
Proportion of annual cost of accountant preparing annual accounts from analysed cash book, settling tax liability, preparing an annual 'profitability' table, giving occasional general and specific advice	25	
Phone, insurance, and water	20	
Wrapping materials, stationery, printing, and postage	15	
Customers' credit, say	10	
Shop and window cleaning, petty cash, trade subscriptions, and other sundries	35	
New ownership promotion, including window displays. (Pharmacists are limited by their profession in how they may advertise, but all other trades will want to make the most of this important opportunity.)	300	2,030

Safety reserve	340

£11,500

The most likely sources of finance to meet this sum are credit from suppliers for stock and new equipment, a bank loan or overdraft, secured at least in part by a life assurance policy, and savings.

Appendix 4. Finding suppliers

When a shopkeeper takes over an existing business it is usual to continue with existing suppliers, at least until the new retailer has settled down and has time to consider carefully whether his selection of merchandise is the best possible. When starting a business from scratch it is necessary to find suitable suppliers. Merchandise for sale is obtainable from wholesalers, certain manufacturers selling directly to retailers, or possibly from voluntary buying groups.

Wholesalers whose delivery area covers the retailer's location can be found by:

1. Consulting a local directory in a near-by public library, such as those issued by Kelly's Directories Ltd, where under headings such as 'Grocers—wholesale', 'Hardwaremen—wholesale', 'Confectioners—wholesale', and so on in the classified 'Trades' section a list usually can be found. Wholesalers occasionally advertise on near-by pages also, giving fuller details of their wares and services.

2. Contacting the manufacturer of the merchandise required, where his name is known, requesting details of the appropriate wholesaler.

3. Asking the retailer's trade association, if he is a member, to provide a list of wholesalers operating in the area.

4. Requesting details from the appropriate trade association for wholesalers.

5. Noting details from various other sources, such as advertisements in the trade press, trade year-book, or local telephone directory, or through recommendation by friends in the trade.

None of these methods guarantees a complete list, but each will provide a sufficient number of wholesalers for the shopkeeper to obtain a wide range of stock. Once the business has started trading, the retailer may well be visited by representatives of other wholesalers serving the district, who, passing or hearing about the shop on their other calls, will see if their own firm can be of assistance.

Manufacturers selling directly to retailers often indicate this fact in their advertisements in the trade press. If a shopkeeper wishes a manufacturer's representative to call to discuss stocking one or more of his lines or granting an agency, he has only to contact the manufacturer. Should it transpire that the manufacturer supplies only through a wholesaler, the request will be passed to the appropriate wholesaler who then calls; no harm stems from this roundabout method of contact.

Voluntary buying organizations exist primarily in the grocery trade. Areas served and other details can be obtained through the trade press, trade association, or local chamber of trade. Many voluntary organizations, in all trades where they exist, and a broad indication of areas served, are listed in the Voluntary Associations section of *The Stores and Shops Retail Directory*, published annually by Newman Books Ltd and available in many reference libraries.

Appendix 5. Trade and similar exhibitions

Trade and similar exhibitions are worth occasional visits. The retailer then can see the latest products in his trade, almost certainly discover established lines which may prove profitable in his own shop, glean useful ideas on displaying merchandise, find out which manufacturers and distributors may have items to interest him at the time or in the future, and renew acquaintance with suppliers and others. Trade exhibitions, sometimes called trade fairs, frequently also include shop and display equipment of particular use to the trade.

There are three types of exhibition likely to interest the retailer professionally: relevant trade exhibitions; large general exhibitions of the Ideal Home type, part of which may be of trade interest; and smaller displays, usually open permanently but with exhibits changed from time to time.

Information about trade and similar exhibitions – when and where they are held, admittance charge, and so on – may be obtained from suppliers, the trade association, or trade paper. The public library also may be able to give this information: many subscribe to the *Board of Trade Journal*, which publishes complete lists of forthcoming trade fairs and exhibitions about every four months, with amendments and additions in intervening issues; alternatively the library may find the information in an appropriate trade year-book. Large general exhibitions are publicized in the national press and similar media.

Permanent displays with changing exhibits are to be found at the centres listed below. Although it is impossible to include every exhibition of this type, the retailer can find such centres by inquiring locally. He should know, however, that several other displays operate under a name suggesting that they are run by impartial trade organizations, and are, in fact, showrooms for a single manufacturer or group, where sales pressure may be exerted on visitors. These, too, may be worth a visit as long as the retailer realizes this fact. All the following are independent of individual manufacturers and admittance is free:

The Design Centre

Haymarket, London, sw1.
Also at Bristol, Manchester, Nottingham, and Glasgow.
Well-designed articles, covering all trades, are included free in the photographic Design Index if they have been selected by experts as of sufficient merit. Some of the actual products, as well as the Index photographs, are displayed: manufacturers pay for this, but the offer is open only to those products already accepted for the Design Index.

The Building Centre

26 Store Street, London, wc1.
Also at Bristol, Birmingham, Nottingham, Manchester, and Glasgow.
Building and allied products of interest to ironmongers, hardware shops, builders' merchants, do-it-yourself shops, etc., are exhibited, and leaflets and similar information are available. Manufacturers rent their space, often showing latest products.

The Glass Industry's Display

19 Portland Place, London, w1.
All products of glass, from delicate cut crystal to items handled by builders' merchants, are on show at the headquarters of the Glass Manufacturers' Federation at this address.

The Craft Centre

43 Earlham Street, London, wc2.
Various articles of hand craftsmanship are displayed, including furniture, woodwork, weaving, embroidery, pottery, metal work, textile printing, bookbinding, and gold- and silversmithing.

The Health Exhibition Centre

90 Buckingham Palace Road, London, SW1.
Products and information of interest to a wide range of retailers
directly or indirectly pertaining to health, from vermin, food,
and the hygienic way to sell ice-cream, to furniture insects and a
variety of building-trade items which make premises healthier or
more convenient. Also displays concerning health in everyday
life such as smoke pollution and the effects of various occupations.

The West End Showroom Centre

1–2 Hanover Street, London, W1.
Household goods in metal and plastic; toys, electrical fittings,
textiles, novelties, gifts, and similar articles in leather, china, and
glass: current lines exhibited by about forty manufacturers or
wholesalers in rented showroom-space, open only to those in the
trade. Exhibitors and their wares vary a little from month to
month.

Appendix 6. The trade press

Every retail trade has at least one trade magazine or paper of its own, and very often two or more. Many appear weekly, others monthly or at various other intervals. These journals exist in such large numbers because retailers realize their value.

They keep retailers up to date by featuring the latest merchandise in both advertising and editorial pages, while advertisements also indicate possible sources of supply, announce special offers from time to time, and forewarn traders of television and press advertising campaigns which, especially if the shopkeeper arranges a corresponding window display or other special promotion, may induce additional business for retailers in the lines concerned. Ideas for improved business efficiency and tips on sales promotion can often be obtained, both from articles written by specialists or the magazine's own staff and through the adaptation of methods used by successful retailers who are written about. Equipment of use to the trade is frequently featured also.

The shopkeeper is kept in touch with trade problems; new legislation and news affecting the trade are always fully discussed. Events at local meetings of relevant trade associations are reported, new books of trade interest reviewed, and most trade magazines include a 'Questions and Answers' feature and a column on legal aspects of retailing. Many trade journals offer a confidential free advice service to subscribers on any trade problem, quite apart from any readers' service which may be available in connection with advertisements or new products mentioned editorially. Inquiries should be addressed to the Subscribers' Information Service, enclosing a stamped addressed envelope. Some magazines also issue a current price list of trade merchandise at regular intervals.

Even more value can be extracted from a trade journal subscription by allowing staff to read each issue: some trade magazines include regular features for assistants but employees can still widen their trade knowledge and improve their sales ability by reading those which do not. It is sometimes convenient to tear out certain pages giving details of new products, tag them together and add them to the 'catalogue corner' referred to on page 130, but not to display publicly the complete magazine because other pages may give details of profit margins and similar trade information.

There are several ways of finding the most suitable trade journal. Probably the best is to visit a good public library and ask, in the reference section if there is one, for any of the following books:

Willing's Press Guide (James Willing Ltd)
The Newspaper Press Directory (Benn Bros. Ltd)
The Writers' and Artists' Year Book (A. & C. Black Ltd)
British Rate & Data (Maclean-Hunter Ltd)
Advertiser's Annual (Business Publications Ltd)

The names in brackets are those of the publishers. Each publication is an annual, except for *British Rate & Data*, which appears monthly. In most cases, details of publications, other journals as well as the trade press, are given in alphabetical order of title, but there is a separate index of titles grouped according to trade from which speedy reference to relevant journals can be made.

The information given in these reference books varies slightly in amount of detail but it is usually possible to find the frequency and day or date of publication together with price and circulation of each relevant trade journal, from which the choice can be made. Alternatively, the retailer can write to the most likely magazines, saying he is considering subscribing, and ask for a specimen copy, which may be free although it is better to offer to pay. He can then decide more easily. The shopkeeper's trade association or friends in the trade may be able to advise if the library cannot produce any of the reference books mentioned, and it is just possible that the library may itself subscribe to the relevant trade journal.

Appendix 7. Trade associations and chambers of trade

Retailers can benefit from membership of an appropriate trade association, which speaks and acts on their behalf at national level and usually provides a number of services useful in the day-to-day running of a shop. In a somewhat similar manner large numbers of retailers belong to their local chamber of trade. Many shopkeepers belong to both a trade association and a local chamber of trade: services of these bodies supplement each other and are not competitive.

Space does not allow a detailed description of all trade associations, but the larger organizations make continuous efforts to maintain retailers' profit margins, watch new legislation carefully to minimize detrimental effects for retailers, and negotiate with manufacturers, government officials and others on behalf of the trade. They also offer representation on wages councils, answers to members' questions, provision of legal advice, organization of meetings, often locally, publication of a bulletin or magazine, compilation of price lists of trade merchandise, operation of a clearing house for joint payment of accounts, and provision of a mathematical calculating service for stock sheets, etc. Many offer a debt-recovery service and hire-purchase financing scheme. In addition, some provide management advice, distribution of publicity material, advice on insurance, usually including provision of insurance services at a discount and private hospital-treatment group schemes.

Membership subscriptions usually vary with the size of the retailer's staff, but are normally only a few pounds a year. Trade associations are always glad to send full details on request about their rates and services.

The retailer can find the name and address of his appropriate trade association by asking the subscribers' information service of any journal in the trade, inquiring of his suppliers, or if he is a member, through his local chamber of trade. Alternatively, he may find the details he seeks at a reference library in *Trade Associations and Professional Bodies of the United Kingdom*, published by Pergamon Press Ltd; in *Directory of British Associations*, published by C.B.D. Research Ltd; or in *Directory of Employers' Associations, Trades Unions, Joint Organizations*, etc., published by Her Majesty's Stationery Office, in the 'employers' associations' section under 'retail distribution'. Unfortunately, none of these reference works gives a complete list.

Most trade associations each represent one trade, though sometimes two or three closely associated trades. For larger retailing concerns there are trade bodies grouped by form of organization instead of by trade merchandise, such as the Retail Distributors' Association, representing many department stores; the Multiple Shops' Federation, and the Co-operative Union. These three bodies have joined with the National Chamber of Trade and the Retail Alliance (itself a federation of about ten major merchandise trade associations) to form the Retail Consortium, an organization aiming to represent a cross-section of the retail trade and to speak on matters where individual policies of these bodies are in agreement.

LOCAL CHAMBERS OF TRADE

Local chambers of trade benefit members and also advance the commercial prosperity of the district. They are self-governing organizations comprising primarily independent retailers, although representatives of department stores and multiple and variety chains trading in the area also often belong, as well as a relatively small number of other individuals, partnerships, and companies carrying on business locally. Occasionally these bodies are misleadingly called chambers of commerce: in some urban areas a chamber of trade and a chamber of commerce exist side by side, the former dealing with retailing matters and the latter mainly with affairs affecting manufacturers.

Activities of local chambers of trade vary. As a minimum, most issue, every few months, bulletins to members about local trading matters, liaise with the local authority and local press, organize local shopping weeks, joint Christmas illuminations and similar sales promoting ideas, cooperate with neighbouring chambers of trade, and arrange some form of social activity. In addition, a journal every two months, booklets on specific trading problems, advice on retailing – including legal – problems, and support at national level for projects beneficial to retailers (and opposition to those detrimental) are provided on behalf of local chambers by the National Chamber of Trade. Improvement of traffic conditions, provision of adequate parking space and public transport, effects of town-planning schemes, and a variety of methods to stimulate business for retailers are typical matters dealt with by chambers of trade.

Larger local chambers often issue their own monthly bulletin to members, provide answers to any retailing problem, keep a watchful eye on local by-laws, actively oppose irregular trading, organize joint appeals against rating assessments, issue questionnaires to parliamentary candidates at general elections, advise members on their legal liability to staff, customers, landlords, and others, secure representation on local civic, social, and welfare committees, and so on.

Many local chambers of trade are served by elected honorary officers. Others have a part-time paid secretary and a few employ a full-time paid official. Subscriptions, which are usually an allowable business expense for tax purposes, vary with the services provided by the local chamber and the number of assistants employed by the retailer. Four pounds a year or less is not uncommon for retailers with three or fewer assistants.

The address of the local chamber of trade can be found through the telephone directory or the National Chamber of Trade, Enterprise House, 3 Hyde Park Place, London, w 2, to which further reference is made on page 284.

Appendix 8. Useful organizations

The more important organizations, other than trade associations, which a retailer may find useful are listed below for his convenience. Most offer to send free, on request, brochures about their activities and advantages of membership. Inquiries should be addressed to the secretary.

The Building Societies' Association

14 Park Street, London, W 1.
Offer information about how building societies work and advise on choosing a building society, giving details of their member societies in the retailer's area.

Business Management Advisory Services

5 Wigmore Street, London, W 1.
One of this country's leading management consultancies, specializing in solving retailers' problems on a fee basis in strictest confidence. The author of this book is the managing director.

City and Guilds of London Institute

76 Portland Place, London, W 1.
The leading examining body in non-food retailing education. See Appendix 10 for further information.

Electricity Council

Trafalgar Buildings, 1 Charing Cross, London, W C 2.
The marketing department promotes full and proper use of electricity. Gives general advice on lighting, issues booklets, some free.

Finance Houses Association

14 Queen Anne's Gate, London, SW1.

One of the trade associations for firms financing instalment credit trading, but has no retailer members. The Association offers to put retailers in touch with suitable members, and undertakes direct collection or block-discounting finance.

The Grocers' Institute

50 Doughty Street, London, WC1.

The leading examining body in food retailing education. See Appendix 10 for further information.

The Hire Purchase Trade Association

3 Berners Street, London, W1.

Includes over 2,000 retailer members and 800 finance-house members. Puts retailers in touch with suitable members; undertakes direct collection or block-discounting finance; offers members advice, practical inexpensive publications on hire purchase, H.P. agreement forms, information about new H.P. legislation, conferences, instruction courses for retailers running their own H.P. schemes, etc. A small additional subscription gives access to the Association's credit-status reporting and debt-collecting services.

Industrial and Commercial Finance Corporation

7 Copthall Avenue, London, EC2.

Details on page 53.

The Institute of Arbitrators

16 Park Crescent, London, W1.

The professional body of arbitrators in Britain which, on request, appoints a suitably qualified arbitrator to judge disputes completely impartially. The Institute's register has eleven categories, one of which is consumer affairs, affecting disputes between retailer and customer, and another commercial disputes, e.g. between retailer and supplier. See details on pages 238 and 264.

The National Chamber of Trade

Enterprise House, 3 Hyde Park Place, London, w 2.
Coordinating body of 800 local chambers of trade (for details
see Appendix 7) and numerous national trade associations,
representing mostly independent traders. Aims to promote the
interests and advance the prestige of all distributive trades.
Membership normally through local chambers, but direct membership of the N.C.T. in addition is possible, conferring appropriate additional benefits.

Registrar of business names

55–71 City Road, London, E C 1 (for England and Wales).
102 George Street, Edinburgh 2 (for Scotland).
64 Chichester Street, Belfast (for N. Ireland).
Part of the Department of Trade and Industry. See page 252
concerning compulsory registration of many businesses.

The Retail Consortium

19–21 Conway Street, London, w1.
Coordinating body of certain trade associations; details on page
280.

Retail Trades Education Council

56 Russell Square, London, w c 1.
Voluntary body promoting and coordinating retail education
and training at all levels. Backed by over forty trade associations
and similar bodies, it is represented on committees of the
Department of Education and Science, Scottish Education
Department, and the City and Guilds of London Institute, and is
an endorsing authority for the Retail Trades Junior Certificate
and the Certificate in Retail Management Principles. Assists in
recruiting and training part-time teachers from various trades,
arranges conferences between retailers and those concerned with
education, organizes study visits for teachers and staff trainers, and
helps larger retailers introduce their own staff-training schemes.

Appendix 9. Variations in the value of the £

The value of £1 varies slightly from year to year. Goods which cost £1 in 1950 would have cost about £2 in 1970, a rise in price coinciding with a corresponding fall in the value, or purchasing power, of money. It can be seen that the more prices rise, the greater the fall in the value of money. The variation from any year to the next is usually small – around five per cent is not uncommon – and in times of general prosperity the fluctuation in value tends to be downwards. However the value of money can also increase, as Table 16 shows.

Table 16. Index of the internal purchasing power of the pound (1963=100)

1914	485	1926	282	1938	310·6*	1958	110·6
1915	394	1927	289	1946	183·5	1959	109·9
1916	332	1928	292	1947	171·8	1960	108·8
1917	275	1929	296	1948	159·5	1961	105·7
1918	239	1930	307	1949	155·8	1962	101·8
1919	225	1931	329	1950	151·5	1963	100·0
1920	195	1932	337	1951	138·9	1964	96·9
1921	215	1933	346	1952	131·1	1965	92·6
1922	265	1934	344	1953	128·9	1966	89·2
1923	279	1935	339	1954	126·6	1967	87·0
1924	277	1936	330	1955	122·4	1968	83·3
1925	275	1937	314	1956	117·2	1969	79·1
				1957	113·6	1970	75·0

* Not calculated during 1939–45 war.

(*Source:* Central Statistical Office)

The fluctuating value of the pound, indicated by variations in general price levels, directly affects the retailer in five ways:

1. Allowance for it must be made in comparing one year's net profit, turnover, or expenses with that of another year if a true

result is to be arrived at. If net profit is two per cent better for one year than for the preceding year and the general price level has risen by three per cent during the same period, the net profit has declined, not improved, in real terms.

2. Allowance for it should be made when buying an established business. If the seller claims to have worked up the trade by, for example, ten per cent in the three years he has owned the shop, during which period the general price level has increased by eleven per cent, the volume of business has declined slightly. This reasoning provides the buyer and his accountant with ammunition for reducing the price of the goodwill.

3. Allowance for it theoretically should be made when setting turnover or profit targets for the coming year, but because of the difficulty for the retailer in forecasting such a complex subject it is perhaps as well to assume that the coming year will repeat the degree of change, and in the same direction, as its previous year.

4. Allowance for it should be made when considering wage increases for staff. If the value of the pound drops substantially one year, indicated by a corresponding rise in general prices, wages should be increased accordingly when they are next reviewed: otherwise employees will find it more difficult to maintain their existing standard of living, will grow dissatisfied, not work as well as they might, and become more likely to leave.

5. Allowance for it must be made when thinking about suitable methods of saving any money not immediately required in the business. Money invested at three and a half per cent per annum is losing its value in real terms, and not increasing as it appears, if at the same time the general level of prices is rising by four per cent per annum. Realization of this fact by investors is one reason why interest rates are normally higher in times of inflation – that is, periods when prices rise relatively steeply. The difficulty is that fluctuations often last only a few months and it may not be convenient to switch savings from one form of investment to another to take advantage of a temporary high rate of interest. The position is further complicated by interest on some investments, such as savings certificates, not reaching the maximum unless left undisturbed. The retailer's best course is to keep in close contact with his bank manager and accountant about such matters.

The index numbers in Table 16 can be used to calculate the change in purchasing power between any two years in the period covered. If the purchasing power of the pound is taken to be 100p in year X, its comparable purchasing power in year Y would be:

$$100p \times \frac{\text{index number for year Y}}{\text{index number for year X}}$$

For example, if the purchasing power of the pound is taken to be 100p in 1962, its comparable purchasing power in 1969 would be:

$$100p \times \frac{79 \cdot 1}{101 \cdot 8} = 77\frac{1}{2}p$$

Variations in the value of the pound are rarely published but fluctuations in the general level of prices can be found from the government publications *Annual Abstract of Statistics* or *Monthly Digest of Statistics* available in the reference section of any good public library. It is necessary to look at only one table, headed 'Index of retail prices' in the chapter on 'Prices' (in the *Annual Abstract*) or on 'Wages and Prices' (in the *Monthly Digest*) (see Table 17).

Table 17. Variations in the level of prices

Annual Abstract and *Monthly Digest* 'All items' column			
16 Jan. 1962 =	100·0		
1962	101·6	1967	119·4
1963	103·6	1968	125·0
1964	107·0	1969	131·8
1965	112·1	1970	145·0
1966	116·5		

Source: Central Statistical Office

If comparing the percentage change in, say, net profit, between any two years the retailer will want to know the percentage change in the general level of prices in the same period so that he can adjust the calculation of his apparent progress to take into account the fluctuating value of money earned. To find the index in one year, say 1968, as a percentage of the index in another year, say 1964, the calculation is $\dfrac{125}{107} \times 100 = 117$ (for practical pur-

poses). The difference between this result and 100 is the percentage change between the years: in this instance, $117 - 100 = 17$ per cent.

It is tempting to deduct directly the index number for 1964 from that for 1968 but this gives a reasonably accurate result only when the index numbers are close to 100 as a number. If the index for the years in which the retailer is interested moved from, say, 200 to 204, the percentage change would not be four per cent but

$$\left(\frac{204}{200} \times 100 \right) - 100 = 2 \text{ per cent.}$$

Once the percentage change between the years has been found it can be applied to the apparent change in net profit. If this had increased by, say, 19 per cent the retailer can deduct the 17 per cent due to downward variation in the general price level and discover that he has improved his trade by only 2 per cent in real terms. Although this simple deduction method is a non-mathematical short cut, it gives correct answers for all practical purposes.

It is usually sufficiently accurate to calculate to the nearest whole per cent in the result. The retailer or his accountant can compute in a similar manner percentage changes in the general price level or value of money between any two years to suit his own purposes.

Appendix 10. Training courses

Training courses are a good method of improving knowledge and skills. Many courses exist, some suitable for the retailer, others for his staff. They fall into three groups: those operated as part of the educational system of the country, those run by merchandise manufacturers to improve knowledge of their own products, and various other relevant courses.

EDUCATIONAL SYSTEM

Assistants can progress in their career by following a continuous scheme of further education in retailing when they leave school. Courses are held at technical and commercial colleges in many parts of the country, sometimes in the evenings, sometimes during the day, when it is usual for the retailer to allow any studying assistants time from work without loss of pay. This is often only half a day a week and sometimes even this coincides with the early closing day. These courses of study, in conjunction with training received in the shop itself, are an excellent way in which assistants can find fulfilment in their career and achieve above-average pay and status, while at the same time providing the retailer with an above-average return for his investment in staff.

The National Distribution Certificate takes two years part-time study, often about five hours a week, normally started at sixteen, on leaving school. This is followed by two further years of part-time study, usually about six hours a week, leading to the Certificate in Distributive Management Principles. Both examinations are conducted by the City and Guilds of London Institute. In addition, a junior course called the General Certificate in Distribution, also started on leaving school at sixteen and involving two years of part-time study, is offered by the City and Guilds of

London Institute and the regional examining bodies listed below. At higher levels, other courses may be available locally, including the Higher National Diploma in Business Studies (Distribution); a diploma course in retail management studies; a course in supervisory management; or short specialized courses run by colleges of further education as local needs demand and facilities permit.

This pattern of courses, introduced in 1971, has superseded the former system outlined below, which nevertheless continues for an overlapping period and is the system under which many present assistants, whom the retailer may be interviewing for a staff vacancy, have studied. The previous pattern of courses began with the Certificate in Retailing course, requiring two years part-time study, often four hours a week, normally started on leaving school. The examination was conducted by the City and Guilds of London Institute and regional examining bodies; the certificate awarded to successful candidates is countersigned by the Retail Trades Education Council.

This was followed in non-food trades by two years' part-time study, often seven hours a week, for the National Retail Distribution Certificate, including study of commodities in the assistant's own trade, general retailing and educational subjects, and discussions on trade topics. This scheme, and the Certificate in Retail Management Principles, detailed below, were run jointly by the Retail Trades Education Council, the City and Guilds of London Institute, and the Department of Education and Science. Assistants leaving school at sixteen were able to take the two year part-time course for the National Retail Distribution Certificate without taking the Certificate in Retailing.

Certain trades have their own educational bodies which hold examinations and award certificates. In the food trades there are the Grocers' Institute and the Institute of Meat, while in non-foods the Booksellers' Association, the National Association of Retail Furnishers, the National Association of Goldsmiths, the National Institute of Hardware, and the British Stationery and Office Equipment Association each issue diplomas to those who qualify. Appenticeship schemes, lasting from three to five years according to trade, exist in butchery, furnishing, ironmongery, stationery and jewellery. Some trades run correspondence courses or a summer school. Cutting across trades, it is possible to study at many colleges for the Diploma of the British Display Society.

Assistants over twenty-one with at least two years practical experience of retailing in either food or non-food trades, and of appropriate educational standards (broadly that of the National Retail Distribution Certificate or above) have been able to take the Certificate in Retail Management Principles course. This took two years part-time study (often five hours a week) or was sometimes studied more intensively. It dealt with merchandising, accounting and similar relatively advanced subjects concerned with retailing, preparing the assistant for managerial duties.

Tuition fees for all these examinations are negligible – a very few pounds a year. Full details of examinations and syllabuses, conditions of entry, and so on, are available from local education offices or colleges, or where applicable, as follows:

General Certificate in Distribution; also Certificate in Retailing

City and Guilds of London Institute
76 Portland Place, London, w 1.
East Midland Educational Union
Robins Wood House, Robins Wood Road, Aspley, Nottingham 8.
Northern Counties Technical Examinations Council
5 Grosvenor Villas, Grosvenor Road, Newcastle-upon-Tyne 2.
Union of Educational Institutions
Norfolk House, Smallbrook, Ringway, Birmingham 5.
Union of Lancashire and Cheshire Institutes
36 Granby Row, Manchester 1.
Yorkshire Council for Further Education
Bowling Green Terrace, Jack Lane, Leeds 11.

Contact should be made with the body above likely to deal with the part of the country concerned.

National Distribution Certificate and Certificate in Distributive

Management Principles; also National Retail Distribution Certificate and Certificate in Retail Management Principles

> City and Guilds of London Institute
> 76 Portland Place, London, WI.

Trade organization examinations

> Booksellers' Association of Great Britian and Ireland, 152 Buckingham Palace Road, London, SWI.
>
> National Association of Retail Furnishers, 42 Sun Street, London, EC2.
>
> National Association of Goldsmiths, 2–4 Carey Lane, London, EC2.
>
> Grocers' Institute, 50 Doughty Street, London, WCI.
>
> National Institute of Hardware, 22 Harborne Road, Birmingham 15.
>
> The Leather Institute, 9 St Thomas' Street, London, SEI.
>
> Institute of Meat, 19–20 Holborn Viaduct, London, ECI.
>
> British Stationery and Office Equipment Association, 6 Wimpole Street, London, WI.
>
> British Display Society, 75 Cannon Street, London, EC4.

MANUFACTURERS' COURSES

Manufacturers of merchandise sometimes run training courses to help retailers and assistants improve their knowledge of the manufacturer's products. More sales can be made by being fully aware of the product's capabilities, advantages over competitors, benefits bestowed on users, and, where mechanical, how they work. Retailers and manufacturers have a common interest in boosting sales, hence these courses which, frequently lasting two or three days, are expensive for the manufacturer but often free to the retailer or his senior staff.

These courses are often held at manufacturers' head office and works and sometimes include free lodging at a near-by hotel for those not near home. Subjects dealt with frequently include a brief historical survey of the industry, a talk on how the articles are made, a tour of the factory, ideas on how to demonstrate the products to customers, display and other merchandising methods and, when applicable, a session on after-sales service.

Courses are usually not too tiring: a friendly affair, with good food (also free) and opportunities for discussion with fellow retailers and manufacturer's senior sales staff. These courses are builders of goodwill to a considerable extent, but the retailer should not lose his sense of perspective: like the manufacturer he will want to sell as much of the product as possible, but not necessarily at the expense of competing lines. One or two manufacturers issue a certificate or so-called diploma to those having attended their course, but these documents should not be confused with the infinitely more valuable certificates and diplomas issued by recognized educational bodies, such as those mentioned in the first part of this appendix.

These courses are run by manufacturers of a wide range of products, such as powered hand-tools, cutlery, electrical appliances, stationery, perfumery, corsetry, piece goods, knitwear, blankets, carpets, linoleum, and shoes. Invitations are not always available because courses are popular and sometimes are held only spasmodically. Retailers interested in attending this type of course can ask suppliers whether any are ever available concerning the lines handled by the retailer and, if so, obtain details.

OTHER METHODS

Other courses cover a variety of activities which may interest the retailer or his assistant.

Further education classes, evening or day, are usually available in English, arithmetic, and writing at various educational levels, while classes may be available also in chairmanship (for local trade meetings, etc.), commerce for traders (advertising, salesmanship, and office methods), debating (to develop confidence when speaking), display, discussion groups (to encourage clear and easy talking), economics, lettering (for showcards, etc.), method study (sometimes called work study), speech training, staff management, and so on. A wide range of other subjects from current affairs to hobbies usually also are available, which help to develop the full personality and powers of retailer and assistant alike.

Details of further education classes are available from local educational offices or colleges. Fees are only a pound or two a year. *Floodlight*, a complete guide to further education classes in the area of the Inner London Education Authority, is published annually for a few pence and is available from bookshops or the I.L.E.A.

Institute of Credit Management, 3 Berners Street, London, W1, regularly holds courses of evening lectures which include retail credit risk assessment, debt collecting, hire-purchase law and practice, and associated subjects. The fee for ten weekly lectures is about £3.

Voluntary chains and groups sometimes organize seminars covering such subjects as shop layout and sales promotion. These are usually held at local centres and last one or two days each. Some are free to members of the organizing voluntary chain or group; others charge a few pounds to cover cost of hiring a hall, etc.

The Co-operative Union runs special short courses for many categories of employees in Co-operative shops throughout the country. Held at its own college in Loughborough, they supplement retailing education courses for Co-operative shops available locally and by post, and lead to certificates or diplomas in aspects of Co-operative retail management.

The National Cash Register Company Ltd, 206–16 Marylebone Road, London, NW1, through its Modern Merchandising Methods department, holds two-day seminars (costing about three pounds) on the principles of modern retailing. It also offers a free shop layout design service.

Appendix 11. Suggested further reading

Books are not priceless heirlooms to be opened only on special occasions, pages turned reverently, and every sentence taken as unchallengeable fact. They are tools to help the retailer become a wiser man, and because this book is a practical work, publications listed here are considered to be useful in helping most retailers run their businesses more easily or profitably.

Books contain the distilled experience of their authors and thus can be a short cut to extremely wide knowledge, practical as well as theoretical. Some books are better than others, but even among good books some are more suited to an individual reader, because they deal precisely with the reader's problems or field of interest, or assume exactly the right degree of previous knowledge held by the reader.

Information in books should be used to suit the reader. Except where a book is wanted as a guide to a completely new field, most of the facts relevant for the reader can be extracted quickly by using the index and chapter-heading details.

Most trades and aspects of retail business management have many books dealing specifically with them. Almost every book is easily obtainable free at a good public library, although some may take a short time to obtain on special request. Libraries and good booksellers are always pleased to advise on books for further reading on any subject. If a book, skimmed through at a library or bookshop, will clearly be of use for reference, it is worth buying.

The range of suitable books is so vast the short list that follows, limited to 50, hardly scratches the surface of what is available. However, they have been very carefully selected and guiding comments added. They are listed in order of title, author and, in brackets, publisher. All are recent or at least reasonably up-to-date in content at the time of preparing this book; should one or two eventually become out of print, copies will be available through the public library service. It is always worth checking that the volume being considered has not been superseded by a later edition: this can be discovered through recent annual volumes of the *British National Bibliography* and associated publications, which will also indicate all other recent books on the subject. A librarian will willingly explain how to use the *British National Bibliography*.

COMMUNICATION, INCLUDING SALESMANSHIP

English Out at Work by W. R. Page (Dent). Also *More English Out at Work* by W. R. Page (Dent).

Written specifically for shop assistants, these excellent books make elementary English grammar and self-expression come alive and interesting, even to those who have never been adept at these subjects at school. The contents aim to help directly in retailing situations, such as describing products, filling in forms, writing letters, and preparing notes. Written by a teacher of English for retail students, the books include many appropriate exercises.

The King's English for Commercial Students, Book 1, by A. R. Moon and G. F. Golding (Longmans).

Admirable for beginners not academically inclined. Includes self-expression, letter writing, and similar subjects.

Write What You Mean by R. W. Bell (Allen and Unwin).

Without trying to teach English, this useful book successfully tackles the difficult subjects of how to compose good letters and similar documents, including how 'tone of voice' can be conveyed in writing and how to decide what to include in a letter.

Usage and Abusage by E. Partridge (Penguin Books).

A readable guide in quick reference form to avoidance of many frequently-encountered errors in spoken and written English.

A Dictionary of Modern English Usage by H. W. Fowler (Oxford University Press).

The standard work on the correct use of English, written and spoken.

The Art of Speaking Made Simple by W. R. Gondin, E. W. Mammen, and J. Dodding (W. H. Allen).

Ideal for retailers and assistants, this thorough book will help immeasurably in sales presentations and the many other occasions when a good voice and wise choice of words bring important benefits.

Better Retail Selling by A. Fiber (Management Books).

A comprehensive practical volume on salesmanship by the author of *The Complete Guide to Retail Management*, for assistants and as a 'refresher' for retailers.

How to Win Friends and Influence People by D. Carnegie (World's Work).

This famous book deals with fundamental techniques in handling people, including ways to win them to the reader's way of thinking, change their views without arousing resentment, how to write effective letters, and suggestions for improving personal relationships in the home.

How to Find Out by G. Chandler (Pergamon Press).

Covers many sources for information, including how to make the best use of books in public libraries.

New Twentieth-Century Encyclopedia (Hutchinson).

A thorough, up-to-date, inexpensive one-volume encyclopedia, ideal for quick reference on the many subjects cropping up in salesmanship, business, and everyday life.

Thinking to Some Purpose by L. S. Stebbing (Penguin Books).

How to avoid common pitfalls in attempting to think clearly.

Straight and Crooked Thinking by R. H. Thouless (English Universities Press).

Reveals dishonest tricks and pitfalls in thinking, discussion and argument; logical fallacies; and similar barriers to arriving at correct conclusions.

The Use of Lateral Thinking by E. de Bono (Cape).

Should stimulate original ideas of everyday application.

DISPLAY AND LAYOUT

The Practical Display Instructor by H. C. Murrills (Blandford Press).

For window and interior display. Covers tools, lighting, colour, lettering, etc., and display of goods from most trades. Well illustrated. Parallel volumes by the same publishers include *Display of Canned, Packed and Bottled Goods*; *Men's Wear Display*, and *Fashion Display Illustrated*.

Notes for Lecturers, No. 10: Window and Interior Display by E. A. W. Simmonds (available only from Retail Trades Education Council, 56 Russell Square, London, WC1).

Useful booklet for retailers and assistants dealing with many aspects of the subject, including ways to arrange goods for various trades, special stands and other equipment, and how to sketch a window for planning a display.

Window Display by N. Kroll (Studio Vista).

Clearly sets out and fully illustrates the principles, covering a wide range of products, especially fabrics, including treatment of showcards and tickets.

Display Dynamics by P. Mytton-Davies (Blandford).

Window and interior display, particularly dealing with arrangements based on geometric patterns.

BUSINESS AND ECONOMICS

The Changing Pattern of Distribution by N. A. H. Stacey and A. Wilson (Pergamon Press).

A wide-ranging survey of the place of retailing within the national economy, including likely trends.

The Livelihood of Man by H. M. Croome and G. King (Christophers).

A good introduction to economics, helping the retailer better appreciate opportunities for increasing profit and to see his business and all worldly affairs in perspective. Includes supply and demand, cost and price, monopoly and competition, the place of State planning in a free society, etc.

Buying by Voluntary Chains by C. Fulop (Allen and Unwin).

 The reasons behind the growth of all forms of retail buying groups and voluntary chains, how the various kinds of organization work, and the advantages and problems they bring.

Be Your Own Boss by A. Fiber (Management Books).

 Includes the kinds of business, often run from home, part-time or full-time, with which retailers may be able to cooperate to advantage, e.g. by selling their products and services for a commission. By the author of *The Complete Guide to Retail Management*.

FINANCE

Accounts for Retailers by A. Fawthrop (Macdonald).

 An excellent elementary book for retailers and staff on how to keep accounts. There are also sections on retail trading documents, including cheques and crossings, commercial terms, business abbreviations, etc., and a useful chapter on the arithmetical background to retailing.

Arithmetic Out at Work, Parts 1 and 2, by W. R. Page (Dent).

 Written expressly for shop assistants, these books deal with both mental and written arithmetical problems encountered in retailing, including fractions, percentages of money, weights and measures, discounts, and calculation of selling prices. Quick methods are included, as well as associated topics such as banking and income tax. Tests and examination papers also incorporated.

Bookkeeping and Accounts by Spicer and Pegler (H.F.L. Publishers).

 For studying bookkeeping in detail, this widely used textbook is comprehensive and clear.

Know Your Accounts by M. Mellor (Macdonald).

 Elementary bookkeeping for the retailer, clearly written, with many examples. Includes chapters on retailing documents and common arithmetical problems.

A Short Guide to Hire Purchase and Instalment Credit Selling by C. M. Greig (Hire Purchase Trade Association).

 A clear and practical booklet. Several companion booklets

include *A Short Guide to the Hire Purchase Acts* and *A Short Guide to Emergency Legislation on Instalment Trading.*

Hire Purchase Credit and Finance by V. R. Fox-Smith (Stevens).

A comprehensive work on hire purchase generally, its financing, law, etc. Includes statistical information, model forms, and other practical detail.

Hire Purchase in a Free Society by R. Harris, M. Naylor, and A. Seldon (Hutchinson, for the Institute of Economic Affairs).

An objective survey providing background reading on the importance of H.P. trading in business today. Parts II and III are probably of greatest interest, dealing with such subjects as how finance houses select their goods, customers, and terms; dealer fraud, and the market for H.P. One appendix outlines the law on instalment credit while another deals with credit protection associations.

How the City Works by O. R. Hobson (Dickens Press).

An impartial account in everyday language of how the stock exchange, banks, commodity markets, hire purchase finance houses, building societies, and similar monetary institutions fit together in British life and how all citizens benefit from their operation. Contents show not only such everyday matters as how cheques are cleared, but help to clarify much about finance, giving background knowledge to newspaper reports and current affairs generally.

Tax Saving for the Business Man by H. Toch (Museum Press).

Useful tax guidance. One chapter deals specifically with the small trader, others with forming a partnership or limited company, corporation and capital gains tax, general tax affairs such as appeals, penalties, errors in past returns, etc.

Daily Mail Income Tax Guide (Associated Newspapers).

An annual summary in simple language of tax matters as they affect most people. Several sections are of particular interest to retailers.

LAW AND INSURANCE

Introduction to English Law by P. S. James (Butterworth).

A comprehensive and lucid panorama of English law for the

beginner. Sections include an outline of how law is administered, the order of events in court proceedings, the legal status of companies, children, and others, as well as chapters on such main branches of law as contract, torts, and property. Reveals the underlying principles of English law, their practical effect, and method of enforcement.

John Citizen and the Law by R. Rubinstein (Penguin Books).

An easy-to-read layman's guide to English law and its administration, covering in sufficient detail all aspects of the subject necessary for general knowledge, from contracts and sale of goods to wills and death duties.

The Retailer's Lawyer by E. Mitchell (Business Publications).

Covers most readably all common legal problems regarding retail trading, staff and tax. Other volumes in this series by the same author include *Your Property and the Law* and *The Personnel Manager's Lawyer and Employer's Guide to the Law*.

The Retailer's Guide to Trading Law by K. R. Bagnall and J. A. Wall (Jordan).

An instructive book on aspects of law, suggesting practical solutions to common legal problems. Includes company formation and partnerships, contracts, sale of goods, credit selling, negligence, matters concerning employees, leasehold premises, shoplifting, etc.

Outline of Law for the Retail Trader by H. M. Croome (National Trade Press).

Usefully deals with contracts and torts, sale of goods, merchandise marks, landlord and tenant, etc.

Law for the Retailer by J. R. Lewis (Allman).

Non-technical guide for students and retailers.

The Legal Aspects of Business by H. R. Light (Pitman).

General principles of law, especially regarding commerce, including contract and sale of goods.

Elements of English Law by W. Geldart (Oxford University Press).

A handy guide for the beginner to the principles of law, including contracts, torts, property, and the sources of law.

Your Job and the Law by L. Sapper (Rapp and Whiting).

Includes chapters on income tax, pensions and trade secrets, as well as conditions of employment, leaving and changing jobs,

injuries at work, etc. Useful for retailers as well as employees.
The Law for Consumers (Consumers' Association).

For better appreciation of the customer's point of view on legal matters.
The Pan Book of Insurance by W. A. Dinsdale (Pan Books).

Insurance for the layman, including householders' comprehensive, 'all risks', motor, personal accident, life assurance, employers' liability, fire, loss of profits, etc.
The Summit Book of Insurance by J. E. Good (Evans Brothers).

An alternative paperback of similar scope to the above.

SALES PROMOTION, STATISTICS, STOCK CONTROL

How to Sell Successfully by Direct Mail by J. W. W. Cassells (Business Publications).

Includes many hints and examples on direct mail, including building and maintaining lists, and writing good selling letters.
Type for Books (Hugh Evelyn).

For comparing appearances of various styles of type when choosing letterheadings, house style, etc.
Your Money's Worth by E. Gundrey (Penguin Books).

For appreciating the customer's point of view concerning consumer protection, what to look for in merchandise, how to complain when necessary, etc.
Statistics for the Distributive Trades by L. Mundy (Macdonald).

The elements of statistics for beginners. Includes calculation of average stocks and stockturn, sales forecasting and budgeting, the 'cost and selling' system of stock valuation, preparation of monthly profit and loss accounts and balance sheet, etc.
Unit Stock and Store Control by H. Dennett (Business Publications).

Several chapters deal with stock control methods for the single-shop retailer, others with systems for larger organizations. Covers the principles, choosing the system, and manual methods. Various proprietary systems are illustrated and discussed, and there is an appendix of equipment suppliers.
Stores Accounts and Stores Control by J. H. Burton (Pitman).

Primarily for the larger firm, especially the manufacturer, but may be of use for detailed study for the larger retail organization. Deals with both physical and financial aspects of stock control.

Retail Stock Management (British Productivity Council).

A series of booklets for specific trades – grocery, footwear, ironmongery, etc. – dealing with basic principles.

Appendix 12. How good a retailer are you?

The quiz that follows will be of interest and help whether you are (or hope to be) an independent shopkeeper, branch or departmental manager, or sales assistant. All the answers are given earlier in this book, but most are less obvious than may appear at first sight, being designed to stimulate wide-ranging thoughts on the whole business of retailing. All the questions are of direct relevance to practising retailers, but the first five may in addition be of special interest to students for the Certificate in Distributive Management Principles and the remainder of particular interest to students for the National Distribution Certificate.

1. Sales assistant Mary Jones, who has been employed eighteen months and works well, threatens to leave unless given a big pay rise. Is this indiscipline? Should the request be rejected, and if so, why? If it should be granted, on what grounds, and to what extent? Where would the money come from to cover the extra wage cost? How should the situation be handled? Should similar requests be allowed to arise in future, from Mary or anyone else? If so, what should be done, and when?

2. Your closest competitor has just started to deliberately undercut you on several major lines. What actions would you take? Why? In which order?

3. Weekly turnover is as high as for the same time in previous years yet profits are declining. What might be the reasons? How would you seek to improve matters?

4. Heavy competition, from existing and new shops, is hitting your shop's sales and profits. What actions would you take? Why? In which order?

5. Your shop is getting many more complaints from customers, on a variety of subjects. There are also more requests to exchange purchases. What might be the reasons? How can the situation be

remedied ? What attitude should be taken with dissatisfied customers ?

6. Your shop has made steadily increasing profits over the five years since you opened in leasehold premises. The new bank manager has given notice that the substantial overdraft so far always allowed will have to be cut by two thirds. What possible rearrangement of business finances would you examine ? When is a big overdraft facility an advantage and when a drawback ?

7. To how many sources can a retailer turn for help to improve profits ? Are such facilities fully used ? If not, why not ?

8. You have never bothered to introduce a system of staff commission on sales but your junior sales assistant asks for it. Your other, senior, sales assistant objects. What actions do you take ? Why ? In what order ? What might you infer from your assistants' attitude ?

9. 'The independent retailer is doomed!' Why, and to what extent, is this statement wrong ?

10. Your district grows rapidly and the shop attracts more people every month yet profits remain the same. What steps would you take to improve profits ? How would you investigate and measure the efficiency of the business ?

Index

Individual retail trades are not listed here because the principles of good management apply to them all and therefore almost all of this book applies to each retail trade. In addition to this index, readers will find the detailed contents listing on pages 7 to 15 very helpful for quick reference. The letter 'n' after a page number in this index refers to a footnote on that page.

layout for, 190–91

Self service, 81, 88, **185–7**
  dispensers for, 192
  layout for, 189–91
  price-marking for, 116
  stores, displays in, 190–91

Seller of shop, dealing with, 58–9, 260, 269

Selling. *See* Salesmanship.

Selling a shop, 46–8, 70, 265
  reasons for, 58, 269
  ways of, 145. *See also* Prospectus *and* Seller of shop.

Servicing. *See* After-sales service

Shelf space, apportionment, 95, 190. *See also* Island shelving.

Shop, alterations to, 41, 53, 63, 183, 186
    surveyor's advice on, 72, 74, 265
  classification of, 89
  cleaning of, 156, 160, 247
  corner, 82
  congregation of, 79–80. *See also* Shopping centres.
  costs, 43, 271
  counter service in, 185–6, 187–90, 191, 192. *See also* Display *and* Layout.
  empty. *See* Premises, vacant.
  equipment for, 40, 47–9, 268–9, 270, 274–7
    valuing, 73, 74–5
    See also Equipment; Merchandise; *and* Stock.
  frontage of, 184. *See also* Shopfront.
  heating, costs of, 43, **271**
    windows in, 203
  interior, appearance of, 83–4, 183–5, 212–13. *See also* Display *and* Layout.
  location of, 25, 41, 43, 69, 80–82, 132, 258
  opening new, 27, 33–4, 54, 76, 85–6, 227–8
  purchasing, 40, 57, 72–3
  restrictions on use, 57, 71, 72, 247, 254
  selling. *See* Seller of shop *and* Selling a shop.
  temperature in, 193, 247
  trading hours for, 23, 101
  trading name of, 71–2, 252

Shopfront, 183, 200–201
  fascia, 201, 224
  See also Shops, frontage of, *and* Windows.

Shoplifting. *See* Pilfering.

Shopping centres, 80, 95, 98
  changes in, 81–2
  as guide to pedestrian flow, 81
  movement of, 49
  multi-storied, 79–80, 98

Shopping expeditions, 80–81
  streets, 77–8. *See also* Market research.
  weeks, 281

Shops Act, 247–8

Shops (Early Closing) Act, 100, 250

Showcards, 142, 191, 205, 209–11, 213, 293, 298

Showcases, lighting for, 203, 204

Showrooms, 192. *See also* Exhibitions *and* Suppliers.

Sick pay, 247

Signs, for shop departments, 191
  outside shop, 224. *See also* Notices *and* Posters.

Sleeping partners, 52–3

Slow-moving lines, 120, 122, 127, 129, 136, 229

Smoking on shop premises, 117, 164. *See also* Fire risk.

Society of Incorporated Accountants, 263

Sole trader, 252

Solicitors, 54, 73, 87, 259, 270
  advice from, 47, 58–9, 170, 263
  choosing, 259–60
  employing, 41, 51–2, 58, 243
  fees of, 58, 71, 259, 263, 270
  professional qualifications of, 59, 259–60
  services of, 70–72

Solvency, 144. *See also* Finance.

Space in shop, utilization of, 95, 183–6, 192

Special events at shops, publicizing, 219

Special offers, by retailers, 43, 225, 227
  by suppliers, 44, 106–7, 110, 225

Special orders, 129–31, 243, 244. *See also* Catalogues, special corner for, *and* Diversification.

Special promotions, 95, 108, 134, 136, 164, 166–7, 237
  by manufacturers, 96
  by suppliers, 109–10
  tied with manufacturer advertising, 277

Staff, 19–20, 64, 154–5, 170–71. *See also* Managers.
  accidents to, 248
  advertising for, 159–60, 168–9
  ambitions of, 156–7, 159, 162
  bonuses on sales by, 160
  changes, 167–8
  commission, 143, 160, 163, 164–5, 169–70
  conditions of work, 23, 160–61, 246–8, 301
  contracts of employment, 246
  cost of, 88, 137, 155, 158, 167–8, 271
  dealing with, 33–4, 154–5, 241–2
  delegation to, 241–2
  deliveries by, 240, 247. *See also* Deliveries.